Year-Round Early Childhood Themes

12 Fun Theme-Based Activity Units

Written by
Vicki Martens

Editor: Heather Butler
Illustrator: Darcy Tom
Designer: Terri Lamadrid
Cover Designer: Barbara Peterson
Art Director: Tom Cochrane
Project Director: Stephanie Oberc

Table of Contents

Introduction

Young children are joyful learners. A high-quality, developmentally appropriate early-childhood program features active, young children enthusiastically participating in a variety of activities. This type of program offers both child-directed and teacher-directed activities. The curriculum is designed to excite the child—to stimulate curiosity, exploration, and imagination.

Thematic teaching is a wonderful way to provide an engaging, exciting curriculum. As children become more actively involved in the learning process, they will experience a wonderful sense of discovery and self-confidence. These experiences, in turn, will foster a love of learning that will last children a lifetime. A theme-based curriculum also allows the teacher flexibility. Themes can be repeated year after year as the children grow and learn. Children build on the skills they achieved the previous year. They approach projects differently due to the physical, emotional, and cognitive growth and development they have undergone.

Year-Round Early Childhood Themes features twelve thematic units and an appendix of art "recipes" designed specifically for young children. Each child-oriented thematic unit provides a variety of hands-on learning activities so teachers can pick and choose the activities that will best meet the needs of their early childhood classroom.

Getting Started

The length of time spent on a themed unit depends on your objectives and goals and children's interest levels. A theme can last anywhere from a few days to several weeks. Children can study the entire broad range of a theme or one specific portion.

Encourage parents to become actively involved by helping in the classroom. This allows the class to be divided into small groups and each child will receive more individual attention.

Each activity includes a materials list and a preparation section. Gather the materials for the chosen activities, and place the items in large boxes or plastic containers that are easily accessible. Review the preparation section, and complete any work that can be done in advance. Store papers, parent letters, and reproducible pages in file folders that are marked with the name of the theme and activity.

The activities in *Year-Round Early Childhood Themes* can be used with the whole class, with a small group, individually, or at a center. Each thematic unit features these elements:

Concepts and Vocabulary—This section introduces key concepts and terms that will be covered within the unit.

Family Letter: Theme Introduction—Photocopy this form letter and send it home to keep in touch with parents so they know what is happening in the classroom. This letter also provides activities for children to try at home to complement what is being taught in the classroom.

Family Letter: Wish List—Photocopy this form letter and send it home to ask parents to help provide some of the materials used in the unit.

Center Ideas—This section lists ideas for materials for classroom centers that tie in to the theme.

Language Development—Use the recommended read-alouds and discussion starters in this section to promote language development. Children can discuss a book, tell a story, or help write a group story. A read-aloud activity idea is also provided.

Math Activities—This section features a variety of activities with the different skills listed at the beginning of each one. The math skills include data collection and display, comparing, ordering, nonstandard measurement, counting, and sorting.

Sensory Activities—Provide children with the activities in this section to encourage them to use all of their senses to explore and discover.

Motor Skills Activities—This section has several activities to improve children's fine and large motor skills.

Alphabet Activities—Use the activities in this section to help foster letter and sound recognition.

Cooking Activities—This section includes cooking activities for the teacher to prepare as well as recipes for children to enjoy making themselves.

Art Activities—Use the activities in this section to have children explore their artistic side as they work on a variety of unique projects.

Fingerplays and Flannel Board Activities—This section includes fun fingerplays and flannel board activities that children will enjoy reciting over and over again.

Songs—This section features several enjoyable songs that tie in with each theme. Many of the songs are sung to the tune of well-known children's songs. A few poems are also included in some of the units.

Reproducibles—Many reproducible pages of patterns and pictures are included for each unit to keep preparation time to a minimum.

All About Me

Concepts

The concepts covered in this unit include the following:
- Everyone is unique and special.
- Everyone grows and changes as they get older.
- Everyone does things differently.
- Everyone has his or her own likes and dislikes.
- People and situations affect how we feel.
- Everyone experiences a wide range of feelings: angry, excited, happy, sad, surprised.
- We express our feelings differently.
- We can often understand how someone feels by looking at his or her facial expressions.
- Feelings can change.
- Feelings have their own words, sounds, and actions such as:
  happy—laugh, smile
  angry—mean words, raised voice
  sad—cry, frown
  confused—"I don't know what to do."
  surprised—gasp

Vocabulary

emotions—strong feelings

feelings—expressed emotions

The feelings discussed in this unit include the following:
- angry
- bored
- confused
- curious
- excited
- embarrassed
- happy
- impatient
- proud
- sad
- scared
- shy
- silly
- surprised

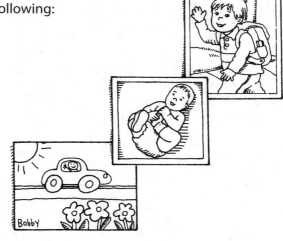

Date _____

Dear Family:

"All About Me" will be the theme for our next unit. We will discuss what makes each of us special and unique, feelings and emotions we have, and what we like and dislike. For this unit we will need some assistance from you. Please send a current photograph and a photograph of your child as a baby. If possible, send 8" x 10" (20 cm x 25 cm) photographs.

Classroom Activities

Children will participate in the following activities:
- Dancing, coloring, and painting to different types of music.
- Talking about how each of us is like other people and how we are unique.
- Matching each child's baby picture to a current photo.
- Listening to and discussing *Glad Monster, Sad Monster: A Book About Feelings* by Ed Emberley.

Home Activities

Here are some activities for your family to try at home to complement what children are doing in the classroom:
- Have your child help you write a letter to the class to tell us all about him or her. For example, you can include some of your child's "favorites" (e.g., favorite food, color, hobby, pet).
- Discuss what makes each member of the family feel happy. Set aside time to do something that everyone enjoys.

Have fun as you explore all of the amazing All About Me activities with your child.

Thank you for all you do!

Sincerely,

Dear Family:

We will use the following items during our All About Me unit. We would appreciate any help you could give us. We will begin this unit on _____, so please sign and return the form below if you can donate items by _____.

- collage material (e.g., feathers, scraps of fabric and wallpaper, glitter, sequins)
- old magazines and catalogs
- plastic shower curtain or tablecloth
- raisins
- roll of green crepe paper
- small containers of assorted types of pasta
- small, unopened box of O-shaped cereal
- small, unopened box of graham crackers
- squeezable jar of jelly
- tennis ball cans or Pringles cans with lid

Thanks!

• •

I would like to contribute the following items for this unit:

_____

Please contact me at _____ (phone number or e-mail)
to let me know how I can help.

_____

(parent's name)

Year-Round Early Childhood Themes © 2006 Creative Teaching Press

Center Ideas

The following are suggestions for different All About Me centers. The various activities provided in this unit can be used or modified for these centers :

- **Art Center**—play dough and face-shaped (teacher- or commercial-made) easel paper

- **Block and Building Center**—unit blocks, Styrofoam blocks, play hammers, bubble wrap

- **Dramatic Play Center**—clothes, puppets, multicultural dolls, mirrors

- **Listening Center**—tapes of stories about feelings, music that expresses different moods and feelings

- **Manipulatives Center**—puzzles of people with various expressions and people involved in various activities, zipping and buttoning boards

- **Math and Science Center**—sensory bottles (see Art Recipes, pages 414–415), mirrors

- **Reading Center**—books about feelings and self (see recommended read-alouds, page 10), stories written in class

- **Sand and Water Tables**—brightly colored pasta (see Art Recipes: Pasta and Rice Dye, page 416), scoops, measuring cups

- **Writing Center**—stamps and stickers representing various feelings

Language Development

Recommended Read-Alouds

A, You're Adorable by Buddy Kaye, Fred Wise & Sidney Lippman (Candlewick Press)

Chrysanthemum by Kevin Henkes (Greenwillow Books)

Feelings by Aliki (Greenwillow Books)

The Feelings Book by Todd Parr (Little, Brown and Company)

Guess How Much I Love You by Sam McBratney (Candlewick Press)

I Like Me! by Nancy Carlson (Viking)

I'm Gonna Like Me—Letting Off a Little Self-Esteem by Jamie Lee Curtis (Joanna Cotler Books)

The Kissing Hand by Audrey Penn (Child & Family Press)

My Many Colored Days by Dr. Seuss (Alfred A. Knopf Books)

That's Good! That's Bad! by Margery Cuyler (Henry Holt and Company)

Things I Like by Anthony Browne (Dragonfly Books)

Today I Feel Silly—And Other Moods That Make My Day by Jamie Lee Curtis (Joanna Cotler Books)

Read-Aloud Activity

Copy pictures from the beginning, middle, and end of a book. Show the copies to children, and ask *Which pictures do you think show what will happen at the beginning, middle, and end of the story?* Read the book to children and check their predictions. Collect three shoeboxes of different sizes to create nesting boxes. Glue the pictures from the beginning of the book on the outside of the largest box, pictures from the middle on the middle box, and pictures from the end on the smallest box. Put the boxes inside of each other. Invite children to take apart the boxes and look at the pictures as they retell the story.

Discussion Starters

Use these suggestions to promote discussions about a read-aloud or to motivate children to tell a story. These ideas can be discussed and then used to write group stories for children to illustrate.

1. Ask children questions about moods (e.g., *What makes you happy? What makes you sad? What makes you grouchy?*), and record their responses on chart paper.

2. Ask children to describe experiences with their friends. For example, ask *What would you do if you went over to see your best friend and he or she was very sad?*

3. Ask children to expand upon their feelings. For example, ask *What might you do when you feel scared?*

4. Ask children how they might feel about the following events. Encourage them to explain their answers:

   • What if you love chocolate ice cream and your mother surprises you with a chocolate ice-cream cone?

   • What if you left your favorite toy truck in the driveway and your dad drove over it and crushed it?

   • What if you just got what you wanted for your birthday?

   • What if your best friend had to move far away?

   • What if you get a kitten or a puppy?

   • What if you are building a giant block tower and someone knocks it over?

   • What if it is raining and you want to go outside to play?

   • What if you have a fight with your friend?

   • What if your little sister or brother takes your toy away from you?

5. Create a "feelings" web on chart paper. Ask children to name different feelings and what makes them feel that way.

6. Ask children to list different things they like or dislike. Write one sentence from each child on a separate piece of paper. Ask children to illustrate their work, and bind their pages together to make a class book.

Math Activities

👦3 Comparing Names

Skills: counting, one-to-one correspondence

M a t e r i a l s
- *Chrysanthemum* by Kevin Henkes
- linking cubes
- chart paper

Preparation

For each child, connect one linking cube for each letter of his or her name.

Directions

Read aloud *Chrysanthemum*. Write on chart paper the names of the children in the story. Draw a box around each letter in each name. Invite children to help you count the number of letters in each name. Give each child the stack of linking cubes that represents his or her name. Invite children to count the number of letters in their name by pulling apart the cubes one by one. Challenge older children to compare the length of their name (in cubes) to the length of other children's names (e.g., *I have one more letter in my name than you do*).

👦3 People Graph

Skills: data collection and display, counting, comparing

M a t e r i a l s
- plastic shower curtain or tablecloth
- permanent marker
- construction paper

Preparation

Use a permanent marker to divide a shower curtain or tablecloth into a grid so the squares are large enough for children to stand in. Write each child's name on a separate sheet of construction paper. Choose a trait to graph (e.g., hair color), and write a different subset of the trait (e.g., brown, black, blond, red) on separate sheets of construction paper (one per grid column). Place each of these papers at the bottom of a different column.

Directions

Give each child the paper with his or her name on it. Invite children to locate the column on the floor graph that best describes their trait, and have them stand on a square in that column. Tell children to place their paper in their square. Invite children to count and compare the number of papers in each column.

🌀 Graphing Birthdays

Skills: data collection and display, counting, comparing

Materials • chart paper

Preparation

Draw a graph with grid squares on a piece of chart paper. Label the columns with the months of the year.

Directions

Record each child's birth month on the graph by writing his or her name in the correct grid square. Help children count the number of birthdays in each month and compare the information in the columns.

🌀 How Big Are Your Feet?

Skills: comparing, ordering, nonstandard measurement

Materials • construction paper
• scissors
• linking cubes

Preparation

Choose three children with feet that significantly differ in size. Trace footprints onto construction paper and cut out each child's footprint.

Directions

Invite children to put the footprints in order from smallest to largest. When the footprints are in order, invite children to use linking cubes to measure each footprint. Trace and cut out a footprint for each of the remaining children. Label each footprint with the correct child's name. Invite children to use linking cubes to measure their own footprint. Place footprints in the math center, and invite children to measure them.

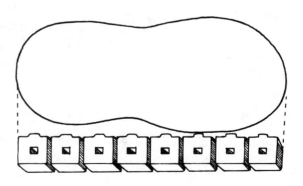

Hand and Foot Flowers

Skills: measurement, data collection and display

M a t e r i a l s
- yellow and green construction paper
- scissors
- pastel colors of construction paper
- current small photograph of each child
- glue
- roll of green crepe paper

Preparation

Cut yellow construction paper into circles to make flower centers.

Directions

Invite children to choose a piece of colored construction paper to make a flower. Draw three outlines of each child's hands (with fingers spread wide) on his or her paper, and draw an outline of his or her shoes on green paper. Help children cut out each hand and footprint. Show children how to glue their six hand cutouts around their yellow circle to make a "flower." Give each child his or her photograph. Help children glue their photo to the center of their flower and then cut a piece of crepe paper that matches their height. Tell children that this is the "stem" of their flower. Staple each crepe-paper stem along the wall, and add the handprint flower and the footprint "leaves" to each stem.

Feelings Sort

Skill: sorting

M a t e r i a l s
- Feeling Cards (page 33)
- scissors
- tape
- small boxes
- magazines

Preparation

Copy and cut apart a set of Feeling Cards. Tape a different Feeling Card to the outside of each box. Cut out several magazine pictures of people's faces with different expressions.

Directions

Show children each feeling card one at a time. Explain what the feeling is, and then invite children to share what makes them feel the same way. Have children sort the pictures into the correct boxes.

Sensory Activities

Feelings Have Special Sounds

Materials
- tape recorder/player
- audiotape

Preparation

Create an audiotape of sounds that represent different feelings (e.g., laughing, crying, cheering, shrieking).

Directions

Have children listen to the tape and identify the feeling represented by each sound. Invite children to make a facial expression that shows each feeling they name. Ask children to explain why each facial expression represents that particular feeling.

How Do You Feel?

Materials
- Feeling Cards (page 33)
- scissors
- hand mirrors
- paper bag (optional)

Preparation

Copy and cut apart a set of Feeling Cards.

Directions

Give each child a handheld mirror. Display each feeling card one at a time. Have children look at the expression on the card, and ask them to recreate each facial expression in the mirror.

Variation

Have a child pick a feeling card out of a bag. Invite the child to make the face on the card, and ask the other children to name which feeling is being expressed.

Do Toes Work as Well as Fingers?

Materials
- play dough (see Art Recipes, page 409)
- crayons
- drawing paper
- simple knob puzzle

Preparation

Set out on the floor each of the items listed above.

Directions

Invite children to use their toes instead of fingers to play with dough, draw, or put together a knob puzzle. Ask children to talk about what it was like to do something with their toes instead of their fingers. Invite children to think of other things they can try doing with their toes instead of their fingers. Select a few for children to try.

 # Who Is That Baby?

Materials
- baby picture of each child

Preparation

In advance, send home a request for each child's baby picture labeled with the child's name on the back.

Directions

Mix up the photographs. Hold up a photograph, and ask children to guess who the baby is. Invite children to compare the picture to the child now. Ask questions such as *Does Ben look the same or different?*

Motor Skills Activities

A Puzzle of Me

Materials
- 8" x 10" (20 cm x 25 cm) current photograph of each child or enlarge a photo to 8" x 10"
- card stock
- scissors
- glue
- 9" x 12" (23 cm x 30.5 cm) envelopes

Preparation

Make two card-stock copies of each child's photograph. Cut one copy into three or more puzzle pieces, depending on the ability of the child. The other copy serves as the base for solving the puzzle. Glue the intact copy onto an envelope and place the puzzle pieces inside.

Directions

Give each child the envelope with his or her puzzle. Invite children to assemble their puzzle on top of the base.

Extension

Send the puzzles home as a Christmas, Mother's Day, or Father's Day gift.

Did You See That?

Materials • none

Preparation

Directions

Gather children on the floor, and invite a volunteer to stand beside you. Whisper to the child a simple direction (e.g., open and close your hands once, close your eyes and count to five before opening them), and ask him or her to demonstrate the action. Invite a child to describe the action. Repeat the activity with a new volunteer and direction.

Put both your hands and feet on the floor.

Feelings Dance

M a t e r i a l s
- music that evokes different feelings on CD/tape
- CD/tape player
- streamers and scarves

Preparation

Directions

Play different pieces of music. Ask children to describe how the music makes them feel. Invite children to use streamers and scarves as they dance the way the music makes them feel.

Pin the Smile on the Face

M a t e r i a l s
- butcher paper
- scissors
- red construction paper
- tape
- blindfold

Preparation

Draw a large face without a mouth on butcher paper, and cut it out. Display the face at a child's eye level on the wall. Cut out a class set of red construction paper smiles. Add a loop of tape to the back of each smile.

Directions

Give a child a smile cutout, and blindfold the child. (Do not spin the youngest children. Spin older children one time.) Invite each child to take a turn trying to place the smile as close as possible to the correct place on the face. Once a child had placed his or her smile cutout, invite the child to share one thing that makes him or her smile.

Alphabet Activities

🔤 Cereal Signature

Materials
- black marker
- card stock
- O-shaped cereal
- glue

Preparation

Use a black marker to write each child's name in large print on a separate piece of card stock.

Directions

Give each child his or her name card and a handful of O-shaped cereal. Help children trace over the first letter in their name with glue. Have them place cereal on top of the glue. Ask children to continue tracing the letters with glue and covering them with cereal one at a time until all of the letters are covered.

🔤 Dot-to-Dot Alphabet Hand

Materials
- Dot-to-Dot Alphabet Hands reproducible (page 34)
- crayons

Preparation

Copy a class set of the Dot-to-Dot Alphabet Hands reproducible. Fold each copy in half on the dotted line to keep the right- and left-hand puzzles separate.

Directions

Give each child a copy of the reproducible and a crayon. Invite children to put their own hand on top of their paper to use as a guide to connect the dots in alphabetical order. Point out that the letters on the left hand are uppercase (capital) and the letters on the right hand are lowercase.

Variation

To simplify this activity, have children complete the dot-to-dot puzzle that they would trace using their dominant hand.

Pudding Names

Materials
- sentence strips
- serving spoon
- vanilla pudding
- waxed paper
- food coloring
- craft sticks

Preparation

Write each child's name on a separate sentence strip.

Directions

Give each child his or her sentence strip and a spoonful of pudding on waxed paper. Ask each child what his or her favorite color is, and add food coloring to the pudding to make the color. Have children use a craft stick to mix the color into the pudding. Invite them to use their craft stick or their finger to trace the letters in their name in the pudding. Have children look at their sentence strip as a reference.

Name Bags

Materials
- permanent black marker
- resealable plastic bags
- card stock
- paper cutter

Preparation

Use a permanent marker to write each child's name on a separate plastic bag. Cut card stock into small squares, and write the letters of each child's name on separate squares. Put the letter squares that make up each child's name in the plastic bag labeled with his or her name.

Directions

Give each child his or her "name bag." Invite children to put the letter squares together to form their name. Have children store their letters inside their bag.

Feeling Puzzles

Materials
- Feeling Cards (page 33)
- card stock
- scissors

Preparation

Make enough card-stock copies of the Feeling Cards so that two children can share one card. Cut each card from top to bottom into two pieces with a unique puzzle cut.

Directions

Give each child one half of a puzzle. Invite children to find the child with the other half of their puzzle. Invite these children to share with each other what makes them have the same expression as the one on their card.

Art Activities

Shake, Rattle, and Roll

Materials
- white paper
- tennis ball cans or Pringles cans
- scissors or paper cutter
- paint (assorted colors)
- Styrofoam bowls
- marbles
- spoons

Preparation

Cut white paper to fit the height of the cans. Wrap the paper around the inside wall of the cans. Pour different colors of paint into separate bowls.

Directions

Give each child two marbles and a paper-lined can. Invite children to place their marbles into their choice of paint. Help children retrieve the marbles with a spoon, put the marbles in their can, and secure the lid. Encourage children to shake the can and roll it across the floor. Help children pour out the marbles into an empty bowl and carefully remove the paper to reveal the unique artwork. Label each child's artwork with his or her name, and display the artwork on a bulletin board.

Where's Your Hair?

Materials
- straight and curly colored pasta
  (see Art Recipes: Pasta and Rice Dye, page 416)
- skin-colored construction paper
- crayons or markers
- glue

Preparation

Follow the directions on page 416 to make red, black, brown, and yellow pasta. Draw a large circle on the matching color of skin-colored construction paper for each child.

Directions

Give each child his or her piece of construction paper and crayons or markers. Have children draw in the circle their facial features. Ask children to pick the color and type of pasta that best represents their hair. Show children how to dab glue around their drawing and attach the pasta or dip the pasta in glue and then place it on their paper to give their self-portrait "hair."

Painting to the Music

Materials
- paint smocks
- paint
- paintbrushes
- white art paper
- music that evokes different feelings on CD/tape
- CD/tape player

Preparation

Directions

Give each child a paint smock, paint, a paint-brush, and a piece of white art paper. Play different types of music. Invite children to paint the way the music makes them feel.

A Collage about Me!

Materials
- magazines and catalogs
- butcher paper
- scissors
- crayons or markers
- glue

Preparation

Remove any inappropriate pictures from magazines and catalogs.

Directions

Have each child lie down on top of a piece of butcher paper, and trace and cut out each child's outline. Ask children to look through the magazines and catalogs and cut out pictures of their favorite things (e.g., toys, colors, foods). Invite children to color in clothes, hair, eyes, and other features on their cutout to show information about themselves. Encourage children to glue pictures of their favorite items on their cutout to create their own unique collage.

Happiness Quilt

Materials
- light-colored construction paper
- scissors or paper cutter
- paint pads in assorted colors (see Art Recipes, page 414)
- crayons and markers
- art collage materials (e.g., feathers; paper, fabric, and wallpaper scraps; glitter; sequins)
- tape

Preparation

Cut four 4" (10 cm) construction paper squares for each child. Make paint pads in assorted colors.

Directions

Give each child four paper squares. Help children press their hands on a paint pad and print their handprints on two squares. On the third square, invite children to draw a picture of themselves or a face that represents their mood. On the last square, invite children to use art materials to create a small collage. Label each square with the child's name. Tape the squares together to create a classroom "quilt."

Cooking Activities

Friendly Food Faces

Ingredients
- graham crackers
- cream cheese
- raisins
- banana slices
- assorted cereal

Other Supplies
- small paper plates
- craft sticks

Directions

Give each child a paper plate with a craft stick and half of a graham cracker. Have children use the craft stick to spread cream cheese on their cracker. Invite children to arrange the remaining ingredients on the cracker to make a face. Ask children to show their friendly food face to a friend before they enjoy their tasty snack.

Cinnamon Initials

Ingredients
- cans of refrigerated biscuits (1 biscuit per child)
- cinnamon
- sugar
- melted butter

Other Supplies
- index cards
- waxed paper
- empty salt shake
- pastry brushes
- baking sheet
- permanent marker

Directions

Write each child's first initial on a separate index card. Give each child the card with his or her initial and an uncooked biscuit on waxed paper. Have children roll their dough into a "snake." Invite them to use their card as a model to shape their snake into their initial. In an empty salt shaker, mix a small amount of cinnamon and sugar. Help children brush their dough with butter and sprinkle the cinnamon-sugar mixture on top of it. Use a permanent marker to write each child's name on his or her piece of waxed paper. Place the biscuits on a baking sheet. Bake the biscuits according to the directions on the package.

Rice Cake Face

Ingredients

- rice cakes
- peanut butter or cream cheese
- raisins
- chocolate chips
- nuts
- banana slices

Other Supplies

- craft sticks

Directions

Give each child a rice cake and a craft stick. Have children use the craft stick to spread peanut butter over the surface of their rice cake. Be mindful of any children with peanut allergies; use cream cheese instead. Invite children to add the remaining ingredients to create their own facial features. Ask children to share something unique about their "face" before they eat their snack.

Thumbprint Cookies

Ingredients

- 2 cups (0.5 L) flour
- 1 teaspoon (5 mL) salt
- ½ cup (118 mL) margarine
- ⅓ cup (79 mL) water
- squeezable jar of jelly

Other Supplies

- bowl
- mixing spoon
- waxed paper
- baking sheet
- permanent marker

Directions

Mix all of the ingredients except the jelly into a stiff dough. Give each child a scoop of dough. Have children use clean hands to shape their dough into a small ball and place it on a waxed paper–lined baking sheet. Use a permanent marker to write each child's name next to his or her cookie. Invite children to use their thumb to press down the middle of each ball. Bake the cookies at 350°F (177°C) for 8 to 10 minutes. After the cookies have cooled, invite children to fill their thumbprint with jelly and then enjoy their treat.

Hands on Shoulders

(Fingerplay)

Perform actions as they are described.

Hands on shoulders,
Hands on knees,
Hands behind you,
If you please.
Touch your shoulders,
Now your nose;
Now your head and now your toes.
Hands up high in the air,
Down to your sides, now touch your hair.
Hands as high as before.
Now clap your hands, one—two—three—four!

I Am Very Special

(Fingerplay)

Point to various body parts as they are mentioned.

I am very special.
Just look at me
And you will see
Two beautiful eyes, one button nose,
Ten talented fingers, ten wiggly toes,
Two little ears, one cute chin,
One little mouth to keep my tongue in,
And two little lips to make a beautiful smile
That can be seen mile after mile.

I Have Something in My Pocket

(Fingerplay)

I have something in my pocket. *(pointing to pocket)*
It belongs across my face. *(pointing to face)*
I keep it very close to me
In a most convenient place.

I bet you could guess it,
If you guessed a long, long while.
I'll take it out and put it on. *(reaching in pocket)*
It's a great big happy smile! *(smiling)*

Poor Little Boy

(Fingerplay)

Poor little boy with sad eyes. *(pointing to eyes)*
See him now how much he cries. *(rubbing eyes)*
He tries to stop with all his might. *(grimacing)*
He doesn't know *(shaking head)*
That tears are all right. *(nodding)*

So Many Parts of Me

(Fingerplay)

I have two hands to clap with *(clapping)*
And one nose with which to smell. *(sniffing)*
I have one head to think with *(tapping head)*
And two lungs that work quite well. *(taking a deep breath)*
I have two eyes that let me see. *(pointing to eyes)*
I have two legs that walk. *(walking in place)*
I have two ears that help me hear *(cupping hands around ears)*
And a mouth with which to talk. *(pointing to mouth)*

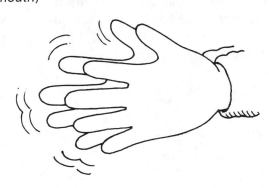

I'm Glad I'm Me

(Fingerplay)

No one looks the way I do.
I have noticed that it's true.
No one walks the way I walk. *(walking in place)*
No one talks the way I talk. *(using hands as mouth puppets)*
No one plays the way I play. *(pretending to play a game)*
No one says the things I say.
I am special, I am me. *(pointing to self)*
There's no one else I'd rather be. *(smiling)*

When I Am . . .

(Fingerplay)

When I am sad, I feel like crying. *(rubbing eyes)*
When I am proud, I feel like trying. *(holding head up high)*
When I am curious, I want to know. *(looking up, wondering)*
When I am impatient, I want to go. *(crossing arms and tapping foot)*
When I am angry, I look this way. *(making an angry look)*
When I am happy, I smile all day. *(smiling)*
When I am confused, my shoulders shrug. *(shrugging shoulders)*
When I am shy, I hide under a rug. *(dropping to knees)*
When I am embarrassed, I turn red. *(hiding face with hand)*
When I am tired, I go to bed. *(pretending to sleep)*

This is Me

(Flannel Board)

Create the following flannel board pieces: body without hands and feet, circle for face, eyes, feet, hands, nose, ears, mouth, cheeks, and other pieces to make a complete child.

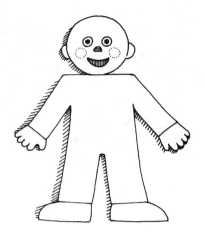

I have two eyes to see with. (*attaching face and eyes*)
I have two feet to run. (*attaching feet*)
I have to hands to wave, (*attaching hands*)
And nose I have but one. (*attaching nose*)
I have two ears to hear (*attaching ears*)
And a mouth to say, "Good day," (*attaching mouth*)
And two red cheeks for you to kiss. (*attaching cheeks*)
And now it's time to play!

Songs

All by Myself

(Sung to the tune of "Three Blind Mice")

All by myself, all by myself,
See what I can do. See what I can do.
I can brush my hair so neat.
I can put my socks on my feet.
I can get a snack to eat.
All by myself, all by myself.

All by myself, all by myself,
See what I can do. See what I can do.
I can ride around on my bike.
I can match pictures that are alike.
I can sing songs that I really like.
All by myself, all by myself.

🎵 The Happy Little Spider

(Sung to the tune of "The Itsy, Bitsy Spider")

Have children sing the song to reflect the feeling described in each verse.

The happy little spider went up the garden spout.
Down came the rain and washed the spider out.
Out came the sun and dried up all the rain.
And the happy little spider went up the spout again.

Additional verses:
The sad little spider
The scared little spider
The mad little spider
The surprised little spider

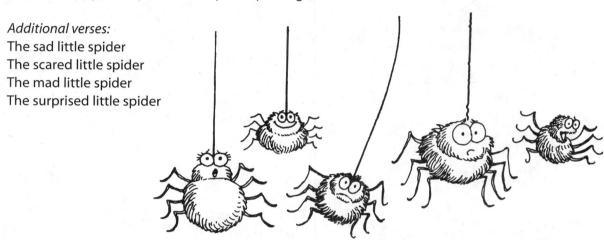

🎵 How I Feel

(Sung to the tune of "Twinkle, Twinkle Little Star")

Sometimes on my face you'll see,
How I feel inside of me.
I am happy.
I am sad.
I am proud.
I am mad.
I have feelings.
Yes, I do.
I just sang about a few.

🎵🎵 I Am Special

(Sung to the tune of "Frère Jacques")

I am special. I am special. (*pointing to self*)
Look and see. Look and see
Someone very special, someone very special.
It is me. It is me! (*pointing to self*)

🎵🎵 If You're Happy and You Know It

(Traditional)

If you're happy and you know it, clap your hands. (*clapping twice*)
If you're happy and you know it, clap your hands. (*clapping twice*)
If you're happy and you know it, then your face will surely show it.
If you're happy and you know it, clap your hands. (*clapping twice*)

Additional verses:
If you're scared and you know it, tell a grown up. (*cupping hands around mouth*)
If you're sad and you know it, wipe your tears. (*pretending to wipe away tears*)
If you're mad and you know it, say, "I'm mad!" (*saying, "I'm mad!"*)

🎵 The Smile on Your Face

(Sung to the tune of "The Wheels on the Bus")

The smile on your face goes ear to ear,
Ear to ear, ear to ear.
The smile on your face goes ear to ear,
All through the day.

Additional verses:
The frown on your face is an upside-down smile.
The surprise on your face makes your mouth like an *O*.
The sadness on your face makes the tears fall down.
The fear on your face makes you shake and shiver.

Feeling Cards

happy

sad

angry

scared

silly

excited

surprised

shy

embarrassed

Dot-to-Dot Alphabet Hands

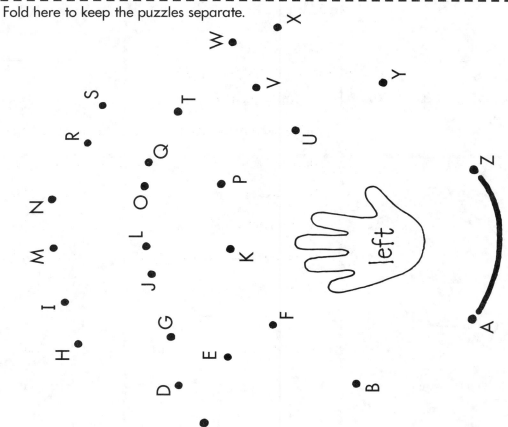

Fold here to keep the puzzles separate.

Year-Round Early Childhood Themes © 2006 Creative Teaching Press

Animals

Concepts

The concepts covered in this unit include the following:
- Different animals live all over the world.
- Zoos allow people to see animals from all over the world.
- We can learn more about wild animals at zoos.
- Some animals lay eggs.
- Baby animals look like their parents.
- Animals have fur, feathers, or special skin to protect them and keep them warm.
- Animals come in many different colors.
- Many animals are camouflaged. Zebras have stripes and leopards have spots.

Vocabulary

camouflage—skin or fur coloring that helps animals blend into their surroundings to hide from other animals

domestic animals—animals that are tame; pets

endangered—species of animals that might soon become extinct (no longer exist) if they are not protected

extinct—species of animal that no longer exists

habitat—a natural place where an animal lives

mammal—a warm-blooded animal that feeds its babies milk that it produces; people are mammals

reptile—a cold-blooded, scaly animal that usually lays eggs

wild animals—animals that are not tame

The animals featured in this unit include the following:
- bear
- camel
- chimpanzee
- crocodile
- elephant
- fish
- giraffe
- hippopotamus
- kangaroo
- leopard
- lion
- monkey
- penguin
- polar bear
- raccoon
- rhinoceros
- seal
- snake
- tiger
- zebra

Date _____

Dear Family:

"Animals" will be the theme for our next unit. We will be learning about animals from all over the world.

Classroom Activities

Children will participate in the following activities:
- Finding out which children are as tall as an emperor penguin.
- Searching for hidden animals.
- Eating "Monkey Bread."
- Listening to and discussing *Dear Zoo* by Rod Campbell.
- Creating zebras with stripes.

Home Activities

Here are some activities for your family to try at home to complement what children are doing in the classroom:
- Visit the zoo or pet store with your child, and discuss the similarities and differences among the animals.
- Find pictures of animals in magazines and on calendars.

Have fun as you explore all of the amazing Animal activities with your child.

Thank you for all you do!

Sincerely,

Year-Round Early Childhood Themes © 2006 Creative Teaching Press

Dear Family:

We will use the following items during our Animals unit. We would appreciate any help you could give us. We will begin this unit on _____, so please sign and return the form below if you can donate items by _____.

- package of animal crackers
- gift boxes (shirt size)
- jelly beans
- nature magazines
- gummy fish
- plastic Easter eggs (the kind that open)
- resealable plastic bags
- can of chow mein noodles
- box of crispy rice cereal
- chocolate or vanilla pudding mix

Thanks!

• •

I would like to contribute the following items for this unit:

_____

Please contact me at _____ (phone number or e-mail) to let me know how I can help.

_____

(parent's name)

Year-Round Early Childhood Themes © 2006 Creative Teaching Press

Center Ideas

The following are suggestions for different Animal centers. The activities provided in this unit can be used or modified for these centers:

- **Art Center**—animal cutouts to paint, animal templates and stencils to trace, play dough, animal cookie cutters, animal sponges

- **Block and Building Center**—plastic animals of various sizes and types, Barrel of Monkeys

- **Dramatic Play Center**—stuffed animals, animal costumes, animal puppets, animal masks

- **Listening Center**—tapes of animal stories, tapes and copies of stories written in class

- **Manipulatives Center**—animal counters

- **Math and Science Center**—animal counters, balance scale, fur, snakeskin, feathers, bird nest, magnifying glasses

- **Reading Center**—animal books (see recommended read-alouds, page 40); flannel board with pieces from stories, puzzles, and other activities; copies of animal stories written in class

- **Sand and Water Tables**—plastic animals, Styrofoam "iceberg," feathers, eggshells, sticks, twigs, straw, birdseed, measuring tools

- **Writing Center**—animal stickers and stamps, animal rubbing plates

Language Development

Recommended Read-Alouds

1, 2, 3 to the Zoo by Eric Carle (Philomel)

Brown Bear, Brown Bear, What Do You See? by Bill Martin Jr. (Henry Holt and Company)

Color Zoo by Lois Ehlert (HarperCollins)

Dear Zoo by Rod Campbell (Little Simon)

Do You Want to Be My Friend? by Eric Carle (HarperCollins)

Down By the Station by Will Hillenbrand (Gulliver Books)

Good Night, Gorilla by Peggy Rathmann (G. P. Putnam's Sons)

If You Give a Moose a Muffin by Laura Numeroff (Laura Geringer Books)

The Mixed-Up Chameleon by Eric Carle (HarperCollins)

Peek-a-Zoo! by Maria Cimarusti (Dutton)

Polar Bear, Polar Bear, What Do You Hear? by Bill Martin Jr. (Henry Holt and Company)

There's an Alligator Under My Bed by Mercer Mayer (Dial Books)

We're Going on a Bear Hunt by Helen Oxenbury (Margaret K. McElderry)

Where's My Teddy? by Jez Alborough (Candlewick Press)

Read-Aloud Activity

Read aloud *Brown Bear, Brown Bear, What Do You See?* by Bill Martin Jr. Have children discuss their ideas, thoughts, and feelings about the book. Follow the format of the story and invite children to add their own animal to the story. For example, you could ask a child *Brown bear, brown bear, what do you see?* and the child could answer *I see a chimpanzee looking at me.*

Variation

After reading aloud a story, have each child be one of the animals and recite the line from the book about his or her animal.

Discussion Starters

Use these suggestions to promote discussions or storytelling. These ideas can be discussed and then used to write group stories for children to illustrate.

1. Tell children that snakes crawl around on their belly all the time. Ask *How do you think the world looks to them?* Have children get down on their stomachs and look around. Discuss with children how a snake's view is different than a person's view. Invite children to draw a picture of how the world looks to a snake.

2. Tell children that we sometimes call many different animals monkeys. Have children compare pictures of gorillas, chimpanzees, orangutans, and spider monkeys. Ask *How are they different? How are they the same?*

3. Explain that monkeys live in jungles. Ask *What do you think a jungle is like? What other animals do you think we might see there?*

4. Take children on a make-believe safari. The following is a suggestion on how to lead the "safari":

    Hurry up! Climb aboard! Fasten your seatbelts. OK. Let's go! Wow, this is a bumpy road. Look on that hilltop over there. I see a big daddy lion with a huge mane and there are some mommy lions, too. Do you see any lion cubs? . . . Oh, wow! There's an elephant right by the road. It looks huge! What animals can you see? . . . Oh, no! There's a rhinoceros in the middle of the road. What can we do? . . .

Math Activities

Are You as Tall as a Penguin?

Skills: measurement, comparing

Materials
- butcher paper
- black marker
- tape

Preparation

Draw on butcher paper a life-size emperor penguin, and mount it on the wall. An emperor penguin can be up to 4 feet (1.1 m) tall.

Directions

Invite each child to stand next to the penguin. Mark the child's height and his or her name on the butcher paper. Encourage children to compare their height to the size of the penguin. Challenge children to compare the size of the penguin to other objects in the room.

123 Animal Crackers in a Jar

Skills: estimating, counting, comparing

Materials
- clear plastic jar
- animal crackers
- chart paper

Preparation

Fill a plastic jar partly full of animal crackers.

Directions

Invite each child to guess how many animal crackers are in the jar. Record the estimates on chart paper. As a class, count the actual number of crackers and compare it to the estimates.

123 Disappearing Animals

Skills: number sense, one-to-one correspondence

Materials
- dice
- small bowls
- animal counters

Preparation

Directions

Divide the class into groups of three to four children. (Depending on ability level, you may want to provide adult assistance for each group.) Give each group a die and a bowl, and give each child ten animal counters. Have the first player roll the die and place that many counters in the bowl. Children take turns rolling the die and placing counters in the bowl. Play continues until one child has placed all of his or her counters in the bowl. (Children must roll the exact number to place their last counter in the bowl.)

 Animal Patterning

Skill: patterning

Materials • animal pictures

Preparation

Create a sound pattern for each animal picture. It could be the noise the animal makes, or the noise it makes when it moves or eats. For example, a giraffe's sound pattern for eating could be *crunch, munch, munch* (an ABB pattern).

Directions

Show children the different pictures of animals one at a time. Tell children the sound pattern that is related to that animal. Help children extend the sound pattern and create a physical pattern to go along with it. For the example in the preparation section, line children up in a row. In order, have each child say one word from the sound pattern. If the child says *crunch*, have that child remain standing. If the child says *munch*, have that child sit down. Invite children to comment on the pattern they notice.

Animal Characteristics

Skills: comparing, sorting

Materials • hula hoops
• paper
• pictures of animals with fur
• pictures of animals with feathers

Preparation

Set two hula hoops on the floor next to each other to create a Venn diagram that does not overlap. Label one piece of paper *Animals with Fur* and another *Animals with Feathers*, and place one paper below each hoop.

Directions

Display an animal picture, and ask children if that animal has fur or feathers. Invite a child to place the picture in the correct circle of the Venn diagram. Repeat the process with the remaining pictures.

Animals with Fur

Animals with Feathers

Sensory Activities

What's Missing?

Materials
- What's Missing? reproducibles (pages 62–63)
- crayons or markers

Preparation

Copy a class set of the What's Missing? reproducibles.

Directions

Give each child a set of reproducibles. Invite children to look at each picture and identify what is missing from the animal's body. Have children describe what needs to be drawn, and challenge them to add it to the picture.

Zoo Molding

Materials
- butcher paper
- tape
- crayons or markers
- play dough (see Art Recipes, page 409)

Preparation

Tape a large piece of butcher paper to a tabletop, and draw on it elements of a zoo (e.g., pathways, trees, shrubs, buildings).

Directions

Give each child a lump of play dough. Invite children to mold animals out of their play dough and add them to the "zoo."

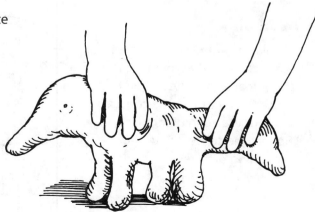

 # Hidden Animals

M a t e r i a l s
- small plastic animals
- sand table
- tongs

Preparation

Hide plastic animals in a sand table.

Directions

Explain to children that many animals hide to keep safe. Have children gather around the sand table and search for the hidden animals. Invite them to use tongs to remove the animals.

 # Icebergs

M a t e r i a l s
- resealable plastic bags
- small plastic polar animals (e.g., penguins, polar bears)
- water table

Preparation

Fill several plastic bags three-fourths full of water, and insert several plastic animals in each bag. Carefully seal the bags, and place them in a freezer.

Directions

Remove the "icebergs" (ice with animals) from the bags, and place them in a water table. Invite children to gather around the water table and explore the icebergs. Ask children questions such as *Do the icebergs float or sink? How do they feel when you touch them? What happens to the icebergs? How long do you think it will take for the animals to get out of the ice?*

Who's Hiding Behind the Door?

Materials
- nature magazines
- scissors
- construction paper

Preparation

Cut out large magazine pictures of different animals. Cut a sheet of construction paper to make several flaps or "doors."

Directions

Place an animal picture behind the paper with the flaps. Invite a volunteer to open the doors until the class can name the animal in the picture. Remove the paper and discuss the animal in the picture. Repeat the process with other pictures.

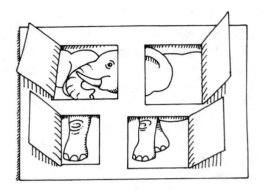

Motor Skills Activities

 # Monkey See, Monkey Do

Materials
- none

Preparation

Directions

Invite one child at a time to be the "monkey" in charge. Ask the monkey to perform an action for the others to copy. Repeat the activity until each child has been the monkey in charge.

Banana Pass

Materials
- music on CD/tape
- CD/tape player
- banana

Preparation
none

Directions
Have children sit in a circle. Start the music, and have children pass a banana around the circle until the music stops. When the music stops, encourage the child with the banana to stand up and act like a monkey.

Move Like a . . .

Materials
- none

Preparation
none

Directions
Invite children to make these animal movements:
- slither like a snake
- jump like a kangaroo
- waddle like a penguin
- run like a tiger
- swing like a monkey

Ask for volunteers to share other animal movements for children to copy.

Preschooler Snake

Materials • none

Preparation

Directions

Have children form a line by holding the waist of the child in front of them. Invite children to try these movements:
- walk around the playground
- move quickly
- move slowly
- wiggle
- move quietly
- move on tiptoes
- stomp
- jump
- the front person tries to catch the last person (i.e., the mouth tries to catch the tail)

Fish Flop

Materials • gummy fish
• fishbowl (with a large opening) or small fish tank

Preparation

Directions

Give each child a handful of gummy fish. Place a fishbowl or small fish tank on the floor. Have children stand a few feet back from the fishbowl or tank and toss their gummy fish back into their home (the fishbowl or tank).

 Kangaroo Hop

Materials
- masking tape
- labels

Preparation

Use masking tape to create a starting line on the floor. Write each child's name on a separate label.

Directions

Explain to children that kangaroos have very strong legs for hopping. Invite children to pretend to be kangaroos and see how far they can hop. Have children stand at the starting line and hop as far as they can. Mark each child's landing spot with his or her label.

Alphabet Activities

 Egg Twist

Materials
- plastic Easter eggs (the kind that open)
- permanent marker
- paper

Preparation

Use a permanent marker to write an uppercase letter on the top half of a plastic egg. Write the lowercase version of the letter on the bottom half of the egg. Write a different lowercase letter on the opposite side of the bottom half. Twist the two halves of the egg so the letters are not aligned. Label slips of paper with each matching pair of uppercase and lowercase letters, and place each paper inside the matching egg.

Directions

Explain to children that some animals lay eggs. Invite each child to choose an egg and twist it so the correct letter pairs are aligned. Encourage children to "crack" open the egg to check their answer. Have children close the egg and twist it so another child can use it.

Variation

For younger children, you may want to have children first "crack" open the egg and remove the paper to use as a guide to match up the correct letters.

Animal Concentration

Materials
- Animal Cards (page 64)
- card stock
- scissors

Preparation

Copy on card stock two sets of the Animal Cards per group of children. Cut apart the cards. (Begin with five pairs of cards per group and increase the number of cards as children's abilities improve.) Place the cards facedown in an array on the floor or a tabletop for each group.

Directions

Divide the class into small groups. In each group, invite a child to turn over one card, then another, attempting to find a pair. If the child finds a pair, he or she picks up the cards. If the cards do not match, the child returns the cards to their location. Have children continue until all of the cards have been matched.

Zoo Animals

Materials
- Animal Cards (page 64)
- Zoo Cards (page 65)
- scissors
- glue

Preparation

Copy a class set of the Animal Cards (only the top two rows of animals) and Zoo Cards.

Directions

Show children the animals on the Animal Cards. Encourage children to name the animals and share information about them. Give each child both sets of cards. Invite children to cut out the animals and glue them in the proper cages by matching the name. Assist younger children as needed.

 Elephant Chain Spelling

Materials
- Elephant Chain reproducible (page 66)
- scissors
- sentence strips
- large resealable plastic bags

Preparation

Make enough copies of the Elephant Chain reproducible so that each child has one elephant for each letter in his or her name. Cut apart the elephants. Write the letters of each child's name on separate elephant cutouts. Write each child's name on a separate sentence strip. Place each name strip and the corresponding "elephant letters" inside a large resealable plastic bag.

Directions

Give each child the bag with his or her name strip and letters. Invite children to put their elephants in a row to spell their name.

Animal Match

Materials
- pictures of mother animals and their babies
- card stock
- glue

Preparation

Mount pictures of mother animals and their babies on separate pieces of card stock. Find a matching pair of mother and child cards. Write the uppercase version of a letter above the mother animal and the lowercase version of the same letter above the baby animal. Repeat the process by writing different letter pairs on the remaining cards.

Directions

Explain to children the different ways that mother animals take care of their babies (e.g., mother kangaroos carry their joeys in a pouch). Invite children to match each mother to its baby and the uppercase to the lowercase letter. Invite children to share what they know about mother animals and their babies.

Art Activities

 ## Making Gray Elephants

Materials
- finger-painting paper
- scissors
- paint smocks
- black and white finger paint
- plastic spoons

Preparation

Cut elephant shapes from finger-painting paper. (You can enlarge and trace the Elephant Chain reproducible on page 66 if needed.)

Directions

Give each child an elephant-shaped paper and a paint smock. Put a spoonful of white and black finger paint on each paper. Invite children to finger-paint their elephant. Encourage them to describe what happens when they mix black and white paint together.

 ## Torn-Paper Giraffe

Materials
- yellow butcher paper
- scissors
- pictures of giraffes
- brown construction paper
- glue

Preparation

Cut out a large giraffe outline from yellow butcher paper.

Directions

Invite children to look at pictures of giraffes and discuss how they look. Give each child a sheet of brown construction paper, and show children how to tear off small "spots" for the giraffe. Invite children to glue on the giraffe the same number of spots as the number of letters in their name (or the number of people in their family or their age). Encourage children to name their giraffe, and display it on a wall.

Marble-Painted Zebra

Materials
- Zebra reproducible (page 67)
- scissors
- shirt gift boxes (1 per child)
- black paint
- shallow paint tray
- marbles (1 per child)
- spoon

Preparation

Copy and cut out a class set of the Zebra reproducible. Write each child's name on a separate zebra cutout. Place each zebra cutout faceup in a gift box. Pour black paint in a shallow paint tray. Place marbles in the black paint.

Directions

Give each child a gift box with a zebra cutout. Use a spoon to drop one marble in each child's box and then place the lid on top. Invite children to roll the marble around by moving each side of the box up and down. (You may need to redip the marble a few times in the paint.) Once the paintings are dry, display the zebras on an "African Animals" bulletin board.

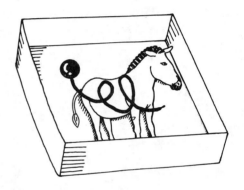

 # Leopard Spots

Materials
- Leopard reproducible (page 68)
- yellow paper
- pictures of leopards
- black paint pads (see Art Recipes, page 414)

Preparation

Copy a class set of the Leopard reproducible on yellow paper. Make black paint pads.

Directions

Invite children to look at pictures of leopards and discuss how they look. Give each child a copy of the reproducible. Show children how to press a finger on a paint pad and use their paint-covered finger to create spots on their leopard.

Leopard

Crispy Lion

Materials
- small paper plates
- yellow paint
- paintbrushes
- markers
- glue
- crispy rice cereal

Preparation

Directions

Give each child a paper plate to paint yellow. After the paint has dried, invite children to draw a lion's face in the center of their plate. Show children how to spread glue around the edges of their plate. Have children sprinkle cereal over the glue to create a furry mane.

Cooking Activities

Zebra Stripe Pudding

Ingredients
- chocolate pudding
- vanilla pudding

Other Supplies
- small, clear plastic cups
- plastic spoons

Directions

Give each child a clear cup. Help children add alternating layers of chocolate and vanilla pudding to their cup to make "zebra stripes."

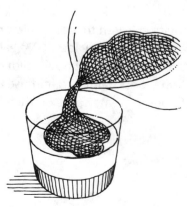

Monkey Bread

Ingredients

- pizza dough
- ½ cup (118 mL) sugar
- 1 tablespoon (15 mL) cinnamon
- 1 cup (237 mL) melted butter

Other Supplies

- mixing bowls
- loaf pan

Directions

Prepare the pizza dough according to the package directions. Mix together cinnamon and sugar in a bowl. Fill another bowl with melted butter. Invite each child to use clean hands to break off a small piece of dough, roll it into a ball, and roll the ball in butter and then the cinnamon-sugar mixture. Place the dough balls in a loaf pan, and bake for 30 to 35 minutes at 350°F (177°C).

Bird's Nest

Ingredients

- ½ cup (118 mL) butter
- 1 cup (237 mL) brown sugar
- 3-ounce (85-g) can chow mein noodles
- jellybeans

Other Supplies

- saucepan
- mixing spoon
- baking cups
- muffin tins
- small paper plates

Directions

Melt the butter in a saucepan. Add the brown sugar, and cook to a boil for 1 minute. Coat the chow mein noodles with the brown-sugar mixture. Put the noodles into baking cup–lined muffin tins. While the noodles are still warm, press them down in the center to form a "nest." Place a nest on a paper plate for each child. Give each child a nest and jellybean "eggs" to put in his or her nest.

 # Zoo Salad

Ingredients

- bananas
- apples
- peanuts
- raisins
- shredded coconut

Other Supplies

- kitchen knife (teacher use only)
- large bowl
- mixing spoon
- small paper bowls
- eating utensils (optional)

Directions

Cut up the bananas and apples into bite-size pieces. Combine all the ingredients in a large bowl and then serve the salad in small bowls. (**Note**: Be mindful of any children with peanut allergies.) Invite children to eat like a raccoon (i.e., with their hands).

Fingerplays

Who Am I?

(Fingerplay)

Of all of the animals in the zoo,
I am the tallest. That is true. (*standing up tall*)
Who am I? I am the giraffe.

My neck is long, I am very tall, (*stretching out neck*)
But I don't have much of a voice at all. (*covering mouth*)
Who am I? I am the giraffe.

I have small horns on top of my head. (*putting fingers on head to resemble horns*)
High up in the air is where I am fed. (*pointing up*)
Who am I? I am the giraffe.

I walk right up to the tallest tree, (*raising arms overhead to form a circle*)
And I eat the leaves that are good for me. (*pretending to chew leaves*)
Who am I? I am the giraffe.

At the Zoo

(Fingerplay)

At the zoo we saw a bear. (*using hand as a visor over eyes*)
He had long, dark fuzzy hair. (*moving like a bear*)
We saw a lion in a cage. (*using hand as a visor over eyes*)
He was in an awful rage. (*growling and showing "claws"*)
We saw a big, long-necked giraffe, (*holding up one arm to mimic giraffe's neck*)
And the silly monkeys made us laugh. (*laughing*)
But my favorite animal at the zoo (*pointing to self*)
Is the **kangaroo**. How about you? (*pointing to a child*)

Repeat the last two lines and invite each child to replace the boldfaced word with his or her favorite animal.

Five Bears Countdown

(Fingerplay)

Five bears were dancing on the floor. (*holding up five fingers*)
One fell down and that left four. (*holding up four fingers*)
Four bears were climbing up a tree.
One found a beehive and that left three. (*holding up three fingers*)
Three bears were wondering what to do.
One chased a bunny rabbit and that left two. (*holding up two fingers*)
Two bears were looking for some fun.
One took a swim and that left one. (*holding up one finger*)
One bear was sitting all alone.
He looked around and then ran home. (*putting hand behind back*)

Five Little Raccoons

(Fingerplay)

Five little raccoons heard a loud cat's roar. (*holding up five fingers*)
One ran away and then there were four. (*holding up four fingers*)
Four little raccoons climbing up a tree.
One slid down and then there were three. (*holding up three fingers*)
Three little raccoons deciding what to do.
One fell asleep and then there were two. (*holding up two fingers*)
Two little raccoons having lots of fun.
One went home so then there was one. (*holding up one finger*)
One little raccoon feeling all alone,
Ran to his mother so then there were none! (*putting hand behind back*)

Five Little Tiger Cubs

(Fingerplay)

Five little tiger cubs (*holding up five fingers*)
Eating an apple core. (*pretending to eat an apple*)
One had a sore tummy, (*rubbing tummy*)
And then there were four. (*holding up four fingers*)

Four little tiger cubs (*holding up four fingers*)
Climbing in a tree. (*pretending to climb tree*)
One fell out, (*having one hand fall into the other*)
And then there were three. (*holding up three fingers*)

Three little tiger cubs (*holding up three fingers*)
Playing peek-a-boo. (*covering eyes with hands*)
One was afraid, (*making a scared face*)
And then there were two. (*holding up two fingers*)

Two little tiger cubs (*holding up one finger on each hand*)
Sitting in the sun. (*using hand as a visor over eyes*)
One ran away, (*placing one hand behind back*)
And then there was one. (*holding up one finger*)

One little tiger cub (*holding up one finger*)
Sitting all alone. (*looking around*)
He saw his mommy, (*pointing with finger*)
And then he ran home. (*running in place*)

Five Little Monkeys Swinging in a Tree

(Fingerplay)

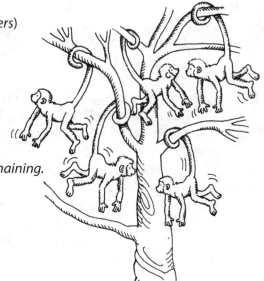

Five little monkeys swinging in a tree, (*holding up five fingers*)
Said to Mr. Crocodile, "You can't catch me!" (*shaking finger*)
Along comes Mr. Crocodile, quiet as can be—
    (*putting palms together to make crocodile's mouth*)
SNAP! (*clapping hands*)
Now there are only four monkeys swinging in the tree.
    (*holding up four fingers*)

Continue in descending order until there are no monkeys remaining.

Songs

🎵 Jungle Animals

(Sung to the tune of "The Muffin Man")

Do you know the striped zebra, the striped zebra, the striped zebra?
Oh, do you know the striped zebra that lives deep in the jungle?

Do you know the chimpanzee, the chimpanzee, the chimpanzee?
Oh, do you know the chimpanzee that lives deep in the jungle?

Do you know the big tiger, the big tiger, the big tiger?
Oh, do you know the big tiger that lives deep in the jungle?

Do you know the fat hippo, the fat hippo, the fat hippo?
Oh, do you know the fat hippo that lives deep in the jungle?

Do you know the tall giraffe, the tall giraffe, the tall giraffe?
Oh, do you know the tall giraffe that lives deep in the jungle?

Invite children to name other jungle animals to add to the song.

🎵 Jungle Row, Row, Row Your Boat

(Sung to the tune of "Row, Row, Row Your Boat")

Row, row, row your boat
Gently down the stream.
If you see a crocodile, don't forget to scream!

*Invite children to name other jungle animals. Repeat the song, replacing **crocodile** with a different jungle animal each time.*

🎵 I'm a Little Joey

(Sung to the tune of "I'm a Little Teapot")

I'm a little joey, oh so small,
Deep in mother's pouch so I won't fall.
When I start to grow up big and tall,
Out I'll hop like a bouncing ball.

🎵 Sally the Camel

(Traditional)

Sally the camel has five humps,
Sally the camel has five humps,
Sally the camel has five humps,
So ride, Sally, ride.
Boom, boom, boom, boom!

Continue in descending order until one hump is left and then sing the final verse:

Sally the camel has no humps,
Sally the camel has no humps,
Sally the camel has no humps,
Because Sally is a horse, of course!

🎵 The Bear Went Over the Mountain

(Sung to the tune of "For He's a Jolly Good Fellow")

The bear went over the mountain,
The bear went over the mountain,
The bear went over the mountain,
To see what he could see.

To see what he could see,
To see what he could see.

The other side of the mountain,
The other side of the mountain,
The other side of the mountain,
Was all that he could see!

Have You Ever Seen a Penguin?

(Sung to the tune of "Did You Ever See a Lassie?")

Have you ever seen a penguin, a penguin, a penguin?
Have you ever seen a penguin swim this way and that?
Swim this way and that way, swim this way and that way?
Have you ever seen a penguin swim this way and that?

Have you ever seen a penguin, a penguin, a penguin?
Have you ever seen a penguin slide this way and that?
Slide this way and that way, slide this way and that way?
Have you ever seen a penguin slide this way and that?

Have you ever seen a penguin, a penguin, a penguin?
Have you ever seen a penguin waddle this way and that?
Waddle this way and that way, waddle this way and that way?
Have you ever seen a penguin waddle this way and that?

What's Missing?

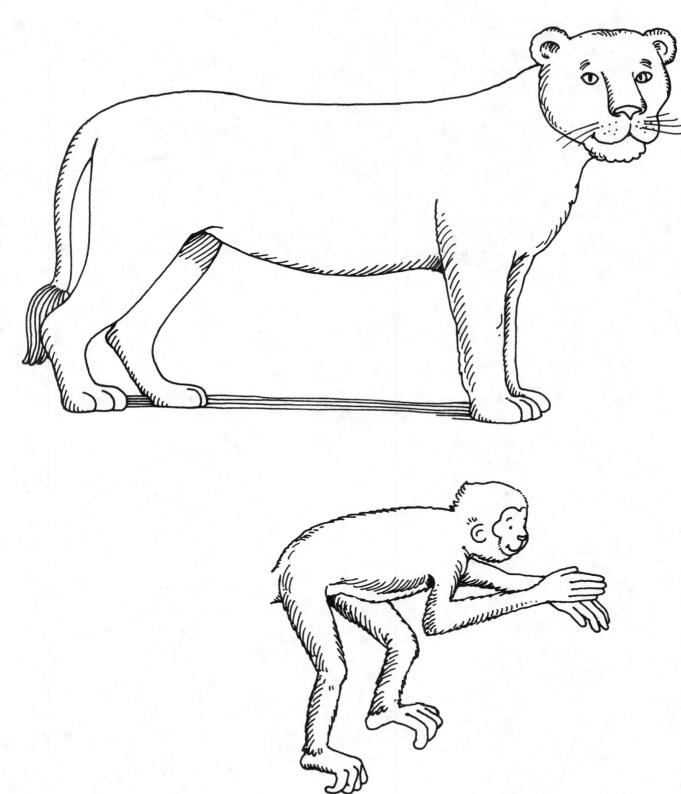

What's Missing?

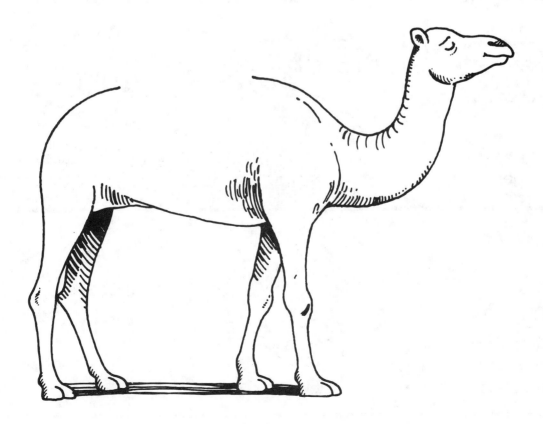

Animal Cards

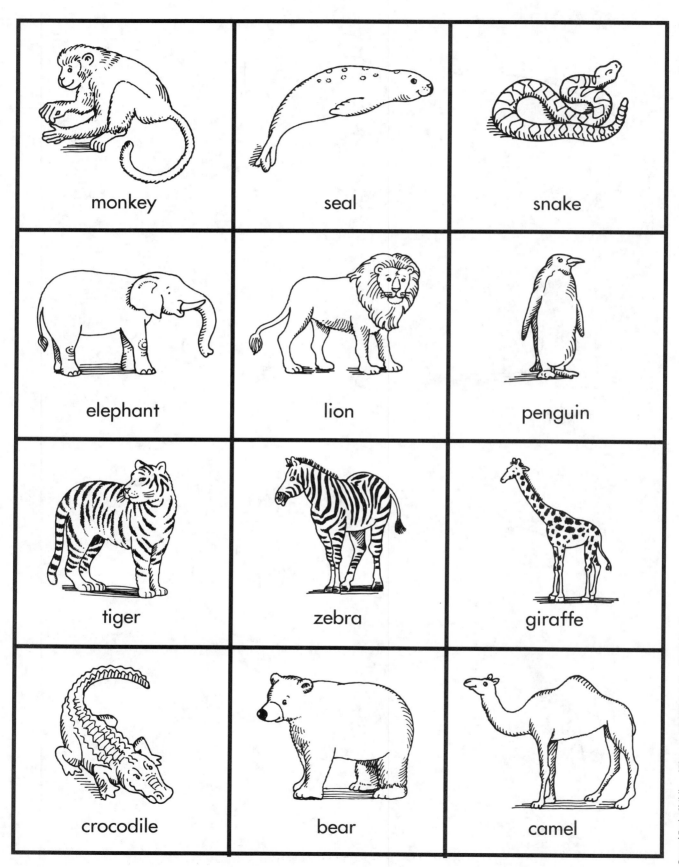

monkey	seal	snake
elephant	lion	penguin
tiger	zebra	giraffe
crocodile	bear	camel

Zoo Cards

Elephant Chain

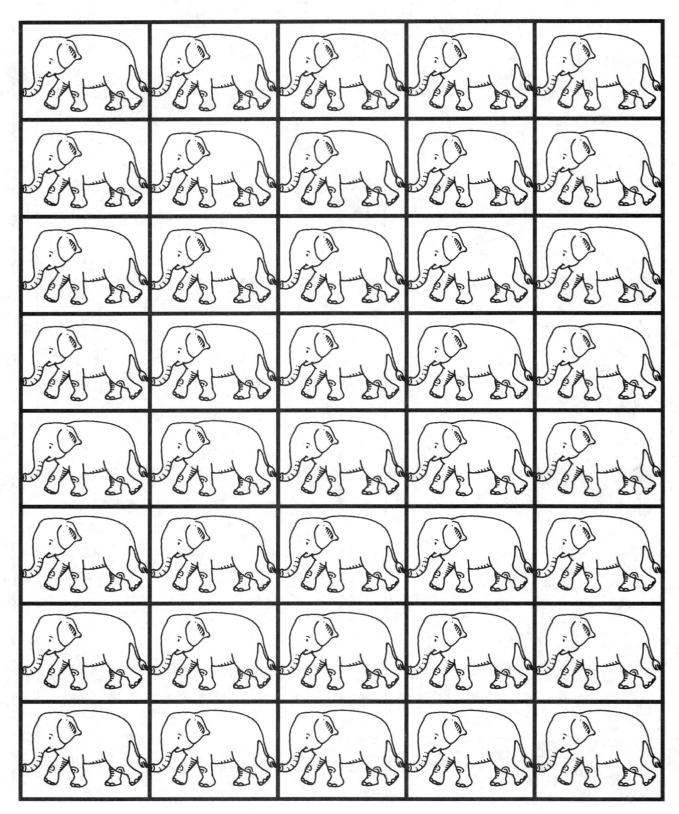

Zebra

Leopard

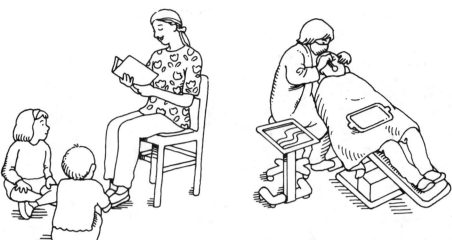

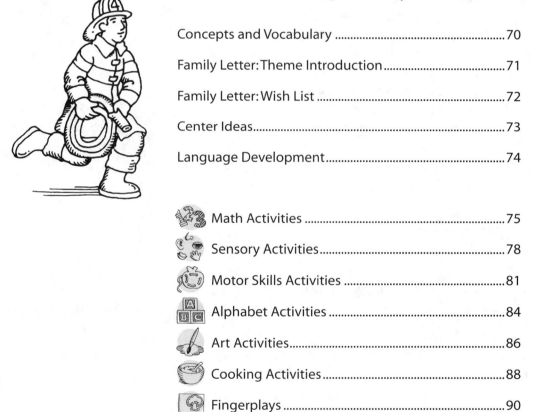

Community Helpers

Concepts

The concepts covered in this unit include the following:
- There are many different kinds of community helpers.
- Community helpers can make life easier and better for everyone.
- Community helpers can be men or women.
- Some community helpers wear uniforms.
- Some community helpers use tools or vehicles to help them do their job.
- Chefs and bakers make us food.
- City workers help our community function and look nice.
- Coaches help us play our games.
- Crossing guards help us cross the street safely.
- Dentists help keep our teeth healthy.
- Doctors and nurses take care of us.
- Firefighters put out fires and help people.
- Hairstylists and barbers help us look and feel good.
- Librarians help us find books to read.
- Mail carriers deliver our mail.
- Police officers are our friends and keep us safe.
- Teachers help us learn new things.

Vocabulary

community—a group of people living in one area

community helper—a person in the community who helps make it a better place to live or visit

occupation—the job a person does to earn money

The community helpers in this unit include the following:
- chef/baker
- city worker
- coach
- construction worker
- crossing guard
- dentist
- doctor
- farmer
- firefighter
- fisherman
- grocer
- hairstylist/barber
- librarian
- mail carrier
- nurse
- painter
- plumber
- police officer
- sanitation worker
- teacher

Date _____

Dear Family:

"Community Helpers" will be the theme for our next unit. Please return the Occupation Bags and Recycled Collage Bags (listed under "Home Activities" below) with your child on _____; we will use them for an activity.

Classroom Activities

Children will participate in the following activities:
- Creating a recycled collage.
- Playing Pin the Bandage on the Boo-Boo.
- Discussing what they want to do when they grow up.
- Listening to and discussing *What Do People Do All Day?* by Richard Scarry.

Home Activities

Here are some activities for your family to try at home to complement what children are doing in the classroom:
- Occupation Bag—Please place in a paper sack some items that relate to your job. The items can be from work, pictures from work, or something with the company's name or logo on it. Talk about the items with your child so he or she can share them with the rest of the class.
- Recycled Collage Bag—Help your child collect recyclable trash or grab bag-type collage items, and send them to school in a bag. Some ideas include foil scraps, newspaper scraps, Styrofoam packing peanuts, toilet and paper towel tubes, fabric or wallpaper scraps, leftover craft items, buttons, and egg cartons. Your trash or clutter is our treasure!

Have fun as you explore all of the Community Helper activities with your child.

Thank you for all you do!

Sincerely,

Dear Family:

We will use the following items during our Community Helpers unit. We would appreciate any help you could give us. We will begin this unit on _____, so please sign and return the form below if you can donate items by _____.

- envelopes
- postage stamps
- shaving cream (non-menthol)
- unopened box of O-shaped cereal
- corn syrup
- Ping-Pong balls
- tennis balls
- feathers

- inexpensive new toothbrushes
- oral medication syringes
- corks
- Styrofoam
- adhesive bandages
- unopened bag of miniature marshmallows
- unopened bag of graham crackers
- unopened package of chocolate sandwich cookies

Thanks!

• •

I would like to contribute the following items for this unit:

_____

Please contact me at _____ (phone number or e-mail) to let me know how I can help.

_____
(parent's name)

Year-Round Early Childhood Themes © 2006 Creative Teaching Press

Center Ideas

The following are suggestions for different Community Helper centers. The activities provided in this unit can be used or modified for these centers:

- **Art Center**—sponge shapes and cookie cutters of community helpers, play dough, easel, paper, paint

- **Block and Building Center**—wooden blocks, nuts, bolts, washers, sturdy glue, tongue depressors, cardboard and fast-food boxes to stack and build with

- **Dramatic Play Center**—clothes, hats, badges, and uniforms from various jobs; doctor's kit; community helper puppets; fast-food and pizza containers; old hair dryers (with cords removed); mixing bowls and spoons, play food

- **Listening Center**—tapes of stories about community helpers, tapes of stories written in class

- **Manipulatives Center**—puzzles featuring different community helpers, sewing cards

- **Math and Science Center**—microscope, postal scale, boxes of varying sizes and weights, stethoscope, cash register or adding machine, graduated spoons

- **Reading Center**—books about community helpers (see recommended read-alouds, page 74), copies of stories written in class

- **Sand and Water Tables**—sawdust, shampoo, sand, water, toy construction equipment, toy emergency vehicles

- **Writing Center**—stationery to write letters, envelopes, cancelled postage stamps, chalk and chalkboard, stickers featuring different community helpers

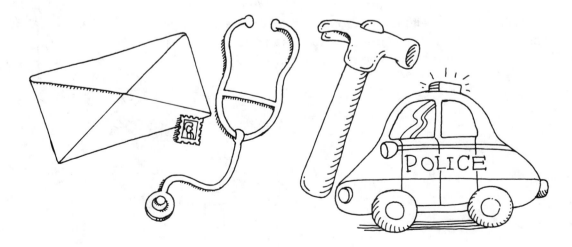

Language Development

Recommended Read-Alouds

Bad Hare Day by Miriam Moss (Bloomsbury Publishing)

Barney and Baby Bop Go to the Grocery Store by Donna Cooner (Barney Publishing)

Corduroy's Busy Street by Don Freeman and Lisa McCue (Viking)

Doctor De Soto by William Steig (Farrar, Straus and Giroux)

Fire! Fire! by Gail Gibbons (Crowell)

I Stink by Kate McMullan (Joanna Cotler Books)

The Jolly Postman by Allen Ahlberg and Janet Ahlberg (Little, Brown and Company)

My Little People Busy Town by Ellen Weiss and Elenor Fremont (Reader's Digest)

Officer Buckle and Gloria by Peggy Rathman (G. P. Putnam's Sons)

Tusk Trouble by Jane Clarke (Hodder Children's Books)

Walter the Baker by Eric Carle (Simon & Schuster)

What Do People Do All Day? by Richard Scarry (Random House Books)

Who Drives This? by Charles Reasoner (Price Stern Sloan)

Read-Aloud Activity

Read aloud a book that features information about several different community helpers. Have children discuss their ideas, thoughts, and feelings about the book. Encourage children to choose which occupation they would want to do. Have children draw pictures of what they would do on that job. Write children's dictation below their picture. Group pictures of the same occupation together, and use them to make a class book. Children can take turns taking home the class book to share with their family.

Discussion Starters

Use these suggestions to promote discussions about a read-aloud or to motivate children to tell a story. These ideas can be discussed and then used to write group stories for children to illustrate.

1. Show children the reproducibles of different community helpers. Point out that some of the workers wear everyday clothes but some wear special uniforms. Ask *Why do they wear special clothes? How do these people help others by doing their job?*

2. Read to children the nursery rhymes listed below. Ask them to think about and discuss whom the characters should call for help.
   • Humpty Dumpty—Whom could Humpty Dumpty call for help?
   • Jack and Jill—Whom would you call if you were Jack and Jill?
   • Old Mother Hubbard—Whom should she call to get a bone for her dog?

3. Display items or pictures of items that doctors and nurses use (e.g., stethoscope, thermometer, adhesive bandages, tongue depressors, cotton balls, syringes, blood pressure gauges, medications). Talk about what each item is used for. For older children, record on chart paper what they say about each item.

Math Activities

Jars of Nuts and Bolts

Skills: estimation, counting, comparing

Materials
• construction worker from the Community Helpers reproducibles (page 96)
• 2 clear plastic jars with lids
• nuts and bolts

Preparation

Put nuts and bolts in each jar, but put noticeably fewer in one than the other. Copy the construction worker from the reproducible.

Directions

Show children the construction worker reproducible, and discuss with them the important job construction workers have. Show children both jars of nuts and bolts together. Ask *Which container has more nuts and bolts? Which one has less?* Invite children to share how they know which one has more and which one has less. For a challenge, assist children in counting how many nuts and bolts are in each jar.

🪙 Coin Rubbings

Skill: sorting

Materials
- several coins of each denomination
- tape
- paper
- unwrapped crayons

Preparation

Directions

Show children the assorted coins, and explain that employees get paid for working at their jobs. Invite children to sort the coins by denomination (i.e., size and color). Have each child pick out an assortment of coins, and tape the coins to the table. Cover each child's coins with a piece of paper, and tape the paper to the table. Invite children to rub the side of a crayon along the coins so they can see the rubbings of the different sizes and the details on their coins.

📮 Weighing the Mail

Skills: weight comparison, estimating

Materials
- *The Jolly Postman* by Allen Ahlberg and Janet Ahlberg
- several boxes of assorted sizes
- items to mail (e.g., cotton balls, marbles, toy cars)
- tape

Preparation

Directions

Read to children *The Jolly Postman*, and discuss with them what a mail carrier's job is. Divide the class into small groups. Give each group a box, a quantity of items to mail, and tape. Ask groups to pack their items in the box, and help them seal the box with tape. Tell children to place their box at the science center. Invite children to visit the center to arrange the boxes from lightest to heaviest. When all children have visited the center, ask the class to guess what is inside each box.

⓵②③ Sorting Grocery Items

Skill: sorting

M a t e r i a l s
- food and nonfood items from a grocery store or the Grocery Store Cards (page 100)
- crayons or markers
- scissors
- paper

Preparation

Copy, color, and cut apart a set of the Grocery Store Cards if you plan to use them.

Directions

Discuss with children why we need grocery stores. Encourage children to share any stories they have about visiting a grocery store. Set out the grocery story items or the Grocery Store Cards for children to look at and discuss. Invite children to sort the items or cards into two categories: food and nonfood. Have children identify other items that would go in either of the categories. Draw pictures of these items on separate pieces of paper, and have children add them to the correct category.

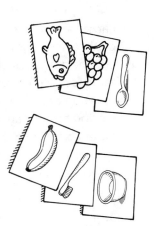

⓵②③ Counting Up the Ladder

Skills: recognizing numerals, counting

M a t e r i a l s
- firefighter from the Community Helpers reproducibles (page 96)
- masking tape
- large die

Preparation

Copy the firefighter from the reproducible. Use masking tape to create a large "ladder" on the floor. There should be at least six rungs, 1 foot (30.5 cm) apart from each other.

Directions

Show children the firefighter reproducible, and explain to them that a ladder is a tool a firefighter uses to fight fires and rescue people and animals. Have children line up at one end of the ladder, and invite the first child in line to roll a die. Have the other children help identify the number. Invite that child to take the corresponding number of steps on the ladder as the rest of the class helps to count. Have the next child in line roll the die and follow the same procedure. The first child will also take that number of steps until he or she reaches the end of the ladder and goes to the end of the line.

Adhesive Bandage Sorting

Skills: sorting, patterning

Materials
- nurse and mail carrier from the Community Helpers reproducibles (page 97)
- adhesive bandages in assorted colors, shapes, and sizes

Preparation

Copy the nurse and the mail carrier from the reproducible.

Directions

Show children an adhesive bandage and the nurse and mail carrier reproducibles. Ask children which community helper they could visit if they had an accident and needed a bandage for a cut or scrape. Place an assortment of adhesive bandages on a table for children to sort by shape, size, color, or any other combination of traits that they choose. Have children discuss their sorting technique and why they chose it. Afterwards, challenge older children to create an AB pattern using the bandages.

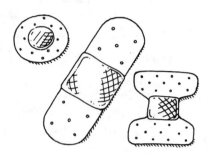

Sensory Activities

 # Toothpaste Putty

Materials
- toothpaste putty (see Art Recipes, page 416)
- waxed paper

Preparation

Make "toothpaste putty" according to the directions on page 416. Tear waxed paper into work-mat sizes.

Directions

Show children the toothpaste putty, and explain that it was made out of toothpaste. Ask children to raise their hand if they brush their teeth two or three times a day. Remind children that another important part of having healthy teeth and gums is to visit a dentist. Give each child a small portion of toothpaste putty on waxed paper, and invite children to use it to make a smiling mouth with several teeth.

 Road Construction

Materials
- city worker from the Community Helpers reproducibles (page 98)
- sand table or tub with sand
- small rocks and pieces of wood
- toy bulldozers, backhoes, cranes, dump trucks, cars, and trucks

Preparation

Arrange the sand at a sand table so it is uneven. Scatter rocks and wood throughout the sand. Place toy bulldozers, backhoes, cranes, and dump trucks on the sand. Copy the city worker from the reproducible.

Directions

Ask children to raise their hand if they rode to school in a vehicle such as a car, truck, or bus. Show children the city worker reproducible, and explain that an important community helper is a city worker who helps build roads for vehicles to drive on. Gather children around the sand table, and invite them to use the vehicles to scoop and move "dirt" and remove rocks and "trees" (wood) to create "roads." Once the roads are constructed, place several toy cars and trucks in the sand table, and invite children to drive the cars and trucks on the roads.

Gone Fishin'

Materials
- fisherman from the Community Helpers reproducibles (page 98)
- water table or tub
- items that float (e.g., toy fish, corks, piece of Styrofoam, aluminum foil)
- fishing nets

Preparation

Fill a water table or tub with water, and set several floating items on the water. Copy the fisherman from the reproducible.

Directions

Show children the fisherman reproducible, and ask them if they know what the person does for a living. Gather children around the water table, and invite them to pretend they are fishermen or fisherwomen. Invite children to use a fishing net to scoop the floating items out of the water.

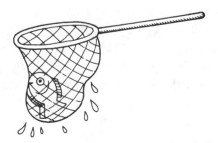

Classroom Chefs

Materials
- chef from the Community Helpers reproducibles (page 99)
- play dough (see Art Recipes, page 409)
- cinnamon
- cookie cutters
- rolling pins
- pans, pie tins, and baking sheets
- chef hats (optional)

Preparation

Mix a small amount of cinnamon into play dough to add a scent. Copy the chef from the reproducible.

Directions

Show children the chef reproducible, and ask them if they know what this person does for a living. Give each child some of the scented play dough and a chef hat, if possible. Have children use the dough and assorted utensils to "make" cakes, breads, pies, pizzas, and cookies.

Work Sounds and Phrases

Materials
- audiotape
- tape player/recorder
- Community Helpers reproducibles (pages 96–99) (optional)

Preparation

Visit various areas in the community to create an audiotape of different work-related sounds or phrases that different community helpers would say (e.g., police siren, jackhammer, a dentist saying, "Let's clean those teeth!"). Photocopy the community helpers that go along with the sounds on the tape. Set the pictures on the chalkboard tray.

Directions

Play the tape for children, and have them identify each sound or phrase. Ask children to select the matching picture and name the community helper that is related to the sound or phrase. Discuss how the community helper is involved with the sound (e.g., police officers use the siren to warn people that they are coming).

Let's clean those teeth!

 What's in the Grocery Bag?

Materials
- plastic grocery bags
- pairs of grocery store items (e.g., empty milk containers, empty egg cartons, cereal boxes)

Preparation

Gather pairs of items, and place one item from each pair inside separate grocery bags. (You may want to double-bag the items so they are not visible.) Tie the handles of the bags shut. Lay the matching items on the floor.

Directions

Invite children to touch the items on the floor. Emphasize words that describe how these items feel and their relative size. Have children sit in a circle around the items. Place a grocery bag with an item in it in front of each child. Invite one child at a time to feel the item in his or her bag without opening the bag. Have the child describe to the rest of the class how the item feels and the size of it. Tell the child to look at the objects on the floor. Ask the child to guess which item on the floor matches the item in his or her bag. Invite the child to pull the item out to see if he or she is correct. Choose a different child to repeat the activity.

Motor Skills Activities

Stop, Drop, and Roll

Materials
- firefighter from the Community Helpers reproducibles (page 96)

Preparation

Copy the firefighter from the reproducible.

Directions

Show children the firefighter reproducible, and discuss how firefighters can help them. Explain to children that sometimes people's clothing can accidentally catch on fire. Demonstrate the Stop, Drop, and Roll technique, and then have children practice it together.

Hair Dryer Locomotion

Materials

- items to attempt to move with hair dryers (e.g., Ping-Pong balls, tennis balls, feathers, leaves, rocks)
- paper
- 2 hula hoops
- hair dryer

Preparation

Place a table near a power outlet. Place items from the materials list on the table. Label one piece of paper *Won't Move* and the other *Will Move*. Set two hula hoops beside each other on the floor, and put one paper above each hoop to create a Venn diagram that does not overlap.

Directions

Explain to children that barbers and hairstylists are community helpers. Gather children around the table, and show them a hair dryer. Explain to children that this is one of the tools a barber or hairstylist uses. Show children the items on the table, and ask them to predict which items they will be able to move with the hair dryer. With supervision, invite children to take turns using the stream of air from the hair dryer to try to move one of the items. Invite each child to place his or her item in the correct circle of the Venn diagram.

 # What Jobs Do Your Parents Have?

Materials

- Occupation Bags (see Family Letter: Theme Introduction, page 71)
- chart paper

Preparation

Send home a reminder with children to return their Occupation Bag.

Directions

Invite one child at a time to empty his or her bag and tell the rest of the group about the objects or pictures in the bag (e.g., what they are and how they are used). Create a list of parents' jobs on chart paper.

 # Fire Ladder

Materials
- Fire Ladder Cards (page 101)
- firefighter from the Community Helpers reproducibles (page 96)
- scissors
- crayons or markers
- masking tape

Preparation

Copy and cut apart a set of Fire Ladder Cards. Copy and color the firefighter from the reproducible. Use masking tape to create a large "ladder" on the floor. The rungs should be about 1 foot (30.5 cm) apart.

Directions

Show children the firefighter reproducible. Explain that sometimes firefighters use ladders to reach people that are high up in buildings. Show children the pretend ladder on the floor, and tell them that they are going to play a game to climb the ladder. Have children stand in a line at one end of the ladder. Ask each child to draw a card. Read it aloud, and invite the child to perform the action.

Put the Bandage on the Boo-Boo

Materials
- white butcher paper
- markers
- tape
- adhesive bandages (1 per child)
- blindfold

Preparation

Draw a child on a large sheet of butcher paper. Color one of the knees so that it looks skinned. Tape the drawing on a wall at children's height.

Directions

Have children line up across from the drawing about 10 feet (3 m) back. One at a time, give each child an adhesive bandage (remove the backing so it will stick), blindfold the child, and have him or her try to put the bandage as close as possible to the "boo-boo." (For older children, spin them once.)

Alphabet Activities

🔤 Community Helper Spelling Puzzles

Materials
- Community Helper Name Strips (pages 102–103)
- scissors
- large resealable plastic bags

Preparation

Copy and cut apart two sets of the Community Helper Name Strips. Set aside one set to be the puzzle base. Cut the second set of words into individual letters. Put each set of letters and the matching name strip in separate plastic bags.

Directions

Give each child a bag with a community helper name and the individual letters of the name. Invite children to reassemble the letters on top of the name to spell the community helper's name.

🔤 Shaving Cream Letters

Materials
- barber from the Community Helpers reproducibles (page 99)
- chart paper
- marker
- non-menthol shaving cream
- paper towels

Preparation

Clear off a table that all the children can sit around. Copy the barber from the reproducible.

Directions

Show children the barber reproducible, and explain that sometimes barbers use shaving cream. Invite children to think of the names of other community helpers, and write their suggestions on chart paper. Say the beginning letter from one of these words as you draw a box around the letter on the chart paper. Ask children to trace the letter with their finger on the table. Squirt some shaving cream on the table in front of each child. Invite children to trace the letter in the shaving cream. (Remind them to keep their fingers away from their eyes and mouth.) Have children smooth out the shaving cream, and repeat the activity with the first letter of the name of a different community helper.

Letter Subtraction

Materials
- Community Helper Name Strips (pages 102–103)
- scissors
- counters
- alphabet cards

Preparation

Copy and cut apart the Community Helper Name Strips. Make enough copies so that each child receives one name.

Directions

Give each child one community helper's name and several counters. Mix up a set of alphabet cards, and choose one card. Show the card to children, and read aloud the letter. Tell children to place a counter over the letter if it appears in their helper's name. Play until each child has covered all of the letters in his or her helper's name.

Alphabet Rubbings

Materials
- Community Helper Tool Cards (pages 104–105)
- card stock
- scissors
- glue
- tape
- white paper
- unwrapped dark-colored crayons

Preparation

Copy the Community Helper Tool Cards on card stock, and cut apart the cards. Create a rubbing plate of each tool by tracing with a thick line of glue the outline of the tool and the letter it begins with, and then set each one aside to fully dry. Tape the rubbing plates to a table.

Directions

Demonstrate how rubbings are done by placing a piece of paper over a rubbing plate, securing the paper with tape to the table, and rubbing the side of a crayon over the paper. Give each child a piece of paper. Help children tape their paper over a rubbing plate. Invite children to use the sides of crayons to make their own rubbings.

Art Activities

 ## Special Delivery: Art

Materials
- envelopes
- construction paper
- markers, crayons, paint
- craft supplies (e.g., sequins, ribbon, glitter)
- glue
- postage stamps

Preparation

Write each child's address on an envelope.

Directions

Invite children to create their own original piece of art.
Tell them they will mail their art to their home. Give each
child his or her envelope and a stamp (or two). Ask older
children to "read" their address. Help children attach the
stamp to the correct place on the envelope. Help children
fold their artwork and place it inside their envelope. Walk
with children to put their mail in a mailbox.

 ## Recycled Collage

Materials
- Recycled Collage Bags (see Family Letter:
  Theme Introduction, page 71)
- poster board
- collage items
- glue

Preparation

Display the items from the recycled collage bags on a table. Add additional items if needed.

Directions

Divide the class into groups of two to four children. Give each group a poster board. Invite groups
to select items from the table to glue on their poster board to
make a collage.

 Brushing Teeth

Materials
- Tooth reproducible (page 106)
- yellow paper
- scissors
- white paint
- silver glitter
- pie tins
- inexpensive new toothbrushes (1 per child)

Preparation

Copy a class set of the Tooth reproducible on yellow paper. Cut apart each tooth. Mix white paint with a small amount of silver glitter in pie tins.

Directions

Discuss with children the importance of carefully brushing our teeth many times each day to help prevent problems. Give each child a toothbrush and a tooth cutout. Invite children to use their toothbrush to paint the tooth with the paint mixture.

Syringe Painting

Materials
- paint in assorted colors
- water
- bowls
- oral medication syringes (1 per child)
- paint smocks
- construction paper

Preparation

In separate bowls, thin out each color of paint with a small amount of water.

Directions

Show children a syringe, and ask them which community helper would use this tool. Give each child a paint smock, a sheet of construction paper, and a syringe. Invite children to put their syringe in the paint. Show them how to pull the plunger on the syringe to fill it with paint. Have children carefully squirt out paint on their paper. Invite them to repeat the process with the same color or different colors as desired to create their painting.

Work-Vehicle Painting

Materials
- toy police cars, trucks, trains, tractors, ambulances, and bulldozers with a variety of treads on the tires (1 per child)
- paint pads in assorted colors (see Art Recipes, page 414)
- construction paper

Preparation

Make paint pads in assorted colors

Directions

Show children the toy vehicles. Ask them which community helper uses each vehicle and how it is used. Give each child a sheet of construction paper. Invite children to choose a vehicle, roll the wheels of their vehicle across the paint pad, and then roll it across their paper to create tire tracks.

Variation

In advance, make a few painted tire track samples from treads that are the most different. Invite children to guess which vehicle made each set of tracks.

Cooking Activities

Firefighter Smoothie

Ingredients
- 1 cup (237 mL) strawberries
- 1½ cups (355 mL) milk
- tray of ice cubes

Other Supplies

- blender
- small plastic cups

Directions

Puree the strawberries and milk in a blender. Add ice and blend until smooth. Pour into cups, and serve immediately.

Apple Smiles

Directions

Wash and slice unpeeled apples into about eight slices. Give each child two apple slices and a craft stick. Invite children to use the craft stick to spread peanut butter on one side of each apple slice. (**Note**: Be mindful of any children with peanut allergies.) On one of the apple slices, have children add miniature marshmallows on top of the peanut butter to create "teeth." Show children how to put the second slice (with the peel facing the same direction as the other slice) on top of the teeth with the peanut-butter side down to make "lips."

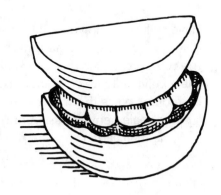

Graham Cracker Fire Truck

I n g r e d i e n t s
- graham crackers
- red frosting
- chocolate sandwich cookies
- black and red string licorice

Other Supplies
- craft sticks

Directions

Give each child a graham cracker and a craft stick. Have children use the craft stick to spread frosting on their cracker. Split sandwich cookies apart, and have children attach the two cookie halves to their graham cracker to make "wheels." Show children how to create a "ladder" with black licorice. Help children roll red licorice into a coil to make a "hose."

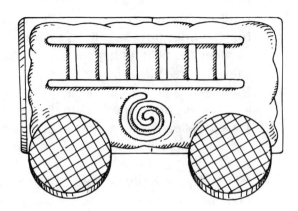

Classroom Delivery

Ingredients
- O-shaped cereal
- raisins
- banana chips
- miniature marshmallows
- pretzels

Other Supplies
- envelopes

Directions

Have children help you address envelopes for "classroom delivery" so each child has one. Hand out each envelope to the correct child (so that child will prepare the snack he or she receives). Invite children to count out five to ten of each ingredient, place them inside their envelope, and seal it. Collect the sealed envelopes. During snack time, have children become mail carriers and help you deliver the "mail."

Gavin
Preschool Rm. 5
Salt Lake City, UT

Fingerplays

Five Little Firefighters

(Fingerplay)

Five little firefighters sit very still, (*holding up five fingers*)
Until they see a fire on top of a hill. (*cupping hands around eyes*)
Number one rings the bell, ding-dong. (*holding up one finger, pretending to ring a bell*)
Number two pulls his big boots on. (*holding up two fingers, pretending to put on boots*)
Number three jumps on the fire engine red. (*holding up three fingers, jumping in place*)
Number four puts a red fire hat on his head. (*holding up four fingers, pretending to put hat on head*)
Number five drives the truck to the fire. (*holding up five fingers, pretending to drive a truck*)
The big yellow flames go higher and higher. (*raising hands over head*)
"Whoo-oooo! Whoo-oooo!" hear the fire truck say, (*cupping hands around mouth*)
As all of the cars get out of the way.
"Shhhh!" goes the water from the fire hose spout, (*pretending to hold hose*)
And quicker than a wink the fire is out! (*winking*)

Five Strong Police Officers

(Fingerplay)

Five strong police officers standing by a store. (*holding up five fingers*)
One became a traffic cop and then there were four. (*holding up four fingers*)
Four strong police officers watching over me.
One took home a lost boy and then there were three. (*holding up three fingers*)
Three strong police officers dressed all in blue.
One stopped a speeding car and then there were two. (*holding up two fingers*)
Two strong police officers. See how fast they run!
One caught a bad man and then there was one. (*holding up one finger*)
One strong police officer saw some smoke one day.
He called the firefighter who put out the fire right away. (*pretending to use hose*)

If I Were . . .

(Fingerplay)

If I were a chef, (*pretending to put on cap and apron*)
What would I do? (*shrugging shoulders*)
Bake lots of yummy food (*rubbing tummy*)
For me and you. (*pointing to self and a friend*)

If I were a librarian, (*pretending to put away books*)
What would I do? (*shrugging shoulders*)
Help find books (*pretending to look for a book*)
That you want to read through.

If I were a crossing guard,
What would I do? (*shrugging shoulders*)
Help you cross the street (*pretending to stop traffic*)
And make it safe for you.

If I were a plumber,
What would I do? (*shrugging shoulders*)
Check all your pipes (*cupping hands around eyes*)
So water will go through.

If I were a coach,
What would I do? (*shrugging shoulders*)
Help you win your game (*pretending to cheer team*)
And smile at you, too. (*smiling*)

Firefighters

(Fingerplay)

Five little firefighters (*holding up five fingers*)
Sleeping in a row. (*resting cheek on hands, closing eyes*)
"Ring" goes the bell— (*pretending to ring bell*)
Down the pole they go. (*pretending to go down pole*)
They jump on the engine (*jumping up*)
And put out the fire. (*pretending to squirt with hose*)
Now they're back home.
My but they're tired! (*stretching and yawning*)

Songs and Poems

Did You Ever See a Firefighter?

(Sung to the tune of "Did You Ever See a Lassie?")

Did you ever see a firefighter, a firefighter, a firefighter?
Did you ever see a firefighter slide down the pole?
Slide this way and that way, and this way and that way.
Did you ever see a firefighter slide down the pole?

Additional verses:
Ride on the truck
Hook up the hose
Put out the fire
Go back to the station

🎵 Did You Ever See a . . . ?

(Sung to the tune of "Did You Ever See a Lassie?")

Did you ever see a builder, a builder, a builder?
Did you ever see a builder saw this way and that?
Saw this way and that way, and this way and that way.
Did you ever see a builder saw this way and that?

Additional verses:
painter ... brush
farmer ... plow
teacher ... read
baker ... toss pizza

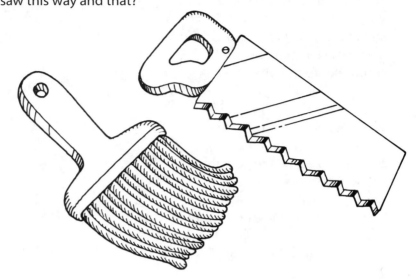

🎵 Construction Worker

(Sung to the tune of "Here We Go Round the Mulberry Bush")

This is the way we saw our wood,
Saw our wood, saw our wood.
This is the way we saw our wood,
So early in the morning.

Additional verses:
This is the way we ...
pound the nails
drill a hole
paint the walls
twist the screw
stack the bricks

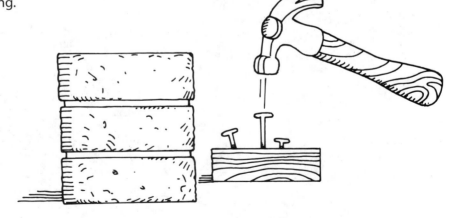

🎵 Our Community Helpers

(Sung to the tune of "Row, Row, Row Your Boat")

Some people bring us food
And drinks fresh and cold.
Some people work in stores
Where many things are sold.

Some people bring us letters
And take more mail away.
Some people stop the traffic
To help us on our way.

Some people take the food
And put it in a van.
Some people take the garbage
And empty every can.

*Invite children to name other community helpers
and identify what they do. Use their responses to
create new verses for the song.*

🎵 The Baker Man

(Poem)

The baker man's truck comes down the street
Filled with everything good to eat.
Two doors the baker man opens wide.
Now, let us look at the shelves inside.
What do you see? What do you see?
Doughnuts and cookies for you and me.
Cinnamon rolls, and pies, and bread, too.
What will he sell to me and you?

🎵 Helpers in Our Community

(Poem)

The helpers in our community help us every day.
Mail carriers bring letters and take some more away.

Construction workers build, and dentists help us smile.
Grocers fill the grocery store, aisle after aisle.

Police keep us safe and tell us when to stop.
Firefighters put out fires, even on rooftops.

Doctors and nurses work hard to do their part.
Teachers and librarians help make us smart.

When you grow up, you can be one, too!
Which community helper's job would you like to do?

Community Helpers

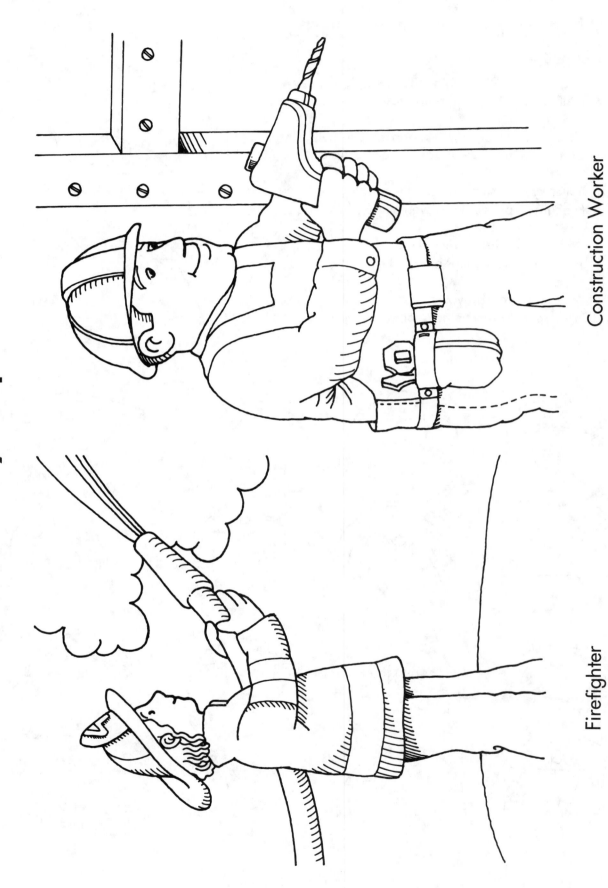

Construction Worker

Firefighter

Mail Carrier

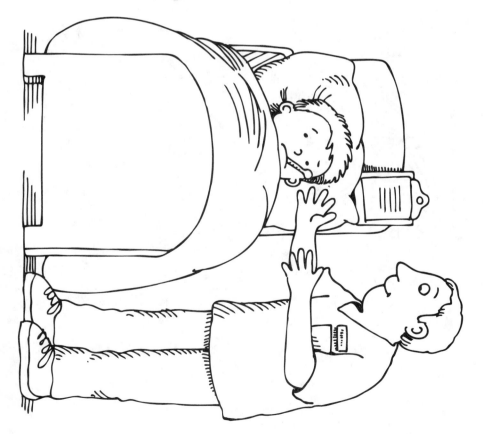

Nurse

Community Helpers

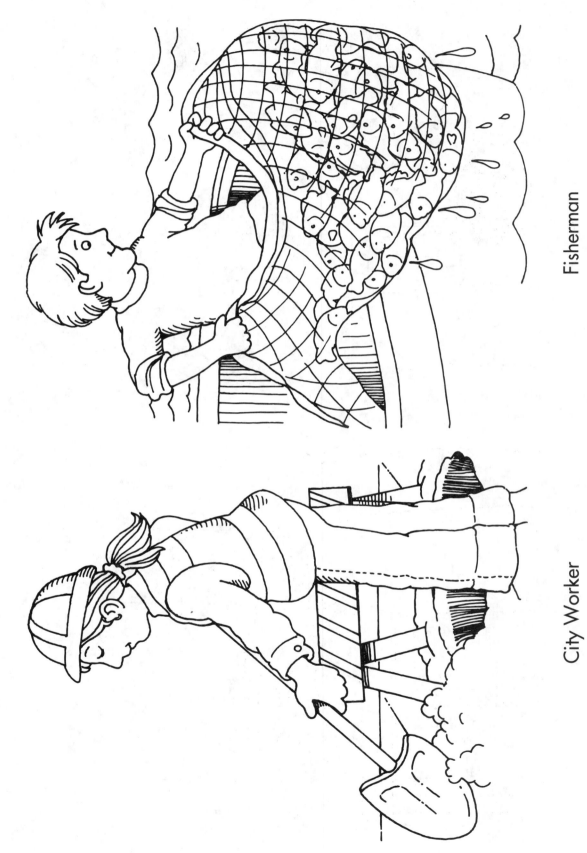

Fisherman

City Worker

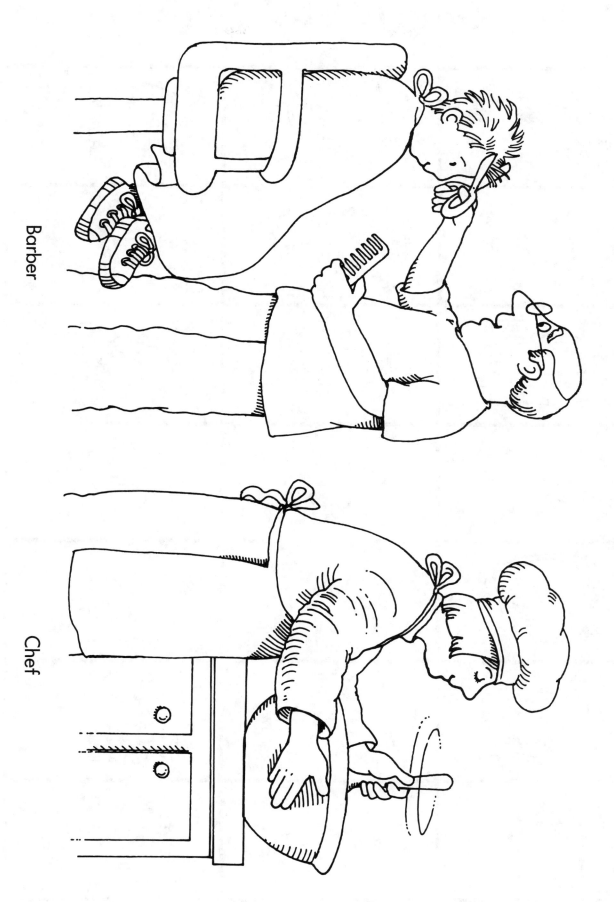

Barber

Chef

Community Helpers

Grocery Store Cards

Year-Round Early Childhood Themes © 2006 Creative Teaching Press

Fire Ladder Cards

Walk along one rail of the ladder.	Step between the rungs.
Walk backward between the rungs.	Jump over the rungs.
Walk with one foot on each rail.	Crawl from one rung to the next.
Step on top of the rungs.	Jump on top of the rungs.

Community Helper Name Strips

Doctor

Nurse

Dentist

Mail Carrier

Barber

Librarian

Painter

Community Helper Name Strips

Plumber

Chef

Grocer

Judge

Teacher

Police Officer

Coach

Community Helper Tool Cards

Community Helper Tool Cards

Tooth

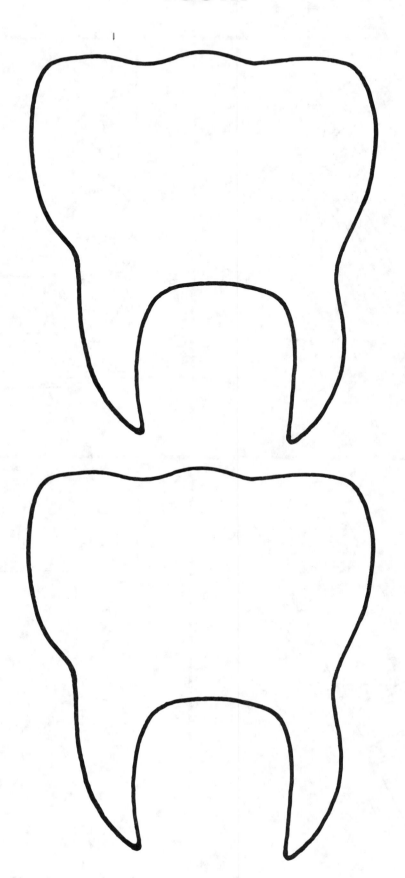

Year-Round Early Childhood Themes © 2006 Creative Teaching Press

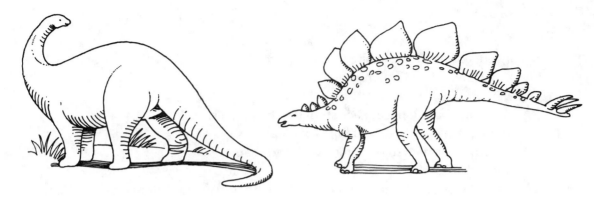

Dinosaurs

Concepts

The concepts covered in this unit include the following:

- Dinosaurs lived long, long ago.
- Dinosaurs are extinct.
- We learn about dinosaurs by studying their fossils.
- There were many different types of dinosaurs.
- Dinosaurs were many different sizes and shapes.
- Some dinosaurs ate plants and others ate meat.
- Some dinosaurs walked on two legs and others walked on four legs.
- Many dinosaurs laid eggs.
- Many dinosaurs attacked other dinosaurs.
- Many dinosaurs protected themselves by using their horns, plates, and spikes.
- We think dinosaurs had scaly skin like reptiles.

Vocabulary

carnivore—an animal that eats meat

extinct—describes an animal species that has died out and no longer exists

fossils—the remains or traces of a plant or an animal that have been preserved or imprinted

herbivore—an animal that eats plants

herd—a group of animals

paleontologist—a scientist who studies dinosaurs and prehistoric fossils

The dinosaurs discussed in this unit include the following:

- Allosaurus
- Apatosaurus
- Baryonyx
- Brachiosaurus
- Iguanodon
- Oviraptor
- Saltopus
- Stegosaurus
- Triceratops
- Tyrannosaurus rex
- Velociraptor

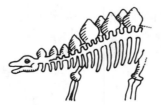

Date _____

Dear Family:

"Dinosaurs" will be the theme for our next unit. We will discuss several different dinosaurs, what they looked like, and what they ate.

Classroom Activities

Children will participate in the following activities:
- Singing songs about dinosaurs.
- Listening to and discussing the book *If Dinosaurs Came Back* by Bernard Most.
- Comparing the size of dinosaurs and dinosaur footprints.
- Creating their own dinosaur.
- Eating a "Dinosaur Diet."

Home Activities

Here are some activities for your family to try at home to complement what children are doing in the classroom:
- With your child, visit a local museum of natural history to see different exhibits about dinosaurs and other prehistoric animals.
- Create a dinosaur puppet by attaching various household items and scraps to a sock. Ask your child to tell you about the dinosaur, such as its name, what it eats, and where it lives. Children are welcome to bring their puppets to school to share.

Have fun as you explore all of the dynamic Dinosaur activities with your child.

Thank you for all you do!

Sincerely,

Dear Family:

We will use the following items during our Dinosaurs unit. We would appreciate any help you could give us. We will begin this unit on _____, so please sign and return the form below if you can donate items by _____.

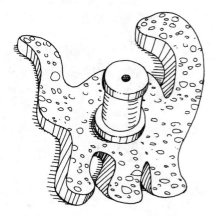

- newspaper
- shells
- shoelaces
- yarn
- plastic Easter eggs (the kind that open)
- unopened jar of peanut butter
- unopened bag of chocolate chips or candy corn
- new sponges (preferably dinosaur shapes)
- empty thread spools
- roll of white paper towels
- variety of pasta—macaroni, rotini, fettuccine, bowtie

Thanks!

• •

I would like to contribute the following items for this unit:

_____

Please contact me at _____ (phone number or e-mail) to let me know how I can help.

_____
(parent's name)

Center Ideas

The following are suggestions for different Dinosaur centers. The activities provided in this unit can be used or modified for these centers:

- **Art Center**—dinosaur cutouts for easel painting, dinosaur templates and rubbing plates, play dough (see Art Recipes, page 409), dinosaur cookie cutters

- **Block and Building Center**—plastic dinosaurs of varying sizes and types, fossil replicas, rocks, and strong glue to create prehistoric scenes (e.g., cave, mountains)

- **Dramatic Play Center**—stuffed dinosaurs, dinosaur puppets, crepe paper (for dinosaur tails)

- **Listening Center**—tapes of dinosaur stories, tapes and copies of stories written in class

- **Manipulatives Center**—dinosaur counters, dinosaur puzzles

- **Math and Science Center**—dinosaur counters and small rocks, scales, fossil replicas, magnifying glass

- **Reading Center**—dinosaur picture books (see recommended read-alouds, page 112), flannel board with flannel-piece characters from stories, puzzles, and copies of stories written in class

- **Sand and Water Tables**—plastic dinosaurs, rocks, fossils, Styrofoam dinosaur "bones"

- **Writing Center**—dinosaur stickers and stamps, dinosaur-shaped paper

Language Development

Recommended Read-Alouds

Bones, Bones, Dinosaur Bones by Byron Barton (HarperCollins)

Can I Have a Stegosaurus, Mom? Can I? Please!? by Lois G. Grambling (BridgeWater Books)

Dinosaur Stomp: A Monster Pop-Up by Paul Stickland (Dutton Children's Books)

Harry and the Bucketful of Dinosaurs by Ian Whybrow (Random House Books)

How Do Dinosaurs Say Good Night? by Jane Yolen (The Blue Sky Press)

If Dinosaurs Came Back by Bernard Most (Harcourt)

Patrick's Dinosaurs by Carol Carrick (Clarion Books)

Saturday Night at the Dinosaur Stomp by Carol Diggory Shields (Candlewick Press)

Ten Terrible Dinosaurs by Paul Stickland (Dutton Children's Books)

What Happened to Patrick's Dinosaurs? by Carol Carrick (Clarion Books)

Read-Aloud Activity

Read aloud a book. Have children discuss their ideas, thoughts, and feelings about the book. Record children's comments on chart paper. Have children draw pictures that represent the book and their reaction to it. Write each child's dictation below his or her picture. Use the pictures to make a class book or mural.

Discussion Starters

Use these suggestions to promote discussions about a read-aloud or to motivate children to tell a story. These ideas can be discussed and then used to write group stories for children to illustrate.

1. Ask children to complete the sentence *If I had a dinosaur, I would ....*

2. Invite children to share their response to *If you could go back to dinosaur times and you met a dinosaur, what would you do? What do you wish you could say to a dinosaur?*

3. Share the following story and ask children to finish it:
   Mom, Dad, and I went out to eat dinner. On the way back to the car, we walked past the museum. We were surprised to hear loud rock music coming from inside. "Sounds like a party," said Dad. "Let's go see." So we listened very carefully and followed the sound to the dinosaur room. To our surprise, the dinosaur skeletons were having a party. They were dancing! I didn't know they could dance! I decided I should ....

4. Invite children to add what they think happened next:
   Early one morning, I was surprised to hear a loud knock at the door. I ran down to see who was there. Who do you think it was? I opened the door and saw a Stegosaurus smiling at me. Well, the first thing I did was ....

Math Activities

 ## Dinosaur Addition and Subtraction

Skills: number sense, predicting, counting

Materials   • dinosaur counters (3 to 5 per child)

Preparation

Directions

Give each child the same number of dinosaur counters. Ask children questions such as *How many dinosaurs will you have if you take away two? How many will you have if you add one?* Have children predict what will happen with each question, and then perform the action and count their counters.

Measuring Bones and Fossils

Skills: nonstandard measurement, comparing

M a t e r i a l s
- Dinosaur Bones and Fossils reproducible (page 135) or replicas of dinosaur artifacts
- card stock
- scissors
- linking cubes

Preparation

Set out the artifact replicas on a table or make enlarged copies of the Dinosaur Bones and Fossils reproducible on card stock. Cut out each object. Place the objects on a table with linking cubes.

Directions

Invite children to line up linking cubes beside one of the objects and count how many linking cubes it takes to cover the length of the object. Encourage children to use the terms *shorter*, *longer*, and *the same* to compare the length of different objects.

Favorite Dinosaurs

Skills: data collection and display, counting

M a t e r i a l s
- Dinosaur Cutouts (pages 136–140) or pictures of dinosaurs
- chart paper
- markers

Preparation

Copy a set of Dinosaur Cutouts, or collect other pictures of dinosaurs for use in this activity. List on chart paper the names of all the dinosaurs children will explore in this activity.

Directions

Invite children to look at the dinosaur pictures and discuss the dinosaurs' similarities and differences. Ask children to name characteristics they like about the different dinosaurs. Ask each child which dinosaur is his or her favorite. Record responses on the chart paper. Help children count and discuss the results (e.g., *Which dinosaur had the most votes? The least votes?*).

23 How Big Was a Dinosaur?

Skills: measurement, data collection and display, counting

M a t e r i a l s
- Dinosaur Size Comparison reproducible (page 141)
- paper
- string (at least 142 feet or 43 m long)
- scissors
- tape

Preparation

Reserve the gymnasium or plan to take the class outside on a nice day. Write *Brachiosaurus*, *Tyrannosaurus rex*, and *Saltopus* on separate pieces of paper. Cut string according to the size of the three different dinosaurs (choose either length or height): Brachiosaurus—85 feet (26 m) long, 50 feet (15.25 m) tall; Tyrannosaurus rex—40 feet (12.2 m) long, 20 feet (6 m) tall; Saltopus—2 feet (61 cm) long, 1 foot (30.5 cm) tall.

Directions

Display the Dinosaur Size Comparison reproducible, and discuss with children the different-sized dinosaurs. Invite six children to come up to the front of the class, and have two children stretch out each piece of string to illustrate the size of each dinosaur. Tape each length of string to the floor, and label each string with the dinosaur's name. Have children compare the different lengths. For example, have children walk from end to end of each string. Ask questions such as *How many giant steps long are they? How many giant steps tall are they? Are they taller or shorter than you?* Invite children to lie down head to toe next to the strings that represent Brachiosaurus and Tyrannosaurus rex. Ask *How many children tall or long is the dinosaur?*

Dinosaur Footprint

Skills: counting, comparing, data collection and display

M a t e r i a l s
- scissors
- butcher paper
- construction paper

Preparation

Cut out of butcher paper an authentic-sized dinosaur footprint. A footprint of a large, carnivorous dinosaur, such as Tyrannosaurus rex, had three large toes and was about 28 inches (71 cm) wide and 33 inches (84 cm) long.

Directions

Trace each child's foot on construction paper, and cut out the footprints. Have children place their footprints on top of the paper dinosaur footprint. Ask *Did we fill the footprint?* (Trace and cut out more footprints if necessary, until the footprint is filled.) Help children count the number of footprints it took to fill the dinosaur's footprint.

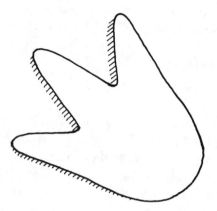

Dinosaur Reconstruction

Skills: number sense, spatial relationships

M a t e r i a l s
- Dinosaur Pair reproducible (page 142)
- card stock
- crayons
- scissors
- dice (1 per pair of children)

Preparation

Copy a class set of the Dinosaur Pair reproducible on card stock.

Directions

Give each child a copy of the reproducible, a crayon, and scissors. Assist children in cutting out both dinosaurs and then cutting apart only one of the dinosaurs into about six different pieces. Invite children to number their pieces. Divide the class into pairs, and give each pair a die. Show children how to set the intact dinosaur in front of them and set the dinosaur pieces faceup so they can see the numbers. Invite partners to take turns rolling the die. Have children count the number of dots on the die, find the body part of the dinosaur that matches the number rolled, and place that piece on the dinosaur in front of them. If a child has rolled the same number a second time, the other child takes his or her turn. Play continues until both children complete their dinosaur.

Sensory Activities

Feely Bag

Materials
- duplicate pairs of silky, furry, and scaly items
- pillowcase

Preparation

Gather pairs of items, and place one item from each pair inside a pillowcase. Display the matching items on a table. (Increase the number and variety of items as children's ability increases.)

Directions

Tell children that we believe dinosaurs had scaly skin like a crocodile or lizard. Invite one child at a time to reach into the pillowcase and touch one of the items. Have the child describe to the rest of the class what the object feels like and the size of it. Ask *Does it feel scaly like a dinosaur would have felt?* Have the child look at the items on the table and guess which object on the table he or she is touching. Invite the child to pull out the item to see if he or she is correct. Choose a different child to repeat the activity until each child has participated.

Dinosaur Artifact Hunt Sand Table

Materials
- Styrofoam
- scissors or a knife (teacher use only)
- sand table or tub of gravel or rice
- variety of plastic dinosaurs, shells, and other "dinosaur artifacts"
- spoons
- small shovels
- paintbrushes
- tweezers or tongs
- crayons or markers
- drawing paper

Preparation

Create "dinosaur bones" by cutting different bone shapes from Styrofoam. Prepare a sand table or a tub of gravel or rice with hidden dinosaur bones and other items (e.g., plastic dinosaurs, shells).

Directions

Explain to children that people who look for and study dinosaur bones and other artifacts are a special kind of scientist called *paleontologists*. Invite children to become paleontologists and use spoons, shovels, and paintbrushes to uncover "dinosaur artifacts." Have children carefully pull out their artifacts with tweezers or tongs. Encourage children to draw pictures of their findings.

 Dinosaur Land

M a t e r i a l s

- clay or play dough (see Art Recipes, page 409)
- small plastic dinosaurs
- twigs
- rocks
- large margarine lids or Styrofoam trays
- resealable plastic bags

Preparation

Gather enough items from the materials list so each child can have a few of each. Place a few items in a resealable plastic bag for each child.

Directions

Give each child a bag of items to explore. Invite children to use the contents of their bag to create their own "dinosaur land" using a margarine lid or meat tray as the base.

 Fossils

M a t e r i a l s

- clay or play dough (see Art Recipes, page 409)
- rolling pin
- variety of plastic dinosaurs
- shells
- leaves
- dinosaur cookie cutters (optional)
- variety of pasta (optional)

Preparation

Roll out clay or play dough on a table. Set out the other objects from the materials list.

Directions

Invite one child to pick an object while the other children are not looking. Have the child create a "fossil" by pressing the object into the clay or play dough and then set it back with the others. Have the other children study the shape of the fossil and guess which object was used to create it. Choose another child to continue the activity.

Variation

Have children use a cookie cutter to make a cutout of a dinosaur in the clay or play dough. Invite children to press different types of pasta into the cutout to create what looks like a "fossilized" dinosaur skeleton.

 # Clean Mud

Materials
- clean mud (see Art Recipes, page 415)
- water table or small tub
- variety of plastic dinosaurs
- rocks
- shells

Preparation

Make "clean mud" according to the directions on page 415, and place the mud in a water table or a tub. Hide plastic dinosaurs, rocks, and shells in the clean mud.

Directions

Give each child a small amount of the mud. Invite children to feel, explore, and experiment with the mud. Encourage children to gather around the water table or tub, close their eyes, and use only their hands to find the hidden objects. When a child finds an object, have him or her describe what it feels like. After children are finished exploring, invite them to build a dinosaur land with hills, mountains, volcanoes, rocks, and dinosaurs.

Motor Skills Activities

 # Dinosaur Egg Hunt

Materials
- plastic Easter eggs (the kind that open)
- small plastic dinosaurs

Preparation

Place a dinosaur inside each egg. Hide the eggs throughout the room.

Directions

Invite children to search for "dinosaur eggs." Encourage children who have found an egg to help someone who has not found one. After all of the eggs have been found, have children open their egg and share one thing they notice about the dinosaur.

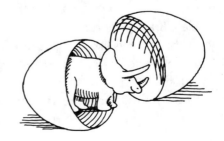

Dinosaur Sewing Cards

Materials
- Dinosaur Cutouts (pages 136–140)
- card stock
- scissors
- hole punch
- tape
- shoelaces
- crayons or markers

Preparation

Copy the Dinosaur Cutouts on card stock. Make enough copies so each child will have a dinosaur. Create sewing cards by cutting out the dinosaurs and punching holes around the edge of each cutout. Tape one end of a shoelace to each cutout.

Directions

Show children how to sew around a sewing card using a shoelace. Give each child a sewing card. Invite children to use the shoelace to sew through the holes. Then have children color their dinosaur.

Dinosaur Movements

Materials • none

Preparation

Reserve the gymnasium or plan to take the class outside on a nice day.

Directions

Invite children to perform the following actions:
- Walk with slow, giant steps and swing your long tail like an Apatosaurus.
- Run with fierceness like a Velociraptor.
- Show your large, pointed teeth like a Tyrannosaurus rex.
- Stretch your neck way, way up to eat the tops of trees like a Brachiosaurus.
- Wave your sharp claws like an Allosaurus.
- Run on two legs and then walk on four legs like an Iguanodon.
- Poke around with the three horns on your head and travel in a herd like a Triceratops.

Pin the Horn on the Triceratops

Materials
- Triceratops from the Dinosaur Cutouts (page 137)
- butcher paper
- construction paper
- scissors
- double-sided tape
- blindfold

Preparation

Draw on butcher paper a Triceratops without horns. Cut out of construction paper "Triceratops horns" (one per child), and label each horn with a different child's name. Place double-sided tape on the back of each horn. Copy the Triceratops from the reproducible.

Directions

As a class, discuss why Triceratops had horns. Relate the "tri" in *Triceratops* to "tri" in *tricycle*. Show children the Triceratops reproducible so they can see where the three horns belong. Display the butcher paper Triceratops on a wall at children's height. Blindfold a child, and have him or her try to place a horn on the Triceratops' head. Repeat the activity with the remaining children.

Dinosaur Path Obstacle Course

Materials
- obstacle course equipment (e.g., wood crates, balance beams, hula hoops)
- large plastic or stuffed dinosaur

Preparation

Create an obstacle course, and place a large plastic or stuffed dinosaur at the end of the "dinosaur path."

Directions

Invite children to follow the dinosaur path. Encourage them to move like a dinosaur (e.g., walk on all fours like a Triceratops, walk on two legs like Tyrannosaurus rex).

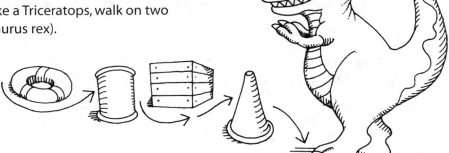

Tyrannosaurus Toss

Materials
- large cardboard box
- markers
- scissors
- beanbag

Preparation

Draw on a cardboard box a Tyrannosaurus rex head with lots of sharp teeth in a big, wide-open mouth. Cut out the mouth, so a beanbag can be tossed through it.

Directions

Have children guess the type of dinosaur the drawing represents. Point out the sharp teeth, and have children guess what a Tyrannosaurus rex might have eaten. Tell children that in this activity the beanbag will be the Tyrannosaurus rex's food. Invite them to throw the beanbag into the dinosaur's mouth to "feed" it.

Alphabet Activities

 # Dinosaur Name Match

Materials
- Dinosaur Name Strips (page 143)
- scissors
- resealable plastic bags

Preparation

Make enough copies of the Dinosaur Name Strips so each child has two copies of one dinosaur's name. Cut apart the letters on one of the matching name strips for each child. Place one intact name strip and the matching letters in a resealable bag for each child.

Directions

Give each child a bag with a dinosaur's name strip and letters. Ask children to match the individual letters to the letters on the strip to create the dinosaur's name.

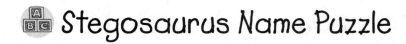 Stegosaurus Name Puzzle

Materials
- Stegosaurus Body reproducible (page 144)
- Stegosaurus Plates reproducible (page 145)
- card stock
- scissors
- glue

Preparation

Copy a class set of the Stegosaurus Body reproducible on card stock. Make multiple copies of the Stegosaurus Plates reproducible on card stock. Label each body with a child's name. Label the plates with the letters needed to make each child's name. Place the plates on a table so the letters are visible. Depending on the ability of the children, you may want to outline the correct number of plates needed to make each child's name or place the plates for only a few children's names at a table.

Directions

Give each child a Stegosaurus body with his or her name printed on it. Ask children if they know why the Stegosaurus had plates on its back and tail. Invite each child to find the lettered plates needed to make his or her name. Have children glue the plates on their dinosaur's back to spell their name.

Dinosaur Alphabet Puzzles

Materials
- Dinosaur Cutouts (pages 136–140)
- scissors
- tape

Preparation

Copy enough Dinosaur Cutouts so there is one for each letter of the alphabet you wish to use. Create "alphabet puzzles" by labeling each dinosaur with a different letter in both uppercase and lowercase. Cut each copy in half between the uppercase and lowercase letter. Use unique puzzle-cuts so there is only one match. Place the alphabet puzzles faceup on a table.

Directions

Invite children to take turns finding matching pairs of letters until all the puzzles have been completed. Have them tape the matching pieces together. Invite children to share what they know about dinosaurs, and provide a few facts (e.g., dinosaurs lived long, long ago and are now extinct).

Dinosaur Letter Subtraction

Materials
- Dinosaur Name Strips (page 143)
- scissors
- counters
- large alphabet cards

Preparation

Copy enough Dinosaur Name Strips so each child has one name. Cut apart the strips.

Directions

Give each child a dinosaur name strip and a handful of counters. Select an alphabet card, display the card, and say the name of the letter. If a child has that letter on his or her dinosaur name strip, the child places a counter over that letter. Continue until children cover all of the letters on their strip.

Art Activities

Stuffed Dinosaur

Materials
- butcher paper
- scissors
- brown and green paint
- paint trays
- paintbrushes
- stapler
- newspaper

Preparation

Cut out from butcher paper two large identical dinosaur outlines. Pour brown and green paint into separate trays.

Directions

Invite children to paint the opposite sides of the dinosaur outlines. Line up the dinosaur outlines, and staple them together around the perimeter until there is only a small opening left. Have children stuff the "dinosaur" with crumpled newspaper. Staple the dinosaur shut. Invite children to give the dinosaur a name and tell about how it lived.

Sponge-Stamped Dinosaurs and Footprints

Materials
- sponge shapes (e.g., dinosaurs, dinosaur footprints)
- empty thread spools
- glue gun (teacher use only)
- paint (assorted colors)
- paint trays
- construction paper
- crayons or markers

Preparation

Glue an empty spool to the top of each sponge to make "sponge stamps." You may have to cut out your own shapes from sponges if you cannot find commercial-made dinosaur shapes. Pour different colors of paint into separate trays.

Directions

Give each child a piece of construction paper. Encourage children to color in a dinosaur landscape. Have children hold a sponge stamp by the spool and dip the sponge in paint. Invite them to print stamps on their construction paper.

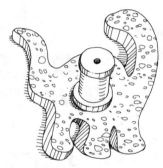

 # Dinosaur Mural

Materials
- Dinosaur Cutouts (pages 136–140)
- scissors
- construction paper (assorted colors)
- white butcher paper
- tape
- paint
- paint trays
- paintbrushes
- book about dinosaurs (see recommended read-alouds, page 112)
- glue

Preparation

Make several copies of the Dinosaur Cutouts (enlarged or reduced, as needed), and cut them out. Cut out trees, plants, fish, and other prehistoric objects from construction paper. Draw an outline of sky, land, lake, and other natural scenery on a large piece of butcher paper. Tape the butcher paper to the floor, and pour different colors of paint into separate trays.

Directions

Invite children to paint the scenery on the butcher paper. Read a dinosaur book to children as the mural dries. Have children glue on a variety of dinosaur cutouts, trees, plants, fish, and other natural scenery.

Paper-Towel Dinosaurs

Materials
- Dinosaur Cutouts (pages 136–140)
- white paper towels
- scissors
- paint or food coloring
- bowls
- water
- eyedroppers (1 per child)

Preparation

Use the Dinosaur Cutouts as templates to cut paper towels into dinosaur shapes. Pour different colors of paint into separate bowls, and thin the paint out with water. If you are using food coloring, add a few drops into a bowl and then add water.

Directions

Give each child a paper-towel "dinosaur" and an eyedropper. Have children use the eyedropper to drop paint or colored water onto their paper towel. They will see the colors run together and make new colors.

 # Dinosaur Bones and Teeth

Materials
- modeling goop (see Art Recipes, page 415)
- large container with lid
- yarn
- scissors
- knitting needle

Preparation

Make "modeling goop" in advance, and store it in a sealed container prior to use. Cut yarn into necklace-length pieces.

Directions

Give each child some modeling goop and some time to explore it. Invite children to create dinosaur "bones" and "teeth" from their modeling goop. Before the modeling goop dries, use a knitting needle to make a hole in each bone and tooth. Set them aside to dry. (This may take a few days.) Once the bones and teeth are dry, string yarn through each hole to make a necklace. Save the remaining teeth and bones for a dinosaur hunt on the playground or in a sand table.

Create-a-Dinosaur

Materials
- Dinosaur Cutouts (pages 136–140)
- scissors
- construction paper
- glue

Preparation

Make several copies of each cutout, and cut each one into separate body parts (e.g., head, legs, arms, body, neck, tail, spikes, plates). Scatter the parts on a table.

Directions

Give each child a piece of construction paper and glue. Invite children to pick the body parts they want to use to create their own dinosaur. Encourage children to arrange the parts into a dinosaur and glue the parts on their construction paper. Invite children to name their dinosaur and describe where and how it lives. Write children's ideas above their dinosaur.

Dinosaur Rubbings

Materials
- commercial or teacher-made dinosaur-related rubbing plates
- card stock
- glue
- tape
- white paper
- unwrapped crayons

Preparation

To make rubbing plates, copy the Dinosaur Cutouts (pages 136–140) on card stock. Use glue to trace the lines on the dinosaurs. Allow the glue to dry completely. Tape the rubbing plates to a table, and set out unwrapped crayons.

Directions

Demonstrate for children how rubbings are done. Give each child a piece of paper. Help children tape it over a rubbing plate. Invite children to use the sides of the crayons to make rubbings.

Cooking Activities

Dinosaur Eggs

Ingredients

- 3 tablespoons (45 mL) margarine
- 1 package (10 oz) marshmallows
  or 4 cups (0.95 L) miniature marshmallows
- 6 cups (1.5 L) crispy rice cereal

Other Supplies

- saucepan
- mixing spoon
- small paper plates

Directions

Melt margarine over low heat. Add marshmallows, and stir until melted. Remove from heat, and stir in cereal. Once the mixture is cool enough to handle, give each child a spoonful on a paper plate to shape into an egg. Invite children to make "dinosaur eggs." Tell children that the shape of dinosaur eggs can be round or oval.

Stegosaurus Tail

Ingredients

- bananas
- peanut butter
- candy corn or chocolate chips

Other Supplies

- kitchen knife (teacher use only)
- paper plates
- craft sticks
- spoon

Directions

Cut bananas in half lengthwise. Give each child a plate with a half of a banana (the tail) flat side down, a craft stick, a spoonful of peanut butter, and several pieces of candy corn or chocolate chips. (**Note**: Be mindful of any children with peanut allergies.) Have children use their craft stick to spread peanut butter over the banana half. Invite children to add to the "tail" four to eight pieces of candy corn or chocolate chips for "spikes."

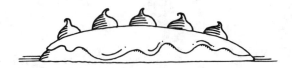

Dinosaur Diets

Ingredients

- shredded lettuce
- celery sticks
- ranch dressing (optional vegetable dip)
- goldfish crackers
- tuna mixed with mayonnaise
- slices of bologna cut into dinosaur shapes
- rock candy
- candy eggs

Other Supplies

- Dinosaur Cutouts: Tyrannosaurus rex and Stegosaurus (page 136), Apatosaurus (page 138), Baryonyx and Oviraptor (page 140)
- card stock

Preparation

Copy each reproducible dinosaur on the bottom half of a piece of card stock. Make "tent cards" by folding each piece in half. Use the questions and answers below to draw a picture on the inside of each tent card to show the food the dinosaur would eat. Place tent cards in a center for children to become familiar with.

Directions

After children familiarize themselves with the dinosaurs and their diets, set out the food items from the materials list and let children help themselves. While children are eating, discuss which dinosaur might eat which food and why. Show the picture of each dinosaur as children discuss these questions:

Q. If you were an Apatosaurus, which food would you eat and why?

   A. Lettuce—because an Apatosaurus was an herbivore (plant eater) with blunt, pencil-like teeth and ate soft-leaved plants (conifers, mosses, horsetails, ferns).

   A. Rock candy—because it swallowed stones to help grind up the plants it ate.

Q. If you were a Stegosaurus, which food would you eat and why?

   A. Celery—because Stegosaurus was an herbivore (plant eater) with a toothless beak and small, rounded teeth. It could eat bushes.

Q. If you were a Baryonyx, which food would you eat and why?

   A. Goldfish crackers and tuna—because Baryonyx was a carnivore (meat eater) that ate fish.

Q. If you were a Tyrannosaurus rex, which food would you eat and why?

   A. Bologna—because Tyrannosaurus rex was a carnivore (meat eater) and ate other dinosaurs, like Triceratops.

Q. If you were an Oviraptor, which food would you eat and why?

   A. Candy eggs—because an Oviraptor's name means "egg stealer."

Some dinosaurs ate fish.

 Dinosaur Sculpture

Ingredients

- 4 cups (0.95 L) peanut butter
- 1 cup (237 mL) dry milk
- ¾ cup (177 mL) honey
- disc-shaped cereal
- pretzel sticks
- raisins

Other Supplies

- large bowl
- mixing spoon
- waxed paper

Directions

Combine in a large bowl the peanut butter, dry milk, and honey to make a dough mixture. (**Note:** Be mindful of any children with peanut allergies.) Give each child a ball of dough on waxed paper. Invite children to shape their dough into a dinosaur. Have them use disc-shaped cereal for plates, pretzels for spikes, and raisins for eyes.

Fingerplays and Flannel Board Activities

 Daring Dinosaurs

(Fingerplay)

Five daring dinosaurs cleaning up the floor, (*holding up five fingers*)
One was swept away and then there were four. (*pretending to sweep*)
Four daring dinosaurs chased by a bee, (*holding up four fingers*)
One got stung and then there were three. (*pretending to get stung on arm*)
Three daring dinosaurs playing with some glue, (*holding up three fingers*)
One got stuck and then there were two. (*pretending that feet are stuck*)
Two daring dinosaurs out for a run, (*holding up two fingers*)
One fell down and then there was one. (*falling down*)
One daring dinosaur, acting like a hero, (*holding up one finger*)
Went to save the others, and then there were zero. (*putting hand behind back*)

Five Huge Dinosaurs

(Fingerplay)

Five huge dinosaurs, looking fierce and mean, (*holding up five fingers*)
The first one said, "I eat things that are green." (*holding up one finger*)
The second one said, "I hatched from an egg." (*holding up two fingers*)
The third one said, "I have big strong legs." (*holding up three fingers*)
The fourth one said, "I can run fast here and there." (*holding up four fingers*)
The fifth one said, "I give everyone a scare." (*holding up five fingers*)
THUMP, THUMP came Tyrannosaurus rex that day, (*patting hands on lap*)
And the five huge dinosaurs all ran away! (*placing five fingers behind back*)

Ten Huge Dinosaurs

(Flannel Board)

Create the following flannel board pieces: ten dinosaurs and a cave for all of the dinosaurs to sleep in.

Ten huge dinosaurs (*placing ten dinosaurs in the cave*)
Sleeping on the floor
Woke on up and started to roar.
"There's no room. No more, no more,
No more room on this cave floor!"
They tossed and turned and pushed galore,
Until one poor dinosaur was shoved out the door. (*removing one dinosaur*)

Continue in descending order until one dinosaur is left and then sing the final verse:

One huge dinosaur
Sleeping all alone on the floor
Woke up and started to roar.
"There is no one, no one, no one,
No one else on this cave floor!"
He tossed and turned and stretched out galore,
Until he rolled right out the door.

Fred the Dinosaur

(Flannel Board)

Create the following flannel board pieces: one large oval (body), four small rectangles (legs), one medium-sized triangle (tail), one medium-sized rectangle (neck), one small oval (head), a smile, and an eye to fit on the small oval.

First, take an oval that looks like an egg. (*placing large oval body on board*)
Then add four small rectangles— (*placing four small rectangle legs on board*)
Each one is a leg. (*pointing to each leg*)
Now for a tail, a triangle. (*placing medium-sized triangle tail on board*)
Not a little speck.
Take a larger rectangle. (*placing medium-sized rectangle neck on board*)
It'll make a sturdy neck.
Now an oval. It's his tiny head. (*placing small oval head on board*)
A smile for a mouth. A dot for an eye— (*adding smile and eye to small oval head*)
It's our dinosaur named Fred!

Songs and Poems

All Around the Swamp

(Sung to the tune of "The Wheels on the Bus")

The Tyrannosaurus rex went, "Grr, grr, grr,
Grr, grr, grr, grr, grr, grr."
The Tyrannosaurus rex went, "Grr, grr, grr,"
All around the swamp.

Additional verses:
Apatosaurus . . . munch, munch, munch
Stegosaurus' tail . . . spike, spike, spike
Triceratops' horns . . . poke, poke, poke

Grrrrr

♫♪ Do You Know . . . ?

(Sung to the tune of "The Muffin Man")

Oh, do you know the Stegosaurus,
The Stegosaurus, the Stegosaurus?
Oh, do you know the Stegosaurus?
He has plates upon his back.

Additional verses:
Apatosaurus . . . He has a very long neck.
Tyrannosaurus rex . . . He is very fierce.
Triceratops . . . He has three sharp horns.

♫♪ Colorful Dinosaurs

(Sung to the tune of "Ten Little Indians")

One red, one blue, one green dinosaur.
One yellow, one orange, one white dinosaur.
One pink, one purple, one black dinosaur.
Nine dinosaurs in all.

♫♪ Herbivore Dinosaurs

(Sung to the tune of "Row, Row, Row Your Boat")

Dinosaurs, dinosaurs
Eating fruits and weeds.
Take a bite and chew it well,
And then spit out the seeds.

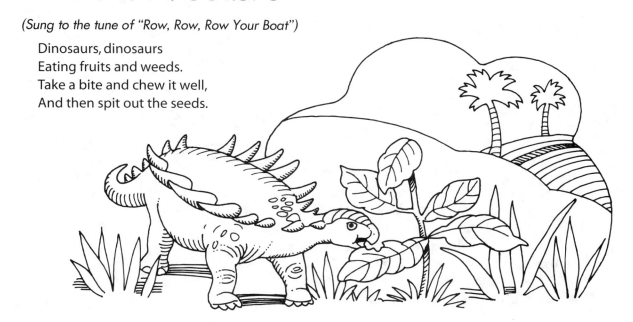

♫ Dinosaurs Went Out To Play

(Sung to the tune of "Five Little Ducks")

One dinosaur went out to play, (*holding up one finger*)
On a bright and sunny day.
He had such enormous fun,
That he called another dinosaur to come.
DI-NO-SAUR! (*calling loudly*)
Thump! Thump! Thump! Thump! (*patting hands on lap*)

Continue in ascending order until you reach five and then sing the final verse:

Five dinosaurs went out to play, (*holding up five fingers*)
On a bright and sunny day.
They had such enormous fun,
That they called another dinosaur to come.
DI-NO-SAUR! (*calling loudly*)
But they heard no thumps!
Instead they heard their mother,
And she was calling, "DINNER!!!"
And they all went home for dinner!
　　　(*thumping hands very fast*)

♫ Dinosaurs

(Poem)

Seven dinosaurs were causing quite a scene—
Stegosaurus said, "I eat things green."
T. rex said, "You can have a head start."
Velociraptor said, "I am very smart."
Triceratops said, "I hatched from an egg."
Apatosaurus said, "I have four strong legs."
Brachiosaurus said, "I eat the tops of trees."
Allosaurus said, "Can I eat you, please?"

Dinosaur Bones and Fossils

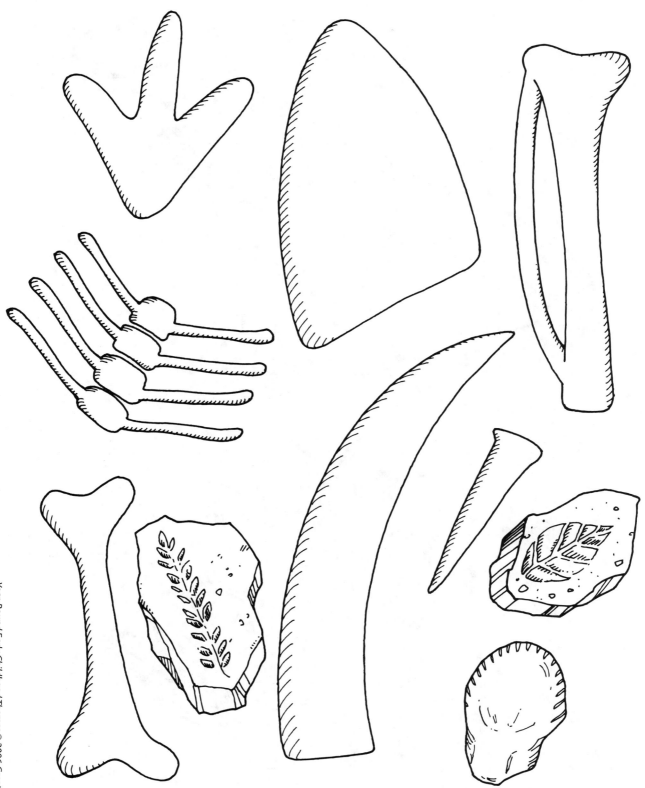

Dinosaur Cutouts

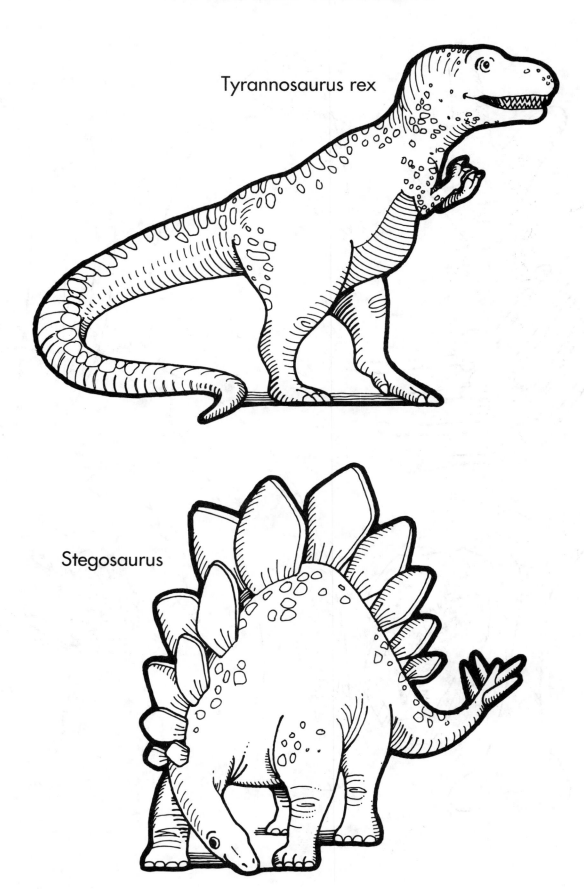

Tyrannosaurus rex

Stegosaurus

Dinosaur Cutouts

Triceratops

Velociraptor

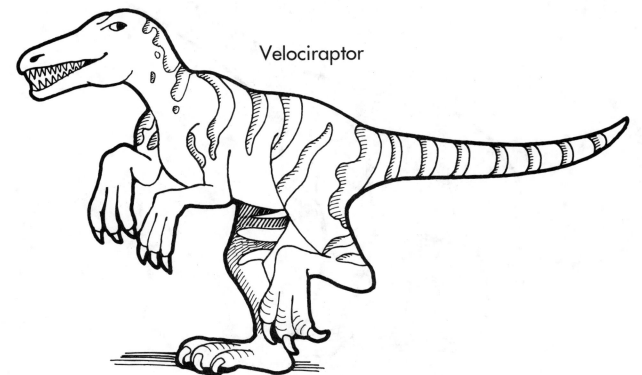

Dinosaur Cutouts

Brachiosaurus

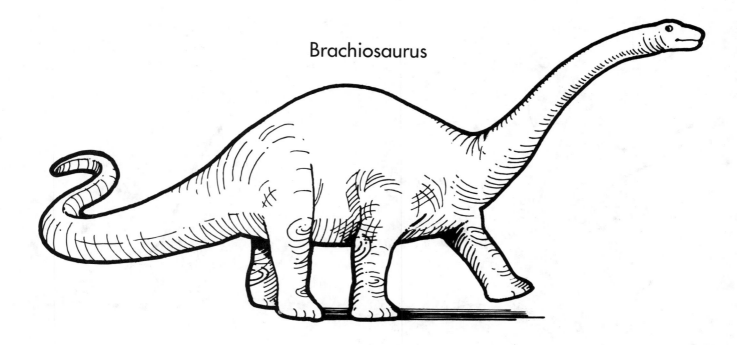

Apatosaurus

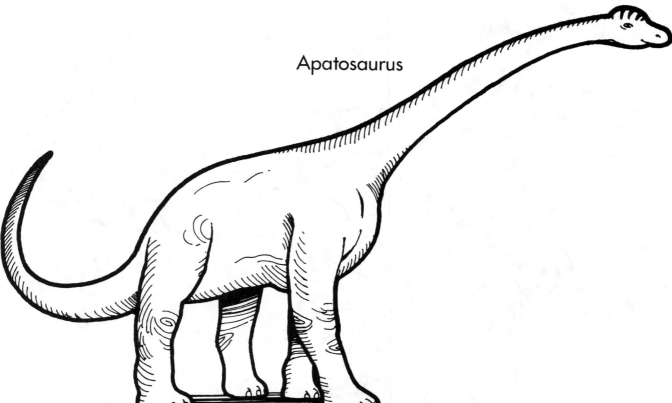

Dinosaur Cutouts

Iguanodon

Allosaurus

Dinosaur Cutouts

Baryonyx

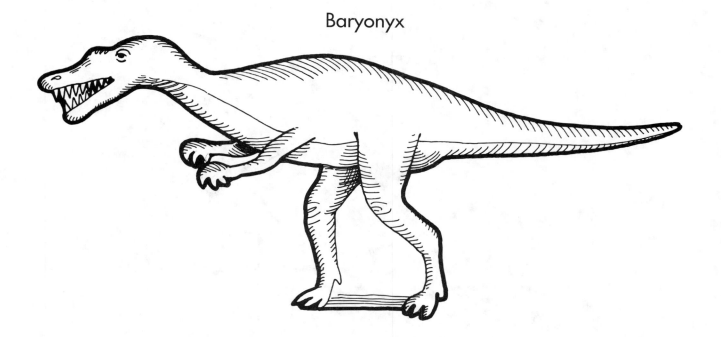

Oviraptor

Dinosaur Size Comparison

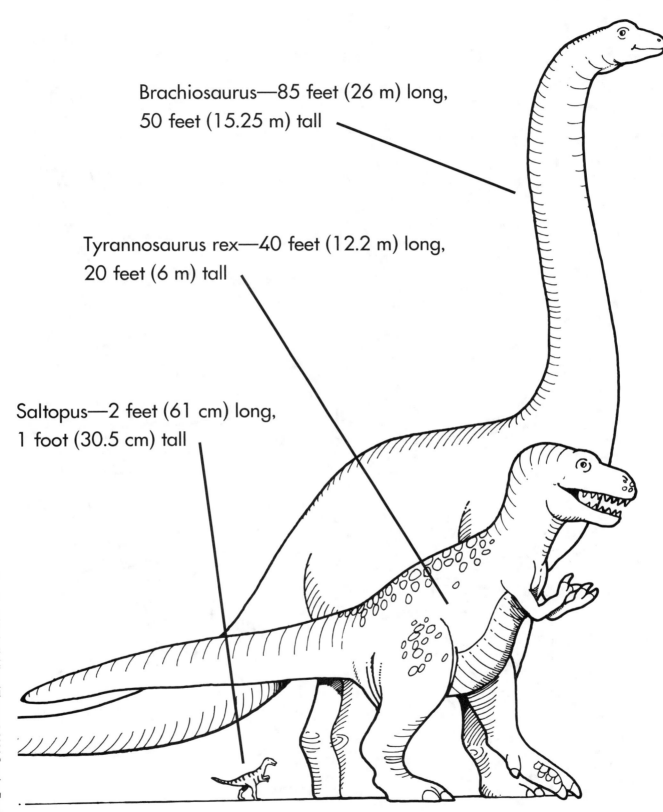

Brachiosaurus—85 feet (26 m) long,
50 feet (15.25 m) tall

Tyrannosaurus rex—40 feet (12.2 m) long,
20 feet (6 m) tall

Saltopus—2 feet (61 cm) long,
1 foot (30.5 cm) tall

Dinosaur Pair

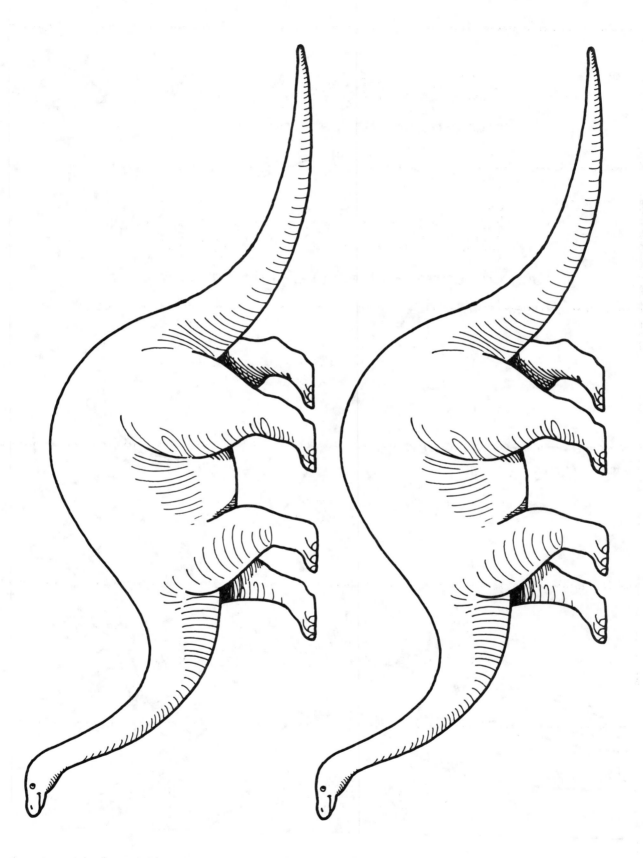

Year-Round Early Childhood Themes © 2006 Creative Teaching Press

Dinosaur Name Strips

Apatosaurus

Brachiosaurus

Oviraptor

Saltopus

Stegosaurus

Triceratops

Stegosaurus Body

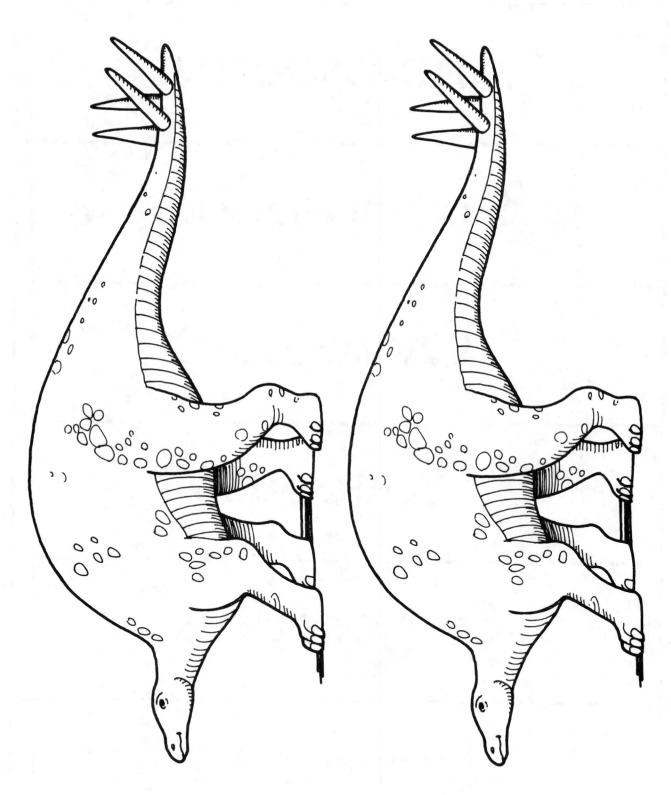

Stegosaurus Plates

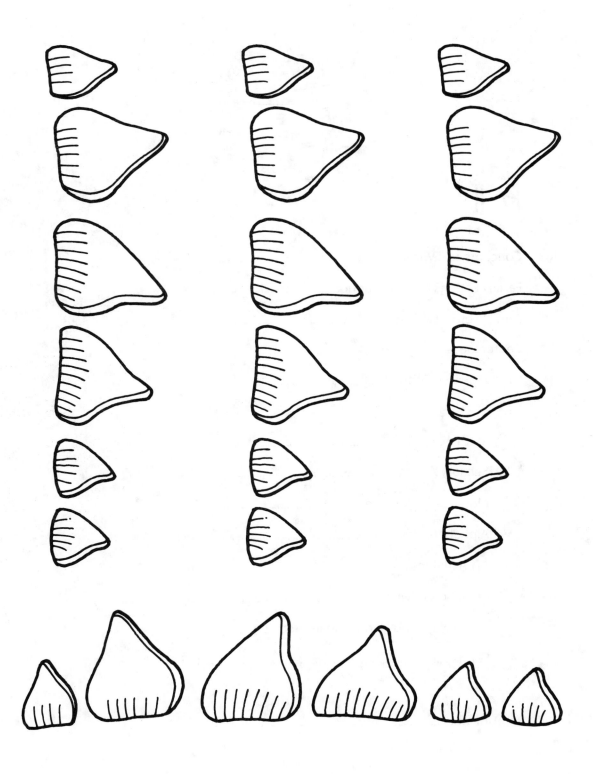

Fall

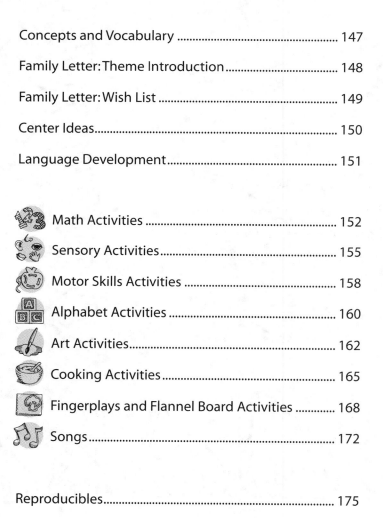

Concepts

The concepts covered in this unit include the following:
- *Fall* and *autumn* are two words for the same season.
- In fall, the leaves on some trees change colors and then fall off.
- Leaves come in many different shapes, sizes, and colors.
- The fall weather in some places is cooler than summer but warmer than winter.
- Some children start a new school year in the fall.
- Flower bulbs are planted in the fall.
- Apples are ready to harvest in the fall.
- Animals get ready for the winter during the fall.
- Some animals eat a lot in the fall so they can sleep all winter (i.e., hibernate).
- Some animals move to a warmer climate during fall (i.e., migrate).

Vocabulary

fall or **autumn**—both refer to the season between summer and winter

harvest—the gathering of a crop when it is ripe

hibernate—to spend part of the winter season sleeping

migrate—to move from one place to another for a season

season—one of four parts of a year characterized by certain weather conditions

Date _____

Dear Family:

The fall season is upon us and "Fall" will be the theme for our next unit. Fall is an exciting time of change, both in the classroom and in the world around us.

Classroom Activities

Children will participate in the following activities:
- Charting and comparing the colors and shapes of leaves.
- Cooking an apple pizza.
- Going on a fall nature walk.
- Listening to and discussing *The Apple Pie Tree* by Zoe Hall, as well as other books relating to the fall season.

Home Activities

Here are some activities for your family to try at home to complement what children are doing in the classroom:
- Take a fall walk in your neighborhood, a field, or the woods. Look for signs of fall. Collect fall items such as nuts, colored leaves, and seed pods. Have your child bring in the items to share with the class.
- Ask your child to talk about his or her favorite things related to fall (e.g., cooler weather, school starts, beautiful leaves, holidays).

Have fun as you explore all of the fabulous Fall activities with your child.

Thank you for all you do!

Sincerely,

Year-Round Early Childhood Themes © 2006 Creative Teaching Press

Dear Family:

We will use the following items during our Fall unit. We would appreciate any help you could give us. We will begin this unit on _____, so please sign and return the form below if you can donate items by _____.

- pie tins
- clean, empty squeeze bottles (like ketchup bottles)
- acorns, nuts, small pinecones, hard berries
- artificial leaves
- sheet protectors
- colorful O-shaped cereal
- brightly colored yarn
- birdseed
- tulip or daffodil bulbs
- shoelaces
- drinking straws
- any type of apples
- can of apple pie filling
- self-adhesive Velcro strips

Thanks!

• •

I would like to contribute the following items for this unit:

_____

Please contact me at _____ (phone number or e-mail)
to let me know how I can help.

_____
(parent's name)

Center Ideas

The following are suggestions for different Fall centers. The activities provided in this unit can be used or modified for these centers:

- **Art Center**—leaf- and pumpkin-shaped cookie cutters and sponges, chart paper cut into leaf and apple shapes

- **Block and Building Center**—nuts, seeds, pinecones, artificial fall leaves, toilet paper tubes to make trees

- **Dramatic Play Center**—light jackets and sweaters, small rakes, artificial fall leaves

- **Listening Center**—tapes of music that represents fall, tapes of stories written in class

- **Manipulatives Center**—fall puzzles and games

- **Math and Science Center**—seeds, pumpkins, Indian corn, scales, leaves, nuts, pinecones, magnifying glass, gourds

- **Reading Center**—fall books (see recommended read-alouds, page 151), books and stories written in class

- **Sand and Water Tables**—popcorn kernels, birdseed, shovels, pails, tweezers

- **Writing Center**—fall stickers and stamps (e.g., leaves, apples, acorns), fall stationery

Language Development

Recommended Read-Alouds

Animals in the Fall by Gail Saunders-Smith (Capstone Press)

The Apple Pie Tree by Zoe Hall (The Blue Sky Press)*

Apples and Pumpkins by Anne Rockwell (Simon & Schuster)

Apples, Apples by Kathleen Weidner Zoehfeld (HarperFestival)

Autumn: An Alphabet Acrostic by Steven Schnur (Clarion Books)

Autumn Is for Apples by Michelle Knudsen (Random House)

Autumn Leaves by Gail Saunders-Smith (Capstone Press)

Clifford's First Autumn by Norman Bridwell (Scholastic)

Every Autumn Comes the Bear by Jim Arnosky (Penguin Putnam)

How Do You Know It's Fall? by Allan Fowler (Children's Press)

In November by Cynthia Rylant (Harcourt)

In the Woods: Who's Been Here? by Lindsay Barrett George (Greenwillow Books)

Leaf Jumpers by Carole Gerber (Charlesbridge)

Nuts to You! by Lois Ehlert (Harcourt)*

Planting a Rainbow by Lois Ehlert (Harcourt)*

Red Leaf, Yellow Leaf by Lois Ehlert (Harcourt)

The Seasons of Arnold's Apple Tree by Gail Gibbons (Harcourt)

When Autumn Comes by Robert Maass (Henry Holt and Company)

Why Do Leaves Change Color? by Betsy Maestro (HarperTrophy)

*Read-alouds used in activities

Read-Aloud Activity

Before reading a book to children, lead them on a "picture walk." Invite children to look at the pictures and describe what they see. Write children's ideas (e.g., the leaves are pretty colors) on sticky notes, and attach each note to the corresponding page. Read aloud the book. Comment on the ideas you recorded for each page. Invite older children to draw a picture of their favorite part of the book. Bind together the pictures to make a class book.

Discussion Starters

Use these suggestions to promote discussions about a read-aloud or to motivate children to tell a story. These ideas can be discussed and then used to write group stories for children to illustrate.

1. Ask children *How can you tell it is fall? What do you do in the fall?*

2. Explain to children what a scarecrow is. Ask *Have you ever seen a real scarecrow? How did it look? Why do you think farmers use scarecrows?*

3. Read aloud *The Apple Pie Tree* by Zoe Hall. Have children pick a tree near the school to observe. Take a picture of it each month. Show children the photographs, and discuss how the tree has changed.

4. Ask *What do you wear in the fall? Do you go out with bare feet and a swimming suit? Do you wear a snowsuit and boots?*

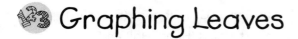 Math Activities

Graphing Leaves

Skills: sorting, counting, data collection and display

Materials
- fall leaves
- overhead projector (or chart paper)
- transparency
- overhead markers (or regular markers for chart paper) in colors to match the leaves' colors

Preparation

Gather several fall leaves that are in good condition and in a variety of colors. Create a graph on a transparency (or chart paper) that lists the colors of the leaves you have collected (e.g., yellow, red, orange, brown). Write the names of the colors in the corresponding color of marker on the graph.

Directions

Give a leaf to each child. Have each child hold up his or her leaf, and ask the child what color it is. Have children sort leaves by color. Count with children the leaves in each pile, and fill in a box for each leaf on the graph. Discuss with children the results. Ask questions such as *Do we have more red leaves or brown leaves? Which color has the biggest number on your paper?*

 Leaf Pairs

Skills: comparing and matching colors and shapes

Materials
- Leaves reproducible (page 175)
- yellow, red, orange, and brown construction paper
- scissors

Preparation

Copy the Leaves reproducible on construction paper. There should only be one match for each color and shape. Cut out all of the leaf pairs.

Directions

Give each child a paper leaf. Invite children to find the classmate with the matching leaf. Once children have found their match, invite them to sit in a circle on the floor. Call out a color. Have children with that color of leaf stand up and switch places with each other.

Fall Leaf Game

Skills: number sense, addition, subtraction

Materials
- Leaves reproducible (page 175) or the leaf cutouts from the Leaf Pairs activity above
- brown butcher paper
- scissors
- yellow, red, orange, and brown construction paper
- tape

Preparation

Cut out a tree from brown butcher paper, and tape it on a wall. Cut 15 leaves from construction paper. Scatter four leaves on the ground below the tree trunk, and tape the remaining leaves on the tree.

Directions

Say to children *I was walking along and I saw four leaves on the ground. Along came a wind and two more fell out of the tree.* (Have children blow and pretend to be the wind as a child pulls off two leaves.) *That means there are now six on the ground. Let's count them.* (Count the leaves with children.) Continue asking children to remove leaves from the tree and count the leaves on the ground until no leaves remain on the tree.

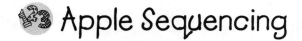 Apple Sequencing

Skills: size comparison, ordering

Materials
- Apple Sequencing reproducible (page 176)
- red paper
- scissors

Preparation

Copy a class set of the Apple Sequencing reproducible on red paper. Cut out the apples.

Directions

Tell children that apples are ready to be picked during the fall. Give each child an apple cutout of each size. (Vary the number of apples used in this activity based on children's ability.) Introduce to children the terms *bigger* and *smaller*. Invite children to put their apples in order from smallest to largest and then largest to smallest. Give each child a piece of red paper. Challenge children to cut out two more apples—one larger than the others and one smaller than the others—and reorder the apples from smallest to largest.

Leaf Sorting and Measurement

Skills: color, size, and shape recognition; nonstandard measurement

Materials
- yellow, red, orange, and brown construction paper
- scissors
- linking cubes

Preparation

Cut leaves of various colors, sizes, and shapes from construction paper. Cut one leaf considerably larger than the others and one considerably smaller.

Directions

Gather a small group of children. Explain to them that leaves come in many different colors, sizes, and shapes. Invite children to sort the leaves by color, size, or shape. (Vary the number and variety of leaves—fewer for younger children; more as their abilities increase.) Have children identify the smallest leaf and the largest leaf. Have children use linking cubes to measure the length and width of the leaves.

Pumpkin and Acorn Patterning

Skills: color recognition, patterning

M a t e r i a l s
- Pumpkin Patterning reproducible (page 177)
- Acorn Patterning reproducible (page 178)
- orange and tan construction paper
- scissors
- sentence strips
- glue

Preparation

Copy the Pumpkin Patterning reproducible on orange paper. Copy the Acorn Patterning reproducible on tan paper. Cut apart the pumpkins and acorns.

Directions

Divide the class into pairs. Give one child in each pair four pumpkin cutouts and the other child four acorn cutouts. Show partners how to take turns laying down their cutout to make an AB pattern. Give each pair a sentence strip. Have children make a pattern together and glue the cutouts on their strip. Use the sentence strips to create a border to decorate the classroom.

 ## Sensory Activities

 # Fall Nature Walk

M a t e r i a l s
- wide packing tape
- scissors

Preparation

For each child make a "bracelet" out of packing tape so the sticky side faces out.

Directions

Explain to children that the class will be going on a nature walk to find fall items. Ask children what they might look for (e.g., leaves, acorns, berries). Put a tape bracelet around each child's wrist. As you go on the walk, invite children to attach different fall items to their bracelet. After the walk, encourage children to share what they found. Invite children to take home their bracelet to share with their family.

Fall Tambourine

Materials
- fall items (e.g., acorns, nuts, small pinecones, hard berries)
- aluminum pie tins (2 per child)
- paintbrushes
- red, orange, brown, and yellow paint
- glue gun (teacher use only)
- music on CD/ tape
- CD/tape player

Preparation

Prepare a display of the fall items from the materials list on a table.

Directions

Give each child two pie tins and a paintbrush. Invite children to paint the outside of each pie tin. Once the paint is dry, invite children to select a few fall items to put inside their pie tins. Use a glue gun to attach the rims of each child's pie tins together to make a "tambourine." Play music, and invite children to shake their fall tambourine.

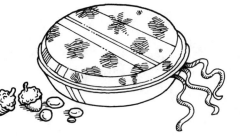

Leaf Rubbings

Materials
- various real or artificial leaves with prominent veins
- smooth sheet protectors
- clipboards (1 per child)
- light-weight, white paper
- unwrapped crayons

Preparation

Prepare the leaves by placing each leaf in a separate sheet protector. Attach each sheet protector to a separate clipboard. Clip a piece of paper over each sheet protector.

Directions

Give each child a clipboard with a leaf. Encourage children to run their fingers over the leaf to feel the veins. Explain to children that the veins are the paths that carry food to the rest of the plant. Invite them to rub the side of a crayon over their leaf to make a leaf rubbing.

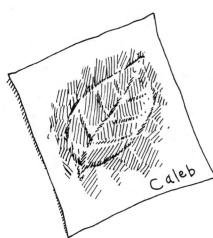

Squirrel Treasure Hunt

Materials
- *Nuts to You!* by Lois Ehlert
- assorted nuts

Preparation

Hide one of each kind of nut somewhere in the classroom. (**Note**: Be mindful of any children with nut allergies.)

Directions

Read aloud *Nuts to You!* Explain to children that many squirrels stay in places where it is cold during the wintertime, so they need to collect nuts during the fall to eat during winter when food is hard to find. Divide the class into small groups of three or four children, and give each each group a nut. Invite children to pretend to be squirrels. Encourage them to find their matching nut somewhere in the classroom.

Birdfeeders

Materials
- brightly colored yarn
- scissors
- colorful O-shaped cereal
- binoculars (optional)

Preparation

Cut yarn into 8-inch (20.3-cm) pieces. Tie a knot around a piece of cereal on one end of each piece of yarn to make a "stopper."

Directions

Give each child a piece of yarn and a handful of O-shaped cereal. Invite children to create "birdfeeders" by stringing the cereal on their yarn. Challenge children to make color patterns with the cereal. Tie each piece of yarn into a loop around a tree branch near the classroom window. Have children use binoculars to watch for birds or squirrels eating from the feeders.

Motor Skills Activities

 Leaf Fishing

Materials
- Leaves reproducible (page 175)
- string
- scissors
- dowel
- strong magnet
- red, orange, yellow, and brown construction paper
- paper clips

Preparation

Cut a 3-foot-long (0.9-m) piece of string. Make a "fishing pole" by tying the string to the end of a dowel. Tie a magnet to the other end of the string. Copy the Leaves reproducible on colored construction paper. Cut out the leaves, fasten a paper clip to each one, and scatter the leaves on the floor.

Directions

Invite children to use the fishing pole to "catch" a leaf. Ask children to identify the color of each leaf they catch.

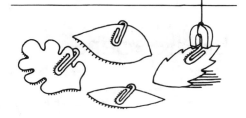

 Fall Planting

Materials
- *Planting a Rainbow* by Lois Ehlert
- tulip and daffodil bulbs (1 per child)
- gardening tools

Preparation

Prepare a small gardening area in a planter or small plot of land outside the classroom.

Directions

Explain to children that some flowers grow from seeds and some grow from bulbs. Read aloud *Planting a Rainbow*, and point out how different flowers grow. After reading the story, invite children to examine and feel tulip and daffodil bulbs. Answer any questions they may have. Invite children to help plant the bulbs in the garden area. Explain that the flowers will not sprout until spring.

 Fall Sewing Cards

Materials
- Fall Sewing Cards (page 179)
- colored card stock
- scissors
- hole punch
- tape
- shoelaces

Preparation

Enlarge the Fall Sewing Cards, and make several copies of them on colored card stock. Laminate the cards for durability. Cut out the sewing cards, and punch holes around the perimeter of each one. Tape a shoelace to each card.

Directions

Show children the different sewing cards, and ask them what each one has to do with fall. Demonstrate how to lace the cards. Give each child a sewing card. Invite children to sew along the edges with the shoelace.

Leaf Blowing Contest

Materials
- drinking straws
- leaves

Preparation

Set up a rectangular table so children can move up and down the longer sides.

Directions

Tell children that they are going to act like the wind. Give each child a straw. Put a pile of leaves on the table, and encourage children to blow through their straw to move the leaves. Discuss with children what happens when you blow softly and when you blow more forcefully. Relate this to how the wind moves leaves. Have each child take a leaf. Arrange children in two lines along either end of the table. Invite children to take turns blowing through their straw to move their leaf from one end of the table to the other.

 # Falling Leaves

Materials
- Leaves reproducible (page 175) or artificial leaves
- red, orange, yellow, and brown construction paper
- scissors

Preparation

Copy the Leaves reproducible on colored construction paper, and cut out the leaves.

Directions

Invite children to sit in a circle. Drop a handful of leaves over the children, and have them catch as many leaves as the can. Repeat until all the leaves are gone. Encourage children, to pick up the leaves that were not caught. Have children sort the leaves by color. Help children count how many leaves of each color there are.

Alphabet Activities

 # Leaf Colors

Materials
- Leaves reproducible (page 175)
- red, orange, yellow, brown, and white construction paper
- black, red, yellow, orange, and brown markers

Preparation

Copy the Leaves reproducible on colored and white construction paper. Each colored leaf should have a matching white leaf. Use a black marker to write the color name on each colored leaf and use the corresponding colored marker to write the color name on each white leaf. (In an older class, use a black marker to label all the leaves.)

Directions

Have children sit in a circle. Scatter the leaves inside the circle so the labels are visible. Invite children to match a colored leaf with the corresponding white leaf and name the color.

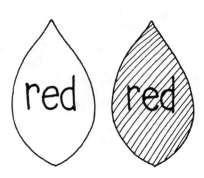

Leaf Letters Search

Materials
- Leaves reproducible (page 175)
- yellow, orange, red, and brown construction paper
- black marker
- scissors

Preparation

Copy the Leaves reproducible on colored construction paper. Write a lowercase letter on the bottom half of each leaf and the matching uppercase letter on the top half of the leaf. (Base the number of letters used on children's ability. This activity can be placed in a learning center with small groups of letters being rotated out daily or weekly.) Cut out each leaf, and then cut apart each leaf between the two letters with a unique puzzle cut. Laminate the pieces, if desired.

Directions

Give each child one half of a leaf. Invite children to search for the child who has the other half of their leaf.

Variation

Put matching leaf halves on a table, and mix them up. Invite a child to choose one leaf half and find the other matching half.

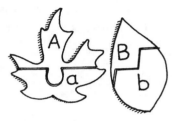

Spell Your Name with Acorns

Materials
- Acorn Patterning reproducible (page 178)
- tan copy paper
- black marker
- scissors
- sentence strips
- glue

Preparation

Copy the Acorn Patterning reproducible on tan paper. Make enough copies to write the letters of each child's name. Use a black marker to write the children's names so there is one letter on each acorn. Cut apart the acorns, and place them faceup on different tables so there are three children's names per table. Write each child's name on a separate sentence strip.

Directions

Give each child his or her name strip. Have children walk around the tables to find the letters in their name. Invite children to form their name with the "acorn letters." Help children glue the acorns on their sentence strip to spell their name.

Apple Attendance Chart

Materials
- red card stock
- scissors
- photograph of each child (optional)
- green and brown butcher paper
- tape
- self-adhesive Velcro strips

Preparation

Cut a red card stock apple for each child. Write each child's name on a separate apple. (For younger children, also attach a photo of each child.) Create a large apple tree and basket out of butcher paper, and tape them to the wall so the leaves of the tree are at the children's height and the basket is at the base of the tree. Attach a piece of Velcro to the back of each apple and the opposite piece of Velcro to a leaf on the tree. Attach to the basket a few strips of Velcro that are opposite the Velcro on the apples.

Directions

Give each child the apple with his or her name printed on it. Have children attach their apple to a leaf on the tree. Tell children to move their apple from the tree to the basket each morning when they arrive at school.

Art Activities

 # Torn-Paper Tree

Materials
- brown butcher paper
- scissors
- red, yellow, and orange construction paper
- glue

Preparation

Cut a large tree trunk and branches out of brown butcher paper.

Directions

Invite each child to tear colored construction paper into leaf shapes. Have children glue their leaves on the tree.

 Apples Everywhere

Materials
- green, red, and yellow paint
- shallow paint trays
- tape
- white butcher paper
- apples (assorted colors, sizes, and shapes)
- kitchen knife (teacher use only)

Preparation

Pour different colors of paint into separate paint trays. Tape butcher paper to the floor. Collect enough apples so each child can have half an apple.

Directions

Show children different apples, and ask them what colors they see. Slice the apples down the center from top to bottom. Invite children to choose an apple half and dip the flat part of the apple in the matching color of paint. Have children print apples on the butcher paper.

Bubbly Cookie Cutter Prints

Materials
- red, orange, yellow, and brown paint
- liquid dishwashing soap
- leaf-shaped cookie cutters
- construction paper

Preparation

Create "bubbly paint" by adding dishwashing soap to the paint until it forms a bubble when the cookie cutter is pulled out of the paint mixture.

Directions

Give each child a piece of construction paper. Show children how to dip a cookie cutter in the bubbly paint and place it on their paper.

Extension

Cut a tree trunk and limbs out of brown butcher paper. Cut out each child's leaf, and have children add their leaf to the tree. Each day, remove one leaf from the tree and have it "fall" to the ground. Invite children to count the remaining leaves. Prepare a culminating activity for the day the last leaf falls (e.g., make Fall Trail Mix, page 168).

Spinning Leaves

Materials

- brown butcher paper
- scissors
- paint (assorted colors)
- squeeze bottles
- red, yellow, and orange construction paper
- salad spinner
- glue

Preparation

Cut a large tree trunk and branches out of brown butcher paper. Pour paint into squeeze bottles.

Directions

Invite each child to cut leaf shapes from colored construction paper. Put the leaves into a salad spinner, and help children drizzle paint on the leaves. Close and spin the spinner. Remove the leaves and set them out to dry. Have children glue the leaves to the tree.

Leaf Prints

Materials

- red, yellow, orange, and brown paint
- jars
- spoon
- cinnamon
- newspaper
- leaves—in good shape (maple and oak leaves work best)
- paintbrushes
- paint smocks
- black construction paper

Preparation

Pour paint into jars, and add a spoonful of cinnamon to each jar to add a scent. Cover the work area with newspaper.

Directions

Show children a leaf that has prominent veins. Point out that veins carry food to the plant. Give each child a jar of paint, a paintbrush, and a paint smock. Invite children to take a leaf and paint over the veined side of the leaf. Give each child a sheet of black construction paper. Show children how to press the painted side of their leaf on top of it. Show them how to gently rub over the unpainted side of the leaf before removing it from the paper. Invite children to choose a new leaf and repeat the activity with another color of paint.

 # Body Stamp Tree

Materials
- brown, orange, yellow, and red paint pads (see Art Recipes, page 414)
- white art paper
- paint smocks

Preparation

Make paint pads per the directions on page 414.

Directions

Give each child a piece of white paper and a paint smock. Help children press the underside of their hand and lower forearm on a brown paint pad. Show children how to press their hand and arm on their paper to create the branches and trunk of a tree. Have children wash off the brown paint. Then, invite children to press each finger on a different colored paint pad. Show children how to press their fingers on top of their tree branches to make leaves.

Cooking Activities

 # Caramel Apple Milkshake

Ingredients
- 2 cups (0.5 L) vanilla frozen yogurt
- ¾ cup (177 mL) milk
- ½ cup (118 mL) applesauce
- 1 teaspoon (5 mL) cinnamon
- ¼ cup (59 mL) caramel topping

Other Supplies

- blender
- small paper cups

Directions

Place the ingredients in a blender. Cover, and blend until smooth. Pour into cups and serve immediately.

Apple Pizza

Ingredients

- prepared pizza crust
- ¼ cup (59 mL) shredded cheddar cheese
- 1 apple, sliced thin
- ½ cup (118 mL) flour
- ½ cup (118 mL) sugar
- 1 teaspoon (5 mL) cinnamon

Other Supplies

- pizza pan
- bowl
- pizza cutter
- paper plates

Directions

Place the crust on a pizza pan. Sprinkle cheese over the crust. Cover with apple slices. Mix flour, sugar, and cinnamon in a bowl. Cover apples with flour mixture. Bake until cheese melts. Cut the pizza into small slices and serve it on paper plates.

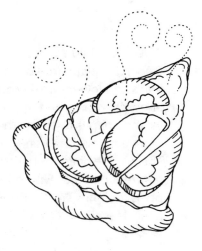

Small Apple Pies

Before making this recipe, read aloud *The Apple Pie Tree* by Zoe Hall.

Ingredients

- refrigerated pie crusts
- apple pie filling
- cinnamon
- sugar

Other Supplies

- large, round cookie cutters
- spoons
- forks
- baking sheet

Directions

Unroll the crusts on a flat surface, and have each child use a large, round cookie cutter (or the rim of a cup) to cut out two circles of dough. Invite children to place a spoonful of pie filling in the middle of one dough circle. Have children place the second dough circle on top of the first. Show children how to use their fingers to pinch the edges closed and how to use a fork to poke a few holes in the middle of their "pie." Mix a small amount of cinnamon into the sugar. Invite children to sprinkle the cinnamon-sugar mixture on top of their pie. Place the pies on a greased baking sheet, and bake for 10–15 minutes at 350°F (177°C).

Apple Ring Sandwiches

Ingredients
- apples
- lemon juice
- peanut butter
- banana slices

Other Supplies

- kitchen knife (teacher use only)
- shallow dish
- craft sticks

Directions

Core and cut the apples into rings. Make enough so each child has two rings. Pour lemon juice in a shallow dish. Dip the apple rings in the juice to prevent browning. Give each child two apple rings and a craft stick. Invite children to use their craft stick to spread peanut butter on one ring. (**Note:** Be mindful of any children with peanut allergies.) Have children add banana slices on top of the peanut butter. Show children how to place the second apple ring on top to make a sandwich.

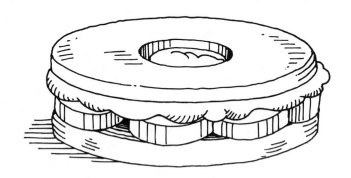

Apple Grahams

Ingredients
- apples
- graham crackers
- peanut butter
- honey

Other Supplies

- kitchen knife (teacher use only)
- craft sticks

Directions

In advance, peel and dice the apples into small pieces. Give each child a graham cracker and a craft stick. Have children use their craft stick to spread peanut butter and then honey on their cracker. (**Note:** Be mindful of any children with peanut allergies.) Give children apple pieces to sprinkle on top of the honey.

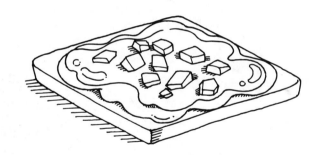

Fall Trail Mix

Ingredients

- popcorn
- assorted nuts
- sunflower seeds
- raisins, banana chips, and other dried fruit

Other Supplies

- large bowl
- small paper cups

Directions

Mix all ingredients in a large bowl. (**Note:** Be mindful of any children with nut allergies.) Serve the trail mix in small paper cups.

Fingerplays and Flannel Board Activities

Raking Leaves

(Fingerplay)

I rake and rake the leaves (*pretending to rake leaves*)
Into a great big heap, (*using hands to represent a large pile of leaves*)
And into the middle I leap. (*jumping into a sitting position*)
I cover myself to hide from you, (*pretending to hide under leaves*)
And then jump out and say, "BOO!" (*jumping up*)

Little Red Apple

(Fingerplay)

One little red apple (*holding up one finger*)
Hung in a tree. (*raising arms overhead to form a circle*)
I looked up at it, (*looking up*)
And it looked down at me. (*looking down*)
"Come down, please," I called, (*cupping hands around mouth*)
And what do you suppose— (*shrugging shoulders*)
That little red apple
Dropped right on my nose! (*covering nose with hand*)

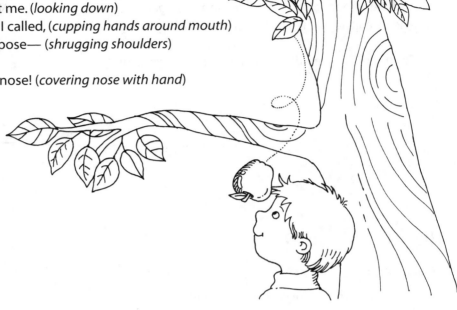

Scarecrow

(Fingerplay)

When all the birds were sleeping, (*laying head on hands*)
And the sun had gone to bed, (*sinking down to the ground*)
Up jumped the scarecrow, (*jumping up*)
And this is what he said:
"I'm a jingle-jangle scarecrow (*stretching tall*)
With a flippy-floppy hat. (*bouncing head*)
I shake my feet like this, (*shaking feet*)
And I shake my hands like that." (*shaking hands*)

Five Little Leaves

(Fingerplay)

Five little leaves up in the tree— (*holding up five fingers*)
They are as bright as can be.
Along came the wind
And blew them all around. (*blowing on fingers*)
And one little leaf fell to the ground. (*taking away one finger*)

Continue in descending order until one leaf remains.

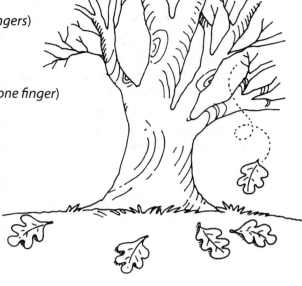

My Poor Back

(Fingerplay)

My poor back will surely break (*rubbing back*)
If one more leaf I have to rake! (*raking motion*)
Crusty, rusty brown leaves,
Dusty, blustery red leaves,
Crunching, bunching, scrunching beneath my feet. (*walking in place*)
In a pile of crispy leaves, I'll find a seat! (*sitting on floor*)

Autumn Day Animals

(Fingerplay)

Four animals on an autumn day— (*holding up four fingers*)
The bird said, "I migrate so I can't stay." (*flapping arms like wings*)
Three animals on an autumn day—(*holding up three fingers*)
The chipmunk said, "I'll go store food and not delay." (*gathering pretend food*)
Two animals on an autumn day—(*holding up two fingers*)
The bear said, "I hibernate," and left to sleep away. (*laying head on hands*)
One animal on an autumn day—(*holding up one finger*)
The fox said, "My fur's white. It's no longer gray!" (*looking shocked*)
All the animals on an autumn day get ready for winter before they play.

Five Apples in a Basket

(Flannel Board)

Create the following flannel board pieces: five apples and a pie tin to hold the apples.

The first apple in the basket (*placing pie tin and one apple on board*)
Was bright and shiny red.
The second apple in the basket (*placing second apple in pie tin on board*)
Said, "What a cozy bed!"
The third apple in the basket (*placing third apple in pie tin on board*)
Said, "Please move over there."
The fourth apple in the basket (*placing fourth apple in pie tin on board*)
Said, "Now we are two pair."
The fifth apple in the basket, (*placing fifth apple in pie tin on board*)
Said, "Oh, dear, me-oh-my!
This basket looks like a pastry.
I think we're apple pie!"

Four Red Apples

(Flannel Board)

Create the following flannel board pieces: four red apples.

Four red apples on an apple tree— (*placing four apples on the board*)
Emily ate one and then there were three. (*removing one apple*)
Three red apples—what did Emma do?
Why she ate one and then there were two. (*removing one apple*)
Two red apples ripening in the sun—
Ethan ate one and now there's just one. (*removing one apple*)
One red apple and now we are done,
Because I ate the last apple and now there are none! (*removing last apple*)

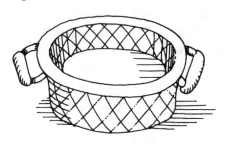

♫ Rake the Leaves

(Sung to the tune of "Here We Go Round the Mulberry Bush")

This is the way we rake the leaves,
Rake the leaves, rake the leaves.
This is the way we rake the leaves
In the middle of fall.

This is the way we jump in the leaves,
Jump in the leaves, jump in the leaves.
This is the way we jump in the leaves
In the middle of fall.

This is the way we throw the leaves,
Throw the leaves, throw the leaves.
This the way we throw the leaves
In the middle of fall.

♫ Apples

(Sung to the tune of "On Top of Old Smokey")

I love to eat apples.
They're juicy and sweet.
The one thing I don't know,
Is which one to eat.

Red, yellow, and green,
They're all good for me.
If you had to choose one,
Which one would it be?

🎵 Ten Little Apples

(Sung to the tune of "Ten Little Indians")

One little, two little, three little apples.
Four little, five little, six little apples.
Seven little, eight little, nine little apples.
Ten little apples to harvest.

🎵 Migrating Ducks

(Sung to the tune of "Ten Little Indians")

One little, two little, three ducks fly away.
Four little, five little, six ducks fly away.
Seven little, eight little, nine ducks fly away.
Ten little ducks migrate.

🎵 Autumn Is Here

(Sung to the tune of "Sing a Song of Sixpence")

Sing a song of autumn
With leaves all falling down.
Sing a song of harvest
With colors gold and brown.
Days are getting shorter;
The nights are cool and clear.
It's almost time to hibernate
Until springtime is here.

🎵 Leaves Are Falling

(Sung to the tune of "Twinkle, Twinkle Little Star")

Leaves are falling from the tree.
They are colors we like to see.
Orange, yellow, and even red—
Catch them before you go to bed.
Leaves are falling from the tree.
They are colors we like to see.

🎵 Back to School

(Sung to the tune of "Frère Jacques")

Kids are coming,
Kids are coming,
Back to school,
Back to school.
Kids are in the classroom.
Kids are in the classroom.
It is fall.
It is fall.

🎵 Leaves Are Turning

(Sung to the tune of "Frère Jacques")

Leaves are turning,
Leaves are turning,
Orange and brown,
Orange and brown.
Leaves are turning colors,
Leaves are turning colors,
All around town,
All around town.

Leaves

Apple Sequencing

Year-Round Early Childhood Themes © 2006 Creative Teaching Press

Pumpkin Patterning

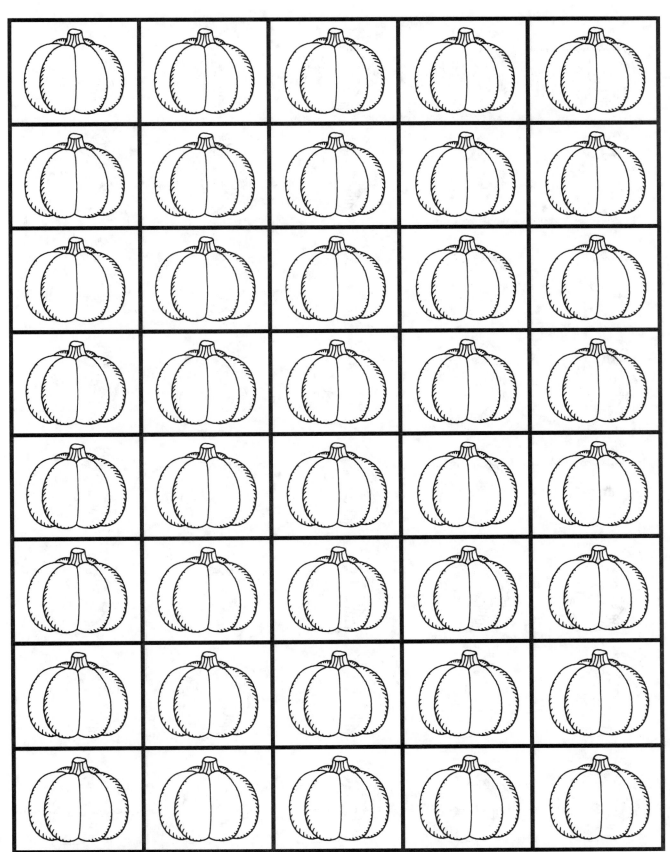

Acorn Patterning

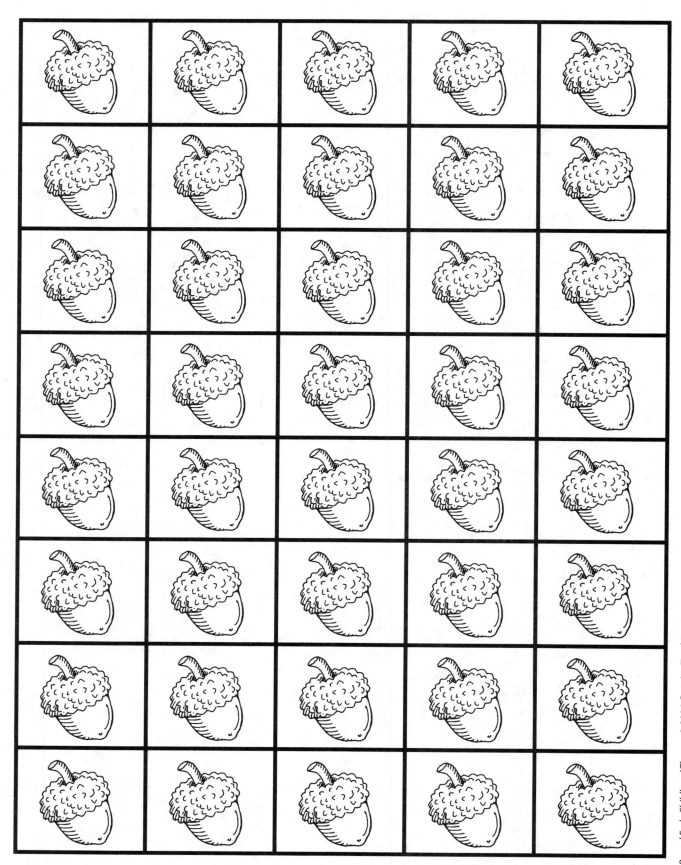

Year-Round Early Childhood Themes © 2006 Creative Teaching Press

Fall Sewing Cards

Family

Concepts

The concepts covered in this unit include the following:
- Families come in all sizes.
- Families love and care for each other.
- There is no right or wrong type of family.
- There are many different types of families: single parent, two parent, combined, and extended.
- Stepparents and stepchildren are also family members.
- Some families have everyone living together and some do not.
- Grandparents, cousins, aunts, and uncles are members of an extended family.

Vocabulary

aunt—sister of a parent

brother—a boy who has the same parents as another child

cousins—children of an aunt and uncle

family—a group of related people

father—a man who has a child or adopts a child

grandparents—parents of a parent

home—where a family lives

mother—a woman who has a child or adopts a child

sister—a girl who has the same parents as another child

uncle—brother of a parent

Date _____

Dear Family:

"Family" will be the theme for our next unit. We invite any family members to come visit our classroom and celebrate all different types of families. For this unit we will need some assistance from you. Please send a photograph of your family and an Art Grab Bag (described under "Home Activities").

Classroom Activities

Children will participate in the following activities:
- Listening to tapes of common household sounds and trying to identify them.
- Listening to and discussing *Guess How Much I Love You* by Sam McBratney.
- Creating a salad of each family's favorite fruits.

Home Activities

Here are some activities for your family to try at home to complement what children are doing in the classroom:
- As a family, create an Art Grab Bag with craft items and scraps of paper, wrapping paper, or wallpaper. Children will be sharing the items with another child and using them to create a collage. Please send the grab bag by _____.
- Set aside one night a week as Family Night. Get all the family together to do a fun activity, play a game, or make something.
- Help your child write a letter to a relative he or she does not see very often.

Have a great time as you explore all of the fun Family activities with your child.

Thank you for all you do!

Sincerely,

Year-Round Early Childhood Themes © 2006 Creative Teaching Press

Dear Family:

We will use the following items during our Family unit. We would appreciate any help you could give us. We will begin this unit on _____, so please sign and return the form below if you can donate items by _____.

- one or two of your family's favorite fruits
- wooden clip-type clothespins
- magazines and catalogs with pictures of adults and children
- small loaf of bread
- American cheese slices
- small round, square, and rectangular crackers
- unopened box of graham crackers
- raisins
- small, unopened box of O-shaped cereal

Thanks!

• •

I would like to contribute the following items for this unit:

_____

Please contact me at _____ (phone number or e-mail)
to let me know how I can help.

_____
(parent's name)

Center Ideas

The following are suggestions for different Family centers. The activities provided in this unit can be used or modified for these centers:

- **Art Center**—people cookie cutters, templates, and stencils; play dough (see Art Recipes, page 409)

- **Block and Building Center**—toy cars and trucks, plastic people of varying ages and sizes, spools, beads, washers, plastic straws cut to different lengths, yarn, pipe cleaner, rocks, glue

- **Dramatic Play Center**—clothes to role-play family members, household tools, puppets, baby dolls and baby equipment, dollhouse

- **Listening Center**—tape of household sounds, books and tapes about the family, tapes of stories written in class

- **Manipulatives Center**—family and home puzzles

- **Math and Science Center**—balance scales, household items to weigh

- **Reading Center**—family books (see recommended read-alouds, page 185), stories written in class, flannel board with story pieces and puzzle pieces, newspapers

- **Sand and Water Tables**—people, blocks, small cars and trucks

- **Writing Center**—stickers and stamps of people and homes

Language Development

Recommended Read-Alouds

The Family Book by Todd Parr (Megan Tingley)

Guess How Much I Love You by Sam McBratney (Candlewick Press)

Horace by Holly Keller (Greenwillow Books)

How Do Dinosaurs Clean Their Room? by Jane Yolen (The Blue Sky Press)

How Many Feet in the Bed? by Diane Johnston Hamm (Simon & Schuster)

Is Your Mama a Llama? by Deborah Guarino (Scholastic)

Mama, Do You Love Me? by Barbara M. Joosse (Chronicle Books)

"More, More, More," Said the Baby by Vera B. Williams (Greenwillow Books)

The Napping House by Audrey Wood (Harcourt)

The Seven Silly Eaters by Mary Ann Hoberman (Gulliver Books)

Ten, Nine, Eight by Molly Bang (Greenwillow Books)

This Is My Family by Mercer Mayer (Golden Books)

Would They Love a Lion? by Kady MacDonald Denton (Kingfisher)

You're All My Favorites by Sam McBratney (Candlewick Press)

Read-Aloud Activity

Read a book to children. Go back to the beginning of the book. Show children the illustrations in order and invite children to tell the story this time. Leave the book in a center for children to practice retelling the story using the illustrations.

Discussion Starters

Use these suggestions to promote discussions about a read-aloud or to motivate children to tell a story. These ideas can be discussed and then used to write group stories for children to illustrate.

1. Make a bulletin board titled *I love my family because* .... Have children complete the sentence, and record their dictation. Invite them to draw a picture of their family to add to the board.

2. Collect things from around the house that various people in the family use (e.g., tie, toothbrush, baby bottle, pencil). Display each item, and discuss who uses the item and what it is used for.

3. Display pictures of different rooms in the house, discuss what you do in each room, and ask silly questions. For example, ask *Could you take a bath in the living room? Do you sleep in the kitchen? Do you eat in the bathroom?*

4. Invite children to complete the sentence *I'm glad I am a big/little sister/brother because* _____.

5. Have each child select a picture (cut from magazines, newspapers, or catalogs) of adults and children involved in an activity. Invite children to dictate a story about what they see in their picture.

Math Activities

How Many People Are in Your Family?

Skills: comparing, counting, data collection and display

Materials
- People reproducible (page 205)
- chart paper
- scissors
- tape or glue

Preparation

Create a chart titled *How Many People Are in Your Family?* Write each child's name along the left side. Copy and cut out the People reproducible. Make enough copies so there is a cutout for each child's family members.

Directions

Ask each child how many people are in his or her family and who they are. Have children count out the number of people cutouts that matches the number of people in their family and attach the cutouts to the chart. Have children compare family sizes by asking them questions about the chart.

Sorting Socks

Skills: sorting, comparing, counting

Materials
- Sock Patterns (page 206)
- Sock Sort Labels (page 207)
- colored paper
- scissors
- tape
- 3 small laundry baskets
- pairs of matching socks (optional)

Preparation

Make several copies of the Sock Patterns on various colors of paper, and cut them out. Place the sock cutouts around the classroom. Copy and cut apart the Sock Sort Labels. Tape each label on a basket. Arrange the baskets in a row.

Directions

Read aloud each label. Invite children to pick up sock cutouts from around the room and place them in the correct basket. Divide the class into three groups. Give each group a laundry basket, and have the children check that the socks were sorted correctly. Help children count the socks in each basket. Ask children which basket had the most and least socks.

Variation

Hide real socks around the room, and invite children to find matching pairs.

How Many People Live Here?

Skills: counting, one-to-one correspondence

Materials
- How Many People Live Here? reproducible (page 208)
- crayons

Preparation

Copy a class set of the How Many People Live Here? reproducible.

Directions

Give each child a reproducible and a crayon. Show children how each home has a different number of dots on it. Invite children to draw the corresponding number of people in front of each home.

🔢 Bargain Shopping

Skill: number recognition

Materials
- index cards
- coupons and newspaper advertisements
- highlighters

Preparation

Write a number from 1 to 9 on separate index cards. Make enough cards so that each child will have one.

Directions

Give each child several coupons and newspaper ads, a highlighter, and a numbered index card. Invite children to look through the coupons and ads to find their number. Tell children to highlight their number each time they find it.

🔢 Child Going Home Game

Skills: counting, one-to-one correspondence

Materials
- file folders
- circle stickers
- plastic game pieces
- dice

Preparation

Place 20 circle stickers on the inside of each file folder to create a game board for each pair of children. Use the stickers to create a path leading from one side of the folder to the other. Draw a child at the beginning of each path and a home at the end of the path.

Directions

Divide the class into pairs, and give each pair a game board, two game pieces, and a die. Have partners put their game piece on top of the drawing of the child. Have partners take turns rolling the die and moving the number of spaces indicated. The game ends when both players reach home.

Sensory Activities

Household Noises

Materials
- tape recorder
- audiotape
- photographs or magazines
- paper
- crayons or markers

Preparation

Create a tape recording of household sounds (e.g., telephone ringing, toilet flushing, water running, doorbell ringing, clock ticking, children laughing). Find a photograph or magazine picture of each sound's source.

Directions

Give each child a piece of paper and crayons or markers. Have children listen to the tape, and encourage them to identify the source of each sound. Ask children to draw a picture of the sound's source. Play the tape again. Display the pictures, and ask children to point to the picture of each sound as they hear it.

Bathtime for Baby

Materials
- water table or baby tub
- water
- baby shampoo
- washable baby dolls
- towels
- doll clothing

Preparation

Fill a water table or baby tub with warm water, and set the other items around it.

Directions

Have children undress baby dolls and give them a bath in the water table or baby tub. Invite children to dry and redress the dolls.

 Shadow Play

Materials
- overhead projector
- various small household items that have a recognizable outline (e.g., spoon, baby rattle, hammer)

Preparation

Set up an overhead projector to project on a screen or plain surface. Hide the household items near the projector so children cannot see them.

Directions

Explain to children that they are going to play a guessing game. Place one of the items on the overhead projector. Point out that this is the shape of something they know. Invite children to guess what this shape might be. (Give them clues as necessary.) After a few guesses, hold up the item so children can see if their guess was correct.

 I Feel . . .

Materials
- paper lunch sacks
- household items (e.g., telephone, toothbrush, hairbrush, toilet paper, shoe, key)

Preparation

Put each item in a separate paper lunch sack.

Directions

Invite a child to pick a sack at random. Ask the child to place his or her hand inside the bag and describe what he or she feels. Ask the class to guess what the object is based on the description. Invite other children to help, if necessary. Invite a different child to choose a new bag, and repeat the activity until each child has participated.

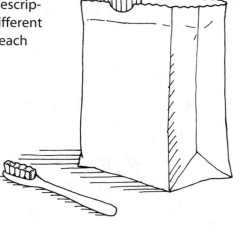

# Play Dough People

Materials
- play dough (see Art Recipes, page 409)
- rolling pins
- gingerbread man or other people cookie cutters
- craft supplies (e.g., pasta, stickers, yarn, fabric scraps)

Preparation

Directions

Discuss with children that families come in all different sizes. Give each child some play dough and a rolling pin. Invite children to roll out the play dough and then use cookie cutters to make play dough people that represent their families. Have children decorate the people in their family with craft supplies (e.g., hair made out of pasta).

What Doesn't Belong?

Materials
- several sets of household items (e.g., baby items, kitchen items, garage items)

Preparation

Directions

Display two or three household items that go together and one that does not belong (e.g., baby bottle, rattle, diaper, and rolling pin). Have children discuss what each item is used for. Invite children to pick the item that does not belong and give the reason.

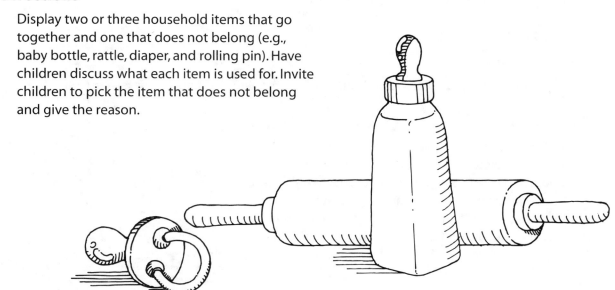

Motor Skills Activities

🐷 Family Puzzle

M a t e r i a l s
- photograph of each child's family, preferably 8" x 10" (20 cm x 25.5 cm)
- white card stock
- scissors
- 9" x 12" (23 cm x 30.5 cm) envelopes
- glue

Preparation

Make two copies (enlarge to approximately 8" x 10") of each child's family photograph on card stock. Cut one copy into three or more puzzle pieces, depending on the abilities of the children. Glue the intact copy on an envelope, and place the puzzle pieces inside.

Directions

Give each child his or her family puzzle. Invite children to use the intact picture as a base to reassemble the puzzle.

🐷 Finding Family Members

M a t e r i a l s
- magazines and catalogs
- scissors
- construction paper
- glue

Preparation

Look through the magazines and catalogs and remove any inappropriate pictures.

Directions

Give each child a magazine or catalog. Invite children to cut out pictures of families or family members and pets. Have them glue their cutouts to a sheet of construction paper. Have children dictate what the families are doing or tell which family member is pictured. Record children's dictation on their paper.

 Family Mazes

Materials
- file folders
- black marker
- dry erase markers

Preparation

Use a black marker to draw a maze on the inside of a file folder for each child. Draw a simple maze for young children and a more complex maze as their abilities improve. Laminate the folders.

Directions

Give each child a dry erase marker and a maze. Invite children to "help a family member return home" (e.g., help your sister get home from school, help your dad get home from work). Show children how to draw a family member at one end of the maze and their home at the other end. Invite children to trace the path with the marker.

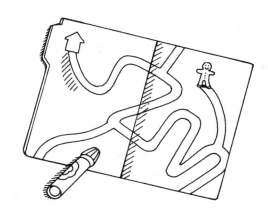

Can You . . . ?

Materials
- none

Preparation

Directions

Ask children to act out different activities that are done in a home or yard such as washing the dishes, brushing their teeth, sweeping the floor, ironing clothes, mowing the lawn, and planting flowers. Invite children to suggest other activities to act out.

Dress-Like-a-Parent Relay

M a t e r i a l s   • adult clothing

Preparation

Directions

Arrange children in two lines that are at opposite ends
of the room. Put adult clothing at the front of one line.
Have the child near the clothes get dressed in the
clothes, race to the other side, and take off the clothes.
The child on the other side puts on those clothes and
races to the other side. Continue until each child has
had a turn.

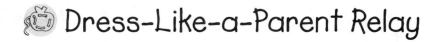
Alphabet Activities

 # "Reading" the Newspaper

M a t e r i a l s   • several newspapers
                        • alphabet cards
                        • red colored pencils

Preparation

Directions

Give each child a page from a newspaper to "read," an alphabet card, and a red pencil. Invite children to find examples of their letter in the newspaper and circle it with the red pencil.

 Name Letters Recognition

Materials
- sentence strips
- counters
- alphabet cards

Preparation

Write each child's first and last name on separate sentence strips.

Directions

Give each child his or her name card. Explain to children that each child's mother and/or father chose his or her first name and that his or her last name is the same as at least one of the parents. Invite children to share stories they know about the origin of their names (e.g., I have my dad's name, John). Give each child a handful of counters. Mix up a set of alphabet cards, and then draw a card. Say the letter's name, and display it. Tell children to cover that letter on their name card with a counter if they have it in their name. Play continues until children cover all of the letters in their name.

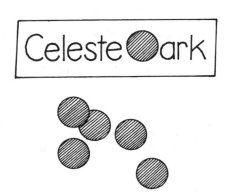

Clothespin Alphabet Match

Materials
- Laundry Letters reproducible (page 209)
- scissors
- 26 wooden clip-type clothespins
- thin black marker
- clothesline

Preparation

Copy and cut apart the Laundry Letters reproducible. Use a black marker to write each upper-case letter of the alphabet on a separate clothespin. Hang a clothesline so children can reach it. Clip each letter clothespin that you wish to use on the clothesline.

Directions

Invite children to hang the laundry letters with their matching uppercase letter clothespin. Then name a letter and invite a child to remove it from the clothesline. (Start with a small number of pairs and gradually increase the number as children's abilities improve.)

🔤 Environmental Print Search

Materials • environmental print such as common store logos (can be printed from Internet) or common traffic signs

Preparation

Directions

Show children examples of environmental print, and ask if they can identify what they see. Ask questions about where they would see this print and what each example means.

🔤 Letter Bingo

Materials • Bingo reproducible (page 210)
• counters
• alphabet cards: b, c, d, f, h, l, m, p, and s

Preparation

Copy a class set of the Bingo reproducible. Write *b*, *c*, *d*, *f*, *h*, *l*, *m*, *p*, and *s* in separate boxes on each card. Make certain no two game cards are the same.

Directions

Give each child a game card and nine counters. Mix up a set of alphabet cards, choose a card, and read aloud the letter. Read the "family words" (listed below) that start with the same letter. Ask children to find the letter on their game card and place a counter over that letter. The game is over when a child has covered three in a row or column.

Family words:
b—brother, baby
c—child, cat
d—dad, dog
f—father, family
h—home, house
l—love
m—mother, mom
p—parent, pet
s—sister, sibling

Art Activities

🖌 Fingerprint Family

Materials
- flesh-colored paint pads (see Art Recipes, page 414)
- construction paper
- markers

Preparation

Make paint pads per the directions on page 414.

Directions

Invite each child to press a finger on the paint pad that matches his or her skin color. Have children press that finger on a sheet of construction paper to make their face outline. Explain to children that they will make the faces of the rest of their family members using their fingerprints. The thumbprint will be grown-ups and the different sizes of fingerprints are for different children. After the fingerprints are dry, invite children to use markers to add facial features and bodies to their family members. Have children dictate the names of their family members as you write each name under the correct person or pet.

🖌 Family Portrait

Materials
- construction paper
- art supplies (e.g., pencils, crayons, paint/paintbrushes)

Preparation

Directions

Give each child a piece of construction paper and art supplies. Invite children to draw or paint a portrait of their family. Record children's dictation about who is in the picture and what they are doing.

Family Puppets

Materials

- Gingerbread Man reproducible (page 211)
- card stock
- scissors
- craft supplies (e.g., buttons, hair-colored yarn, sequins)
- glue
- craft sticks

Preparation

Copy a class set of the Gingerbread Man reproducible on card stock, and cut out the gingerbread men.

Directions

Give each child a gingerbread man. Have children use the craft supplies to make a family member. Show children how to glue a craft stick to the back of their cutout to make a puppet.

Grab Bag Art

Materials

- Art Grab Bags (see Family Letter: Theme Introduction, page 182)
- large sheets of construction paper
- glue

Preparation

Send home a note with children to remind them to bring in their Art Grab Bags.

Directions

Invite children to exchange grab bags with a partner. Give each child a sheet of construction paper and glue. Have children create a collage by gluing items from their grab bag to their paper.

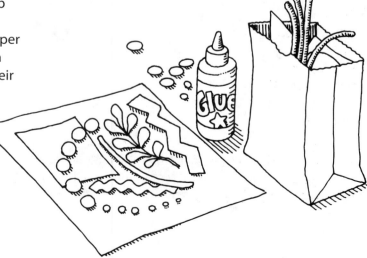

Cooking Activities

🥣 Building a House and Yard

Ingredients
- loaf of bread
- sliced American cheese
- small square and rectangular crackers
- parsley
- broccoli florets
- celery stalks

Other Supplies
- kitchen knife (teacher use only)
- paper plates

Directions

In advance, slice bread in half diagonally and clean the vegetables. Set out all of the ingredients. Give each child a paper plate. Invite children to create the shape of a house using the bread (roof) and cheese. Encourage them to add cracker windows and doors and vegetables for plants in the yard.

🥣 Family Favorite Fruit Salad

Ingredients
- 1 or 2 favorite fruits from each family
- whipped topping

Other Supplies
- kitchen knife (teacher use only)
- large bowl
- mixing spoon
- small paper plates

Directions

In advance, cut washed fruit into bite-size pieces, and place them in a large bowl. Use whipped topping as a fruit dip, or add whipped topping to fruit and thoroughly mix. Chill until time to serve.

Food Faces

Ingredients
- graham crackers
- cream cheese
- raisins
- banana slices
- O-shaped cereal

Other Supplies
- craft sticks

Directions

Have children use a craft stick to spread cream cheese on a graham cracker. Invite them to use the remaining ingredients to create a family member's face.

Variation

Ingredients
- round crackers
- peanut butter
- raisins
- miniature marshmallows

Directions

Have children use a craft stick to spread peanut butter on a cracker. (**Note**: Be mindful of any children with peanut allergies.) Invite children to use the remaining ingredients to create a family member's facial features.

Tasty Family Tree

Ingredients
- round crackers
- green frosting
- small red candies
- graham crackers

Other Supplies
- craft sticks

Directions

Have children use a craft stick to spread frosting on a round cracker. Invite them to add a small red candy for each family member. Have children complete the "family tree" by adding a fourth of a graham cracker as the trunk.

Fingerplays and Flannel Board Activities

🍄 Families

(Fingerplay)

Some families are large. (*spreading arms out wide*)
Some families are small. (*bringing arms close together*)
But I love my family best of all! (*hugging self*)

🍄 Where Should I Live?

(Fingerplay)

Where should I live?
In a castle with a moat? (*making points with hands over head*)
On a river in a boat? (*waving motion with hands*)
Maybe an igloo made of ice? (*pretending to pack snow*)
All of these places sound so nice.
I like apartments made of stone, (*stretching tall*)
But I'd like to live in a mobile home. (*shortening up*)
A cabin would give me lots of space, (*stretching wide*)
But I guess my home is the very best place! (*pointing to self*)

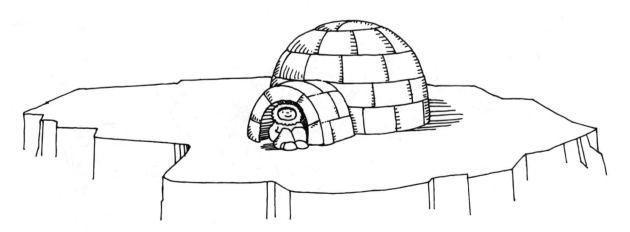

 Knock on the Door

(Fingerplay)

Knock, knock on the door. (*knocking twice*)
Who's inside? (*shrugging shoulders*)
One knock more. (*knocking once*)
Now the door's open wide. (*opening door*)
Step once. Step twice. (*stepping two times*)
What do you see? (*holding hands around eyes like glasses*)
People who are nice. (*crossing hands over heart*)
They're my family!

A Family

(Flannel Board)

Create the following flannel board pieces: large heart, mother, father, sister, baby, and dog.

This is a family—let's count them and see (*placing large heart as background on board*)
How many there are and who they might be.
This is the mother who loves everyone, (*placing mother on board*)
And this is the father who is lots of fun. (*placing father on board*)
This is the sister. She helps and she plays. (*placing sister on board*)
And this is the baby. He's growing each day. (*placing baby on board*)
But who is this one? He's there all alone.
Why it's Prince, the dog, and he's chewing a bone. (*placing dog on board*)

Songs and Poems

🎵 I Love Mommy

(Sung to the tune of "Frère Jacques")

I love Mommy. I love Mommy.
Yes, I do. Yes, I do.
And my mommy loves me,
And my mommy loves me,
Loves me, too. Loves me, too.

*Repeat song, replacing Mommy
with Daddy, sister, brother, and so on.*

🎵 Families

(Sung to the tune of "Ten Little Indians")

Some have fathers.
Some have mothers.
Some have sisters.
Some have brothers.
In some houses,
There are others.
Every family's special.

🎵 Family Time

(Sung to the tune of "Mary Had a Little Lamb")

Tell me what you like to do, like to do, like to do.
Tell me what you like to do with your family.

Mary likes to **make cookies**, **make cookies**, **make cookies**.
Mary likes to **make cookies** with **her** family.

*Replace the boldfaced text with a different child's name
and what he or she likes to do with his or her family and
repeat this section for each child.*

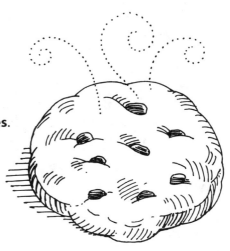

🎵 Good Night

(Poem)

If you peek into my room at night,
My family you will see.
They kiss my face and tuck me in tight.
Why? Because they love me.

🎵 Family

(Poem)

We read and talk and work together —
Just to name a few.
Eat and grow and stick together—
Some more things that we do.

We spend time and celebrate.
We could laugh and play all day.
My family is so special to me.
I love them in every way.

🎵 My Family

(Poem)

This is my family.
It's filled with love.
We fit together
Like a hand in a glove.
We laugh. We play.
We work. We share.
We know many ways
To show that we care.

People

Sock Patterns

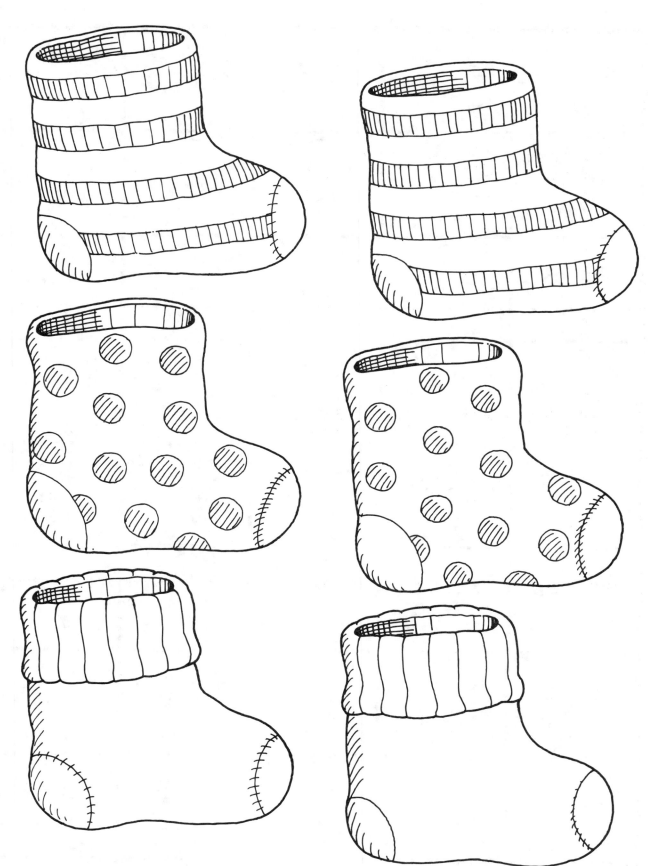

Sock Sort Labels

Striped socks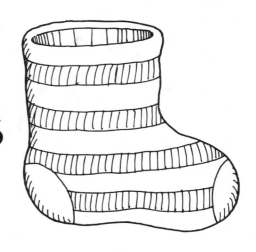

Polka-dotted socks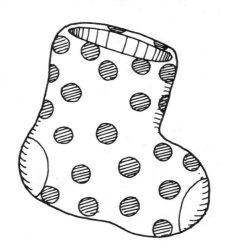

Solid socks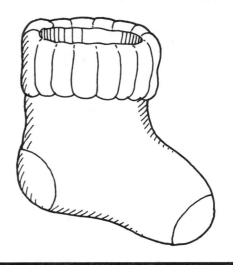

How Many People Live Here?

Year-Round Early Childhood Themes © 2006 Creative Teaching Press

Laundry Letters

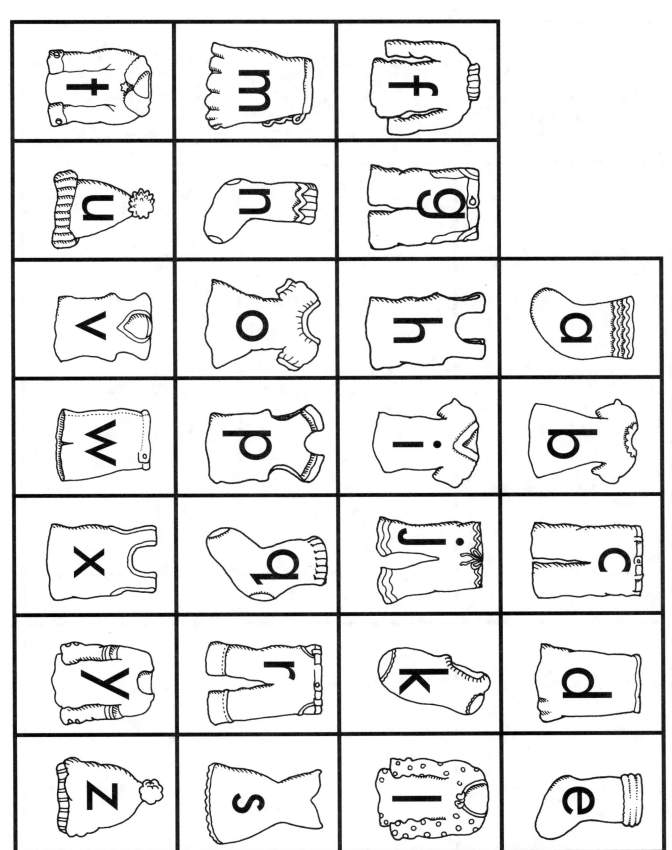

Bingo

BINGO

Year-Round Early Childhood Themes © 2006 Creative Teaching Press

Gingerbread Man

Five Senses

Concepts

The concepts covered in this unit include the following:
- People have five senses: touch, taste, smell, sight, and sound.
- People use their five senses to learn about the world around them.
- People have two ears for hearing.
- People have two eyes for seeing.
- People have a mouth and tongue for tasting.
- People have a nose for smelling.
- Frequently, we use more than one sense at a time to explore and enjoy the world around us.

Vocabulary

senses—a living being's knowledge about itself and its surrounding by using touch, taste, smell, sight, and sound

sensory—having to do with the senses

Date _____

Dear Family:

"Five Senses" will be the theme for our next unit. This will be a very enjoyable unit since children are so fond of exploring the world around them with their senses.

Classroom Activities

Children will participate in the following activities:
- Using their sense of hearing to identify sounds on a tape.
- Comparing the taste of the same foods prepared in different ways.
- Creating sweet-smelling flowers.
- Listening to and discussing *The Listening Walk* by Paul Showers.

Home Activities

Here are some activities for your family to try at home to complement what children are doing in the classroom:
- Discuss each family member's favorite things and what senses he or she uses to enjoy those things (e.g., homemade cookies—see, smell, taste; movies—see and hear; music—hear).
- Sit outside on a warm day. Close your eyes. Discuss what you hear. Open your eyes. Can you find the things that you heard while your eyes were closed?

Have fun as you explore all of the fascinating Five Senses activities with your child.

Thank you for all you do!

Sincerely,

Year-Round Early Childhood Themes © 2006 Creative Teaching Press

Dear Family:

We will use the following items during our Five Senses unit. We would appreciate any help you could give us. We will begin this unit on _____, so please sign and return the form below if you can donate items by _____.

- 35 mm film canisters with lids
- toilet paper tubes
- bubble wrap
- small buttons
- wooden clip-type clothespins
- plastic Easter eggs (the kind that open)
- bag of potpourri
- sugarless drink mix packets
- coarse sandpaper
- cinnamon sticks

- green pipe cleaners
- corrugated cardboard
- cotton balls
- large baking cup liners
- perfume samples
- textured fabric scraps (e.g., burlap, faux fur, nylon net, velvet, terry cloth, denim, satin)

Thanks!

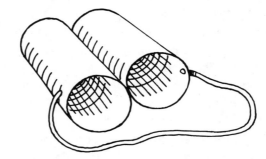

• •

I would like to contribute the following items for this unit:

_____

Please contact me at _____ (phone number or e-mail) to let me know how I can help.

_____
(parent's name)

Center Ideas

The following are suggestions for different Five Senses centers. The activities provided in this unit can be used or modified for these centers:

- **Art Center**—sensory paint and play dough (see Art Recipes, page 409), scented nonmenthol shaving cream, cookie sheet

- **Block and Building Center**—variety of blocks (e.g., unit blocks, snap blocks, bristle blocks, Styrofoam blocks), golf tees, plastic hammers, bubble wrap secured to the wall, plastic hammer to pop bubbles

- **Dramatic Play Center**—puppets/dolls with changeable features, clothes and equipment to role-play sensory experiences (e.g., going out to eat at a restaurant)

- **Listening Center**—story tapes, sound tapes, music tapes

- **Manipulatives Center**—sensory puzzles

- **Math and Science Center**—items that change the way things look (e.g., magnifying glass, binoculars, prism, kaleidoscope, colored cellophane glasses, sunglasses); "listening tubes" (paper towel tubes); pictures of body parts we use to sense things; pictures of things children enjoy seeing, hearing, smelling, feeling, and tasting

- **Reading Center**—books on any of the five senses (see recommended read-alouds, page 217), flannel board activities

- **Sand and Water Tables**—tubs or tables filled with sensory items such as cotton balls, water with colored ice cubes, colored water, pebbles, sand, buttons, dirt and plastic worms (look in fishing supply section of store), ice or snow, colored pasta or rice (see Art Recipes: Pasta and Rice Dye, page 416)

- **Writing Center**—colorful stickers, variety of stamps, sensory letters and numbers (e.g., letters or numbers covered with sand, birdseed, or other rough material)

Language Development

Recommended Read-Alouds

Barnyard Banter by Denise Fleming (Henry Holt and Company)

Brown Bear, Brown Bear, What Do You See? by Bill Martin Jr. (Henry Holt and Company)*

Is It Rough? Is It Smooth? Is It Shiny? by Tana Hoban (Greenwillow Books)

The Listening Walk by Paul Showers (HarperTrophy)

Look Book by Tana Hoban (Greenwillow Books)

Mr. Brown Can Moo, Can You? by Dr. Seuss (Random House)

My Five Senses by Margaret Miller (Alladin)

My Five Senses (Let's-Read-and-Find-Out Science 1) by Aliki (HarperCollins)

Polar Bear, Polar Bear, What Do You Hear? by Bill Martin Jr. (Henry Holt and Company)

Sounds All Around (Let's-Read-and-Find-Out Science 1) by Wendy Pfeffer (HarperTrophy)

Touch and Feel: Dinosaur by Dave King, Andy Crawford, and Ray Moller (DK Children)

You Can't Smell a Flower With Your Ear!: All About Your 5 Senses by Joanna Cole (Grosset & Dunlap)

You Can't Taste a Pickle With Your Ear!: A Book About Your 5 Senses by Harriet Ziefert (Chronicle Books)

*Read-aloud used in an activity

Read-Aloud Activity

Read to children a book about the senses. Discuss with children the senses mentioned in the book. Invite them to use the sense or senses discussed in the book to explore the classroom (e.g., for a book about the sense of touch, encourage children to find many different textures in the room and make a crayon rubbing).

Discussion Starters

Use these suggestions to promote discussions about a read-aloud or to motivate children to tell a story. These can be discussed and then used to write group stories for children to illustrate.

1. Discuss with children things they like and dislike to feel, see, touch, taste, or hear. Write their ideas on a chart.

2. Tell children this story: *Once there was a little boy named Jared who liked to smell everything he saw. He smelled his clothes. He smelled his food. He even smelled his baby brother. He smelled just about everything. But last week, he learned a lesson: it's not always good to smell everything you see. On Monday, he took off his socks after playing hard all day and took a big sniff. Boy, was that a mistake! On Tuesday, he smelled some stinky cheese in the refrigerator. But Wednesday was the worst day of all. He saw a funny-looking animal that was black with a big, white stripe down its back. He thought it might be a cat. So he walked right up, grabbed it by the tail, and took a big sniff. That black and white animal wasn't a cat, it was a _____. Then he _____.* Invite children to tell the end of the story.

3. Ask children *Do you always use one sense at a time or do you sometimes use more than one? Which sense or senses do you use when you sit down to eat dinner? What about when you watch TV or talk on the telephone?*

Math Activities

Favorite Food Chart

Skills: counting, data collection and display

Materials
- chart paper
- sample of food items (optional)

Preparation

Create a chart with food items (name and picture) for each of these categories: sweet, sour, salty, and bitter. A sample of each type of food can also be provided for children to taste before they choose their favorite.

Directions

Explain to children that *taste* is one of the five senses. Ask children which of the foods is their favorite to taste and why. Ask children questions such as *What's good about them? Do you eat them often or are they special treats?* Chart children's favorite foods. Compare the results. Ask *Which food got the most votes? Which got the least votes?*

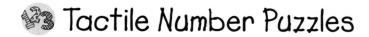

Tactile Number Puzzles

Skills: number sense, counting

Materials
- coarse sandpaper
- scissors
- large index cards
- glue
- hole punch

Preparation

Cut the numerals from 1 to 10 out of sandpaper. Glue each cutout to the left side of separate index cards. Use a hole punch to make 55 small circles out of a different piece of sandpaper. Find the card with the numeral one and glue one sandpaper circle to the right of it. Repeat for the remaining cards. Cut the number apart from the set of dots on each card. Make the cut on each card unique to make ten different puzzles.

Directions

Demonstrate for children how to match two pieces together to make a puzzle. Invite children to take turns finding matching number pairs. Encourage children to trace over the numeral and dots with their finger.

Dominoes

Skills: counting, matching

Materials
- large dominoes

Preparation

Collect only the dominoes with zero to six dots on either half.

Directions

Give each child five dominoes, and place the remaining dominoes facedown on a table. (This game is recommended for four or fewer children.) Turn over one of the dominoes. Ask a child if he or she has a domino that has the same number of dots on one side as the domino you just turned over. If the child has a match, ask him or her to place it beside the domino with the matching set of dots touching. If the child does not have a domino that matches, tell him or her to draw one domino from the table. Play continues with the next child. Tell children to play until a child has used all of his or her dominoes.

 Pizza Math

Skills: number sense, subtraction, fractions, counting

Materials
- pieces of red, orange, and tan flannel
- flannel board

Preparation

Create from the pieces of flannel a "pizza" with six slices. Set the pizza on the flannel board.

Directions

Ask children to raise their hand if pizza is one of their favorite foods. Have children point to the body part they use to taste pizza. Invite them to count the total number of slices on the board. Tell a story about children sharing the pizza. For example, ask *How many slices will be left if (child's name) eats two?* (Give that child two slices.) *Then, (child's name) comes along and eats one slice.* (Give that child one slice.) *How many slices will be left?*

Variation

Materials
- white, uncoated paper plates (1 per child)
- black marker
- scissors
- colored construction paper
- crayons or markers
- glue

Preparation

Create from the paper plates a "pizza" for each child. Use a black marker to draw lines to divide the plate into six "slices." Cut out shapes from construction paper to represent various pizza toppings (e.g., small red circles for pepperoni).

Directions

Give each child a pizza. Invite children to use crayons or markers to add sauce to their pizza. Give children "toppings" to glue on their pizza. Read a book to children from the recommended read-alouds (page 217) while the glue dries and an aide cuts each pizza into six slices. Invite children to count how many slices their pizza has. Ask children questions about their pizza such as *If you ate two slices, how many would be left?* (Encourage children to pretend to eat two slices and put the eaten slices on their lap.) *If your dog ate one slice when you weren't looking, how many slices would you have left?*

Weighing Bells

Skills: counting, estimating, weighing, comparing

Materials
- medium-sized bell
- small craft bells (enough so combined they can weigh as much as the medium-sized bell)
- chart paper
- balance scale

Preparation

Directions

Allow each child to take a turn holding a medium-sized bell and a smaller bell. Ask children *Which bell is heavier? How many little bells do you think it will take to weigh as much as the bigger bell?* Invite children to estimate how many small bells equal the weight of the larger bell. Record the estimates on chart paper. Put the larger bell on one side of a balance scale. Ask children to put small bells on the other side of the scale one at a time until the two sides balance. Encourage children to count aloud as each bell is added. At the end of the activity, let children ring the bells. Ask children questions such as *Which sense do you use to hear the bells ring? Which bell rings the loudest? Which bell rings the softest?*

Sensory Activities

Listening Tape

Materials
- audiotape
- tape recorder/player

Preparation

Create a tape of several easily recognizable sounds (e.g., doorbell ringing, horn honking, people talking, dog barking), or ask the children to make some of the sounds and record them.

Directions

Invite children to find a comfortable place on the ground, and ask them to lie down and close their eyes. Play the recording. Encourage children to listen carefully. Stop the tape after each sound, and ask children to identify it. After all of the sounds have been identified, have children think of other sounds they have heard (e.g., paper ripping, children laughing), and add these sounds to the tape recording.

Shadow Shapes

Materials
- overhead projector
- various small items with recognizable outlines (e.g., pencil, light bulb, CD, leaf)

Preparation

Set up an overhead projector to project on a screen or plain surface. Hide the items near the projector so children cannot see them.

Directions

Explain to children that they are going to play a guessing game using their sense of sight. Place one of the items on the overhead projector. Point out to children that this is the shape of an object they know. Invite children to guess what this shape might be. (If needed, give children clues.) After a few guesses, hold up the item so children can see if their guess was correct.

What Does Your Nose Smell?

Materials
- 35 mm film canisters with lids
- Phillips screwdriver (teacher use only)
- various items with a distinct scent (e.g., onions, banana slices, coffee grounds, vanilla extract, vinegar, rubbing alcohol, lemon oil, peppermint extract, perfume, aftershave, cinnamon)
- cotton balls
- pairs of matching stickers (optional)

Preparation

Use a screwdriver to puncture the lids of several film canisters. Put the liquid items on cotton balls. Place the scented cotton balls and other items in separate containers and secure the lids.

Directions

Encourage children to smell through the hole in each lid, describe the smell, and guess what the smell is. Invite children to separate items into the smells they like and dislike.

Variation

Make canisters of matching items. Place matching stickers on the bottom of the canisters of the same items for self-checking. Invite children to pair up the canisters with the same scents.

 Sound Shakers

Materials
- several plastic Easter eggs (the kind that open) or 35 mm film canisters
- identical pairs of small household items (e.g., rice, pennies, cotton balls, beads, paper clips, marbles, gravel)

Preparation

Place identical items in two plastic eggs or canisters. Repeat with another set of plastic eggs or canisters and a different item to make additional "sound shakers."

Directions

Explain to children that they are going to play a sensory game using their ears. Ask child which sense they will be using. Demonstrate how to play the game. Pick up a plastic egg, and shake it near your ear. Describe the sound you hear. Pick up another egg, shake it, and tell children whether you think it is the same or different sound. Invite children to repeat the process to find each matching pair of eggs. Challenge older children to guess what is inside each sound shaker.

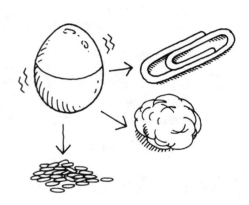

Guess What's Inside

Materials
- opaque rubber gloves
- sensory materials (e.g., gelatin dessert, rice, beans, cotton balls, sand, beads, water, flour)
- heavy-duty tape
- resealable plastic bags (optional)

Preparation

Fill separate gloves with different sensory materials. (Chill gelatin dessert and freeze ice until ready to use.) Tape each glove securely shut. (You may want to place each glove in a resealable plastic bag to prevent spills.)

Directions

Explain to children that today they will not be putting on the gloves to feel things. Tell children they will be feeling the gloves to figure out what is inside. Invite children to feel the gloves and guess what each one is filled with. Encourage children to use descriptive phrases to tell about what they feel (e.g., *This one feels hard and cold*).

Motor Skills Activities

 Scented Dough

Materials • Jell-O play dough (see Art Recipes, page 411)

Preparation

Make batches of Jell-O play dough with different flavors of gelatin to make different scents. Divide the dough into balls.

Directions

Give each child a ball of dough to manipulate. Encourage children to use sensory phrases (e.g., *It feels*, *It smells*, *I see*) to describe colors and scents.

Let's Feel

Materials
- large sheet of plastic
- tape
- items with various textures (e.g., carpet squares, textured fabric scraps, tissue paper, waxed paper, nylon netting, corrugated cardboard, bubble wrap, pans of pudding or shaving cream)
- bucket
- liquid dish soap
- water
- towels

Preparation

Tape down a large sheet of plastic to protect the floor. Place various items on top of the plastic for children to feel. Fill a bucket with warm, soapy water, and set it near the edge of the plastic.

Directions

Invite children to feel each item with their hands. Encourage children to describe the items they do and do not like to feel. Have children use soapy water and towels to clean their hands.

Potpourri Pictures

Materials

- bag of potpourri
- large bowl
- tweezers
- small bowls
- rubber gloves (for children with allergies)
- construction paper
- glue

Preparation

Pour potpourri into a large bowl.

Directions

Invite each child to use tweezers to sort the items in the potpourri into small bowls. Give each child a sheet of construction paper. Invite children to glue sorted potpourri pieces on their paper to make a scented, textured picture.

Bubble-Wrap Walking

Materials

- bubble wrap
- tape

Preparation

Tape bubble wrap to the floor.

Directions

Have children remove their shoes and socks. Invite children to walk across the bubble wrap in different ways (e.g., as light as a bird, as heavy as an elephant, as fast as a racehorse, as slow as a turtle, crawling like a baby). Invite children to share the different sensations they experienced.

Listening Walk

Materials
- tape recorder/player
- audiotape
- drawing paper (optional)
- crayons or markers (optional)

Preparation

Directions

Discuss with children what they might hear on a walk through the hallway of the school or on a walk outside the building. Take children on a walk. Use a tape recorder to tape the sounds children identify along the way. When you return to the classroom, have children listen to the tape. Encourage them to name what made each sound. Challenge older children to choose one of the sounds and draw a picture of its source.

Alphabet Activities

Play Dough Letters

Materials
- play dough (see Art Recipes, page 409)
- laminated alphabet cards

Preparation

Directions

Give each child a ball of play dough and one alphabet card. Invite children to roll play dough into a "snake." Tell children to arrange their snake into the shape of the letter either off to the side or on top of the alphabet card. Have children trade alphabet cards with each other, and repeat the activity.

 Tactile Name Cards

Materials
- card stock
- butcher paper
- sand, birdseed, and cornmeal
- glue
- bowls
- paintbrushes

Preparation

Write or type in large block letters each child's name on card stock to create "tactile name cards." Cover tables with butcher paper. Put glue, sand, birdseed, and cornmeal in separate bowls, and place the bowls on the tables.

Directions

Give each child a paintbrush and his or her name card. Show children how to paint with glue inside the first letter of their name and then how to sprinkle sand, birdseed, or cornmeal over the glue. Encourage children to continue until they have covered all of the letters. Allow the glue to dry, and then shake the excess material into the garbage can. Encourage children to practice saying the letters of their name as they trace over each letter with their finger.

 Name Hunt

Materials
- sentence strips
- photograph of each child
- double-sided tape

Preparation

Write each child's name on a separate sentence strip, and attach a photograph of each child to his or her strip. Hide these name cards around the classroom.

Directions

Invite children to find a classmate's name card and return it to the child whose name is on it. Once children have their card, challenge them to find another child that has one of the same letters in his or her name.

 # Letter Safari

M a t e r i a l s
- toilet paper tubes (2 per child)
- glue gun (teacher use only)

Preparation

Use a glue gun to attach two toilet paper tubes together to make a pair of "binoculars" for each child.

Directions

Tell children that the class will go on a "letter safari." Explain that they will observe different letters in their "natural surroundings." Give each child a pair of binoculars. Invite children to use their binoculars to find different letters. Encourage children to share the sounds or names of the letters they locate.

Variation

Take children on a letter safari for a particular letter. Encourage children to find things that begin with that letter. For example, go on a letter *b* safari. Help children identify things such as balls and backpacks and use adjectives starting with *b* to describe things they see (e.g., *That's a **big** car!*).

 # Whisper the Letter

M a t e r i a l s
- none

Preparation

Directions

Have children sit in a circle. Invite a child to whisper the name of a letter in your ear. Challenge the child to help you give the other children clues about the letter he or she named (e.g., the sound it makes, words that start with that letter, describe or draw in the air the shape of the letter) until someone guesses correctly. Continue until each child has had a turn to whisper the name of a letter in your ear.

Art Activities

 ## Textured Sponge Painting

Materials
- textured fabric scraps (e.g., burlap, nylon net, corduroy) large enough to wrap around sponge pieces
- sponges
- wooden clip-type clothespins
- paint pads in assorted colors (see Art Recipes, page 414)
- construction paper

Preparation

Wrap each piece of fabric around a sponge, and secure it with a clothespin to make textured sponges. Make paint pads in assorted colors.

Directions

Show children how to press a sponge on a paint pad and use it to make a print on construction paper. Give each child a piece of construction paper. Encourage children to use different sponges and paint pads to make a picture. Once the paint is dry, encourage children to feel the different textures of the dried paint.

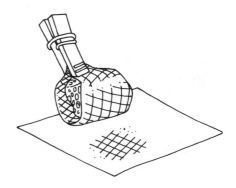

 ## Scented Art

Materials
- glue
- packets of sugarless drink mix (assorted flavors)
- bowls
- construction paper
- paintbrushes

Preparation

In separate bowls combine glue with the drink mix to make scented paint. Make a variety of scented paint.

Directions

Give each child a piece of construction paper and a paintbrush. Encourage children to use the scented paint to make a design or picture on their paper. Tell children that when the paint dries, it will still have its scent.

Sweet-Smelling Flowers

Materials

- perfume samples
- cotton balls
- green and light blue construction paper
- scissors
- green pipe cleaners
- glue
- large baking cup liners

Preparation

Put approximately three drops of different perfumes on separate cotton balls.

Directions

Give each child a sheet of green construction paper. Have children cut out two leaves. Give each child a sheet of light blue construction paper and a green pipe cleaner. Show children how to glue their pipe cleaner and leaves to their light blue paper to make a flower stem. Have children flatten a baking cup liner and glue it to the top of their stem. Invite children to choose a scented cotton ball and glue it to the center of their baking cup liner.

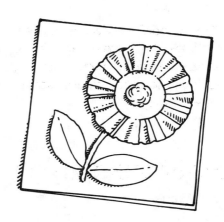

Handy Collage

Materials

- large piece of butcher paper
- paint pads in assorted colors (see Art Recipes, page 414)
- textured materials (e.g., sandpaper, bubble wrap, sponge pieces, faux fur, corrugated cardboard, aluminum foil)
- glue

Preparation

Label the top of a piece of butcher paper *Things We Like to Feel*. Make paint pads in assorted colors.

Directions

Give children materials with various textures to feel. Invite them to decide which one they like to feel the best. Have children press their hand on a paint pad and print their handprints along the edges of the butcher paper. Ask each child to make one handprint in the center of the paper. Write each child's name below his or her handprint. Invite children to glue a piece of their favorite material to their handprint.

🖌 Sensory Painting

Materials

- butcher paper
- tape
- finger paint
- bowls
- plastic spoons
- salt
- rice
- small pieces of pasta
- cornmeal
- sand

Preparation

Tape a large sheet of butcher paper to a table. Pour finger paint into separate bowls. Stir salt, rice, pasta, cornmeal, and sand into separate bowls of paint to make "sensory paint."

Directions

Put a spoonful of each type of sensory paint on the butcher paper. Invite children to finger-paint. Encourage children to describe how each mixture feels as they work.

🖌 Gingerbread Men

Materials

- Gingerbread Man reproducible (page 211)
- card stock
- scissors
- coarse sandpaper
- cinnamon sticks (1 per child)
- small buttons
- wiggly eyes
- glue

Preparation

Make one copy of the Gingerbread Man reproducible on card stock, and cut it out. Trace the card stock template on the back of sandpaper to make a classroom set of gingerbread men. Cut out each gingerbread man.

Directions

Give each child a sandpaper gingerbread man, a cinnamon stick, a few small buttons, two wiggly eyes, and glue. Encourage children to "color" their gingerbread man with their cinnamon stick. Invite children to glue on the buttons and wiggly eyes.

Cooking Activities

🥣 English Muffin Pizza

Ingredients

• For 8 pizzas:
  • 4 English muffins, halved
  • pizza sauce
  • pizza toppings (e.g., cheese, pepperoni, salami, ham, sausage, pineapple, vegetables)

Other Supplies

• plastic spoons
• baking sheet
• waxed paper
• permanent marker

Directions

Invite each child to use a plastic spoon to spread pizza sauce on a muffin and then add desired toppings. Place the pizzas on a baking sheet lined with waxed paper. Use a permanent marker to write each child's name beside his or her pizza. Bake the pizzas at 350°F (177°C) for about 5 minutes or until the cheese melts. Encourage children to describe the different types of flavors they taste as they eat their pizza (e.g., *The pineapple is sweet and juicy and the pepperoni is spicy*).

🥣 Food Comparison

Ingredients

• applesauce
• apple slices
• cheddar cheese
• cottage cheese
• mashed potatoes
• french fries
• pickles
• cucumber slices

Other Supplies

• paper plates

Directions

Give each child a plate with a bite-size portion of each item. (**Note**: This activity can use any of the same type of food that is prepared differently.) Ask children which sense they will use the most in this activity. Invite children to taste a pair of similar foods (e.g., applesauce and apple slices) at a time. Encourage children to compare the tastes of each pair of foods. Ask them questions such as *What is the same about the taste? What is different?*

Fresh Popcorn

Ingredients
- 1 cup (237 mL) popcorn kernels

Other Supplies
- hot-air popcorn popper
- large bowl
- small paper cups

Directions

Show children the unpopped kernels, and ask them how much popcorn they think it will make. Pop the corn in the air popper. Invite children to use a small cup to scoop out some popcorn. Ask children what senses they used while making and eating the popcorn: sight—see unpopped and popped corn, hear—listen to it pop, smell—smell it while it cooks and after, touch—feel the popcorn as they eat it, taste—taste the popcorn as they eat it.

Hand-Shaped Sugar Cookies

Ingredients
- rolls of refrigerated sugar-cookie dough
- frosting
- sprinkles

Other Supplies
- rolling pin
- plastic knife
- baking sheet
- craft sticks

Directions

Use a rolling pin to roll out the cookie dough. Invite each child to put a clean hand on the dough. Trace around each hand with a plastic knife and use the knife to press each child's initials into his or her cookie. Place each dough hand on a baking sheet. Bake according to the directions on the package. Have children use a craft stick to spread frosting on their cookie. Invite them to use sprinkles to decorate it.

Blindfolded Taste Test

Ingredients • assorted flavors of jellybeans or baby food

Other Supplies
• blindfold
• spoons

Directions

Blindfold a child. Ask the child to hold his or her nose. Have the child taste each food item. Ask the child if he or she can tell the difference between the different flavors. Ask if he or she can name the flavor. Repeat the activity with other children.

Fingerplays and Flannel Board Activities

Happy Senses

(Fingerplay)

Stand and point to the body parts as they are mentioned.

Eyes, eyes—they can see.
Nose, nose—it can smell.
Fingers, fingers—they can touch.
Hip, hip, hooray! I'm happy! *(dancing and spinning)*

Teeth, teeth—they can chew.
Tongue, tongue—it can taste.
Fingers, fingers—they can touch.
Hip, hip, hooray! I'm happy! *(dancing and spinning)*

Five Senses

(Fingerplay)

I have two ears to hear with. (*holding up two fingers*)
I have two eyes to see. (*holding up two fingers*)
I have two hands to touch things. (*holding up two fingers*)
They're all a part of me.

I have a mouth to taste with. (*holding up one finger*)
I use it also when I speak,
And a nose I use to smell things. (*holding up one finger*)
All my parts make me unique.

These are my five senses. (*holding up five fingers*)
I use them every day.
They help me understand my world
In a very special way.

What's on a Face?

(Flannel Board)

Create the following flannel board pieces: a circle for the face, two ears, a nose, a chin, a mouth, two eyes, and bushy eyebrows.

Here's a face. Now let's begin. (*placing circle on board*)
It has two ears, a nose, and a chin. (*adding ears, nose, and chin*)
A mouth, two eyes, with a bushy brow. (*adding mouth, eyes, and eyebrows*)
What's on a face? We all know now.

What Do You See?

(Flannel Board)

*Create flannel board pieces of various colored animals. Do this activity after reading **Brown Bear, Brown Bear, What Do You See?** by Bill Martin Jr.*

Teacher: **Tara**, **Tara**, what do you see? (*attaching a purple hippo*)
Tara: I see a **purple hippo** looking at me.

Continue the activity by replacing the boldfaced name and colored animal until each child has had a chance to answer.

I see a green turtle looking at me.

Songs

🎵 The Senses that I Have

(Sung to the tune of "The Farmer in the Dell")

The senses that I have,
The senses that I have,
I have five senses,
And I use them every day.

I taste with my tongue,
I taste with my tongue,
I taste the yummy food I eat.
I taste with my tongue.

I feel with my skin,
I feel with my skin,
I feel the things around me.
I feel with my skin.

I hear with my ears,
I hear with my ears,
I hear noises—loud and soft.
I hear with my ears.

I see with my eyes,
I see with my eyes,
I see shapes and colors.
I see with my eyes.

I smell with my nose,
I smell with my nose,
I sometimes smell my stinky toes!
I smell with my nose.

♫♪ Five Senses Songs

(Sung to the tune of "Old MacDonald Had a Farm")

Teach this song one verse at a time. Teach as many verses as desired.

On my face I have two eyes.
I use them every day.
They are used to help me see,
When I work and play.
With a look, look here,
And a look, look there.
Here a look. There a look.
Everywhere a look, look.
On my face I have two eyes.
I use them every day.

On my face I have one nose.
I use it carefully.
I just sniff, then I can tell
When something is smelly.
With a sniff, sniff here,
And a sniff, sniff there.
Here a sniff. There a sniff.
Everywhere a sniff, sniff.
On my face I have one nose.
I use it carefully.

In my mouth I have one tongue.
I use it when I eat.
Tasting with it I can tell
The sour from the sweet.
With a lick, lick here,
And a lick, lick there.
Here a lick. There a lick.
Everywhere a lick, lick.
In my mouth I have one tongue.
I use it when I eat.

On my head I have two ears
That listen all day long.
And if I didn't have them there,
I couldn't hear this song!
With a listen here,
And a listen there.
Here a listen. There a listen.
Everywhere a listen, listen.
On my head I have two ears
That listen all day long!

On my body I have skin
That feels the cold and heat.
It stretches from atop my head
Way down to my feet.
With a touch, touch here,
And a touch, touch there.
Here a touch. There a touch.
Everywhere a touch, touch.
On my body I have skin
That feels the cold and heat.

 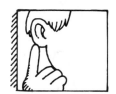

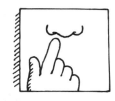 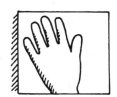

 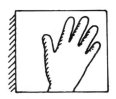

🎵 The Five Senses

(Sung to the tune of "Where is Thumbkin?")

The five senses, the five senses,
We have them. We have them.
Seeing, hearing, touching,
Tasting, and smelling.
There are five. There are five.

🎵 I'm Smelling

(Sung to the tune of "It's Raining, It's Pouring")

I'm smelling. I'm smelling.
My nose is busy smelling.
This is the song I like to sing
When I smell most anything!

Friends

Concepts

The concepts covered in this unit include the following:
- A friend is someone you like and who likes you back.
- Friends can be children in your neighborhood or school.
- Family members can be friends.
- It is good to have friends.
- Some very special friends who spend lots of time together are called best friends.
- In some ways, we are the same as our friends, but in many ways, we are different.
- Sometimes friends don't get along with each other.
- Friends play together, share, and cooperate.

Vocabulary

cooperate—to work together to help each other

friends—others whom you like and respect who feel the same way about you

friendship—the relationship between friends

share—to take turns using or doing something

Date _____

Dear Family:

"Friends" will be the theme for our next unit. We will be learning all about what friends are and how to be a good friend. For this unit we will need some assistance from you. Please send a snack (described under "Home Activities").

Classroom Activities

Children will participate in the following activities:
- Going on a group scavenger hunt.
- Working in pairs on string art.
- Sharing puzzles of themselves.
- Listening to and discussing *The Rainbow Fish* by Marcus Pfister.

Home Activities

Here are some activities for your family to try at home to complement what children are doing in the classroom:
- Please send a small resealable plastic bag to school containing your child's favorite dry snack (e.g., crackers, popcorn, M&M's, pretzels, cereal, fruit, cheese). Please send the snack by _____.
- Arrange playtimes for your child with different children in the classroom.

Have fun as you explore all of the fantastic Friendship activities with your child.

Thank you for all you do!

Sincerely,

Dear Family:

We will use the following items during our Friends unit. We would appreciate any help you could give us. We will begin this unit on _____, so please sign and return the form below if you can donate items by _____.

- inoperable cellular phones
- small box of tube-shaped pasta
- empty thread spools
- fabric and wallpaper scraps
- magazines and catalogs
- craft supplies—buttons, sequins, pipe cleaners, yarn, feathers
- packets of unflavored gelatin
- unopened box of graham crackers

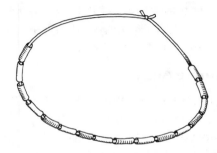

Thanks!

• •

I would like to contribute the following items for this unit:

_____

Please contact me at _____ (phone number or e-mail) to let me know how I can help.

_____

(parent's name)

Year-Round Early Childhood Themes © 2006 Creative Teaching Press

Center Ideas

The following are suggestions for different Friends centers. The various activities provided in this unit can be used or modified for these centers:

- **Art Center**—play dough (see Art Recipes, page 409), people cookie cutters, person-shaped easel paper

- **Block and Building Center**—selection of plain wood blocks, rocks, glue, paint (children can glue items together and paint it to make a paper weight to give to a friend)

- **Dramatic Play Center**—dress-up clothes, multicultural dolls, dollhouse, play phone, class phone book

- **Listening Center**—tapes of stories about friends, tapes of children in class having conversations or telling stories, tapes of stories written in class

- **Manipulatives Center**—pictures of children playing alone and together made into puzzles

- **Math and Science Center**—stethoscope, ink pads (materials to create finger prints)

- **Reading Center**—books about friendship (see recommended read-alouds, page 244), flannel board activities about friendship

- **Sand and Water Tables**—shovels, pails, and sandcastle molds (for children to work together to build a sandcastle)

- **Writing Center**—friend stickers, folded construction paper (to make friendship cards), stationery and envelopes

Language Development

Recommended Read-Alouds

The Best Friends Book by Todd Parr (Little, Brown and Company)

Brown Bear, Brown Bear, What Do You See? by Bill Martin, Jr. (Henry Holt and Company)*

Chester's Way by Kevin Henkes (Greenwillow Books)

Do You Want to Be My Friend? by Eric Carle (Philomel)

The Doorbell Rang by Pat Hutchins (Greenwillow Books)

A Friend is Someone Who Likes You by Joan Walsh Anglund (Harcourt)

Friends by Helme Heine (Aladdin)

My Best Friend by Pat Hutchins (Greenwillow Books)

A Porcupine Named Fluffy by Helen Lester (Walter Lorraine Books)

The Rainbow Fish by Marcus Pfister (North-South Books)

Swimmy by Leo Lionni (Alfred A. Knopf Books)

This Is My Friend by Mercer Mayer (Golden Books)

We Are Best Friends by Aliki (Greenwillow Books)

Will I Have a Friend? by Miriam Cohen (Aladdin)

*Read-aloud used in an activity

Read-Aloud Activity

Copy pictures from the beginning, middle, and end of a book. Show the copies to children, and ask *Which pictures do you think show what will happen at the beginning, middle, and end of the story?* Read the book to children, and check their predictions. Collect three shoeboxes of different sizes so they can fit inside each other to create nesting boxes. Glue the pictures from the beginning of the book on the outside of the largest box, pictures from the middle on the middle box, and pictures from the end on the smallest box. Put the boxes inside each other. Have children take apart the boxes and look at the pictures as they retell the story.

Discussion Starters

Use these suggestions to promote discussions about a read-aloud or to motivate children to tell a story. These ideas can be discussed and then used to write group stories for children to illustrate.

1. Ask children *What do you like about your friends? What do they do that makes you happy?*

2. Discuss with children their role as a friend. Ask *How can you be a good friend?* Record children's answers on chart paper.

3. Help children understand what they can do to make new friends. Ask questions such as *What would you do if you saw your friend sitting alone and looking sad?* Write children's answers on separate pieces of paper and bind the pages together to make a class book.

4. Chart children's favorite things with pictures (e.g., flavor of ice cream, color, food). Have children look at the charts, and point out that children have some likes in common with each other, but they have differences, too.

5. Display pictures of children playing together in class. Discuss what they are doing and what other things they could do with friends.

Math Activities

123 Friendship Bingo

Skills: comparing and matching pictures

Materials
- Bingo reproducible (page 210)
- individual class photographs
- scissors
- glue
- counters

Preparation

Make several copies of each child's individual class photograph, and cut out the photos. Copy a class set of the Bingo reproducible. Glue children's photographs to separate boxes of the game boards to make different bingo cards. Keep one set of the photos to lead the game.

Directions

Give each child a bingo card and several counters. Place children's individual class photos facedown in a pile. Draw a photo from the pile, and show it to children. Tell children to place a counter on the same photo if they see it on their card. Repeat with another child's photograph. Play continues until each child has covered all the photos on his or her card.

Class Phone Book

Skill: number recognition

Materials
- individual class photographs
- paper
- glue
- inoperable cellular phones

Preparation

Glue each child's photograph to a separate sheet of paper. Write each child's name and phone number below his or her photo. Bind the pages together into a class book titled *Our Friends' Phone Numbers*.

Directions

Place the class phone book with several telephones in the dramatic play center. Invite children to use the phones to "call" their friends.

Pattern Pals

Skills: matching, patterning

Materials
- 9" x 12" (23 cm x 30.5 cm) sheets of construction paper
- scissors
- resealable plastic bags
- shaped blocks

Preparation

Cut construction paper into 2" x 9" (5 cm x 23 cm) strips. Draw an AB or AABB pattern using block shapes on separate strips. Place each strip in a separate plastic bag with the blocks needed to create the pattern.

Directions

Divide the class into pairs. Give a bag with the patterning items to each pair, and invite children to use the blocks to make the pattern shown on the strip in their bag. Ask children to place their pattern strip and blocks back in the bag and give it to another pair of children.

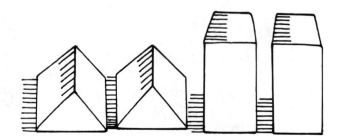

Counting Friends

Skills: counting, one-to-one correspondence

M a t e r i a l s
- Counting Friends reproducible (page 265)
- scissors

Preparation

Copy and cut apart a class set of the Counting Friends reproducible.

Directions

Give each child a set of the numerals and pictures from the reproducible. Invite children to match each numeral card with the number of children playing in each picture.

Making Friends

Skills: number sense, spatial relations

M a t e r i a l s
- Making Friends reproducible (page 266)
- card stock
- scissors
- dice

Preparation

Copy a class set of the Making Friends reproducible on card stock. (As an option, label the body parts before making copies.) On half of the copies, cut out the outline of the body and the different body parts.

Directions

Divide the class into pairs. Tell children they will be "making" friends out of pieces of paper. Give each pair a die, a reproducible, and a set of the reproducible's body parts. Invite children to take turns rolling the die and placing the body part with the matching number on top of the body. Have children play until they have placed each body part on their reproducible.

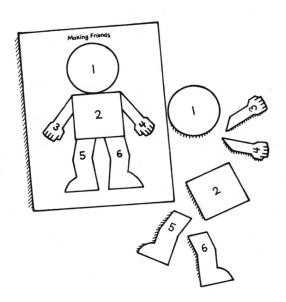

Sequencing Hearts

Skills: size comparison, sequencing

Materials
- red paper
- scissors

Preparation

Cut out three hearts of different sizes from red paper for each child.

Directions

Give each child a set of heart cutouts. Invite children to put their hearts in order from smallest to largest. Give each child a piece of red paper and scissors. Challenge children to cut out two hearts—one larger and one smaller than the others.

Sensory Activities

Friendship Hug

Materials
- none

Preparation

Directions

Have children sit in a circle and hold hands. Tell children that you are going to start a "friendship hug." Explain that you will squeeze the hand of the child to your left, and that child should squeeze the hand of the child to his or her left. Encourage children to continue until the hug returns to the person who started it.

 # Hearing Heartbeats

Materials • stethoscope

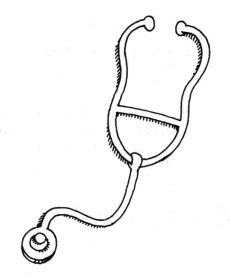

Preparation

Directions

Discuss with children the similarities they have with their friends (e.g., Daren and Stephanie both like sea creatures). Remind children that they often choose friends based on similarities. Tell children that one thing that everybody has in common is that their heart beats. Invite children to listen to their classmates' heartbeats.

Mirror, Mirror on the Wall

Materials • full-length mirror

Preparation

Directions

Invite two children to stand in front of a mirror. Ask them to tell what they see that is the same and different about each other. Encourage children to describe one thing they like about each other. Repeat the activity with a new pair of children.

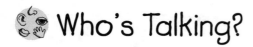 # Who's Talking?

M a t e r i a l s
- tape recorder/player
- audiotape

Preparation

Create a tape of each child saying, *I'm a great friend because _____.*

Directions

Play the tape for children, and invite them to guess who is talking. Discuss with children all of the ways that they are good friends.

Friendship Stories

M a t e r i a l s
- magazines and catalogs
- scissors
- construction paper
- glue
- paper

Preparation

Cut from magazines and catalogs pictures of friends playing and doing different activities together. Make sure there are enough pictures so each child can have one. Glue each picture on a separate sheet of construction paper.

Directions

Invite each child to select a picture. Ask children to dictate why they think the children in their picture are friends. Record children's dictation on a separate sheet of paper. On a different day, display all of the pictures on a wall or ledge. Read aloud a child's dictation, and ask children to point to the picture that is being described. Repeat with other children's papers.

Friendship Book

Materials
- photographs of groups of children from class playing together
- bookbinding materials (e.g., card stock, scissors, glue, hole punch, yarn)

Preparation

Use the photographs to make a class book.

Directions

Encourage children to find themselves in the class book. Ask children to dictate a sentence or two about what they are doing in their picture, and write their words below their picture. Place the book in the reading center.

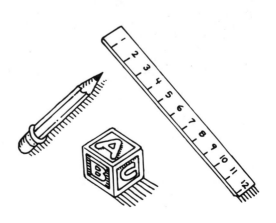

Motor Skills Activities

Scavenger Hunt

Materials
- Scavenger Hunt Lists (page 267)
- scissors

Preparation

Copy and cut apart the Scavenger Hunt Lists.

Directions

Divide the class into four teams. Give each team a different list of items to find. When the teams find their items, ask them to bring the items back to the circle and sit down. Have each group share with the rest of the class what they found and how they worked together.

Balancing Friends

Materials • 2 balance beams

Preparation

Set up balance beams parallel and approximately 1 foot (30.5 cm) apart.

Directions

Invite two children to hold hands and walk across the beams at the same time. Make positive comments as the children walk across (e.g., *Look how these friends are helping each other*).

Friendly Musical Shares

Materials
• class set of chairs
• music on CD/tape
• CD/tape player

Preparation

Set up chairs as you would for Musical Chairs. Make sure there is one for each child.

Directions

Invite children to play a game similar to Musical Chairs. Have each child stand next to a chair. Remove a chair, and start the music. Show children which direction they should walk in until the music stops. Stop the music, and have children find a chair to sit on. Encourage a sitting child to share his or her chair with the child left standing. Invite the children sharing a chair to name each other. Remove another chair, and start the music again. Repeat the game until every child is sharing a chair with a friend.

Friendship Necklace

Materials
- colored tube-shaped pasta (see Art Recipes: Pasta and Rice Dye, page 416)
- yarn
- scissors
- tape

Preparation

Use the Pasta and Rice Dye recipe on page 416 to color pasta. Cut yarn into necklace-length pieces. Tape one end of each strand and tie a piece of pasta to the other end to make a "stopper."

Directions

Give each child a piece of yarn and some pasta. Show children how to string the pasta on their piece of yarn. Tie the ends of the string together to make a necklace. Encourage children to give their necklace to a friend.

Friendly Ball Roll

Materials
- medium or large-sized ball

Preparation

Directions

Have children sit in a circle. To start, say something similar to *My name is **Miss Holly**, and my friend is **Lance**.* Roll a ball to that child. Invite the child to use the name of a different child to repeat the activity. Continue until all children have been named.

Alphabet Activities

Name Hunt

Materials
- sentence strips
- photograph of each child
- tape

Preparation

Write each child's name on a separate sentence strip, and attach the matching photograph. Hide the name strips around the room.

Directions

Invite children to look for a name strip. When they find a strip, have them give it to the child it belongs to. (Remind children to say *Thank you* and *You're welcome.*)

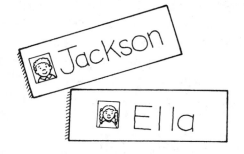

Who Do You See?

Materials
- Who Do You See? reproducible (page 268)
- *Brown Bear, Brown Bear, What Do You See?* by Bill Martin Jr.
- photograph of each child
- glue
- bookbinding materials

Preparation

Copy a class set of the Who Do You See? reproducible.

Directions

Read aloud *Brown Bear, Brown Bear, What Do You See?* Tell children that they are going to create a story that is similar to the one they just heard. Invite a child to start the story by saying something similar to *John, John, who do you see?* Prompt the child to follow the format of *I see Jessica looking at me.* Write the child's name on a copy of the reproducible. Repeat for each child in class. Attach each child's photograph to his or her page, bind the pages together, and put the book in the reading center for children to enjoy.

 # Alphabet Switch

Materials
- large index cards
- hole punch
- yarn
- scissors

Preparation

Label each index card with a different letter so each child will have one. Punch two holes in each index card at the top corners. Cut yarn into necklace-length pieces, and string a piece through the holes in each index card to make a letter necklace for each child.

Directions

Have children sit in a circle on the floor. Give each child a letter necklace, and review as a class each letter's name. Call out two letters, and invite the children with the letters named to skip across the circle and switch places with each other. Repeat the activity until each child has switched places a few times.

 # Alphabet Hearts

Materials
- pink construction paper
- scissors

Preparation

Cut construction paper into heart shapes. Label each heart cutout with a different uppercase letter written on one half and the corresponding lowercase letter on the other half. Cut each heart into two pieces between the letters with a unique puzzle cut. Mix up the heart halves, and place them faceup on a table.

Directions

Show children the different halves of the hearts. Show children how the halves go together to make a heart. Remind children that a heart is a symbol for love, and when we love our friends it means we like and care for them. Invite children to pick up one half of a heart and search for the matching half.

Friendly Letters

Materials • large alphabet cards

Preparation

Directions

Divide the class into small groups. Show children a set of alphabet cards one at a time. Challenge groups to work together to use their bodies to form the letters of the alphabet.

Five-Letter Friends

Materials
- large alphabet cards
- large index cards
- hole punch
- yarn
- scissors

Preparation

Select the alphabet cards you want to use (at least five). Write one letter from the selected alphabet cards on each index card. Punch two holes in each index card at the top corners. Cut yarn into necklace-length pieces, and string a piece through the holes in each index card to make a letter necklace.

Directions

Give each of five children a different letter necklace. Review with the class the name and sound of each letter. Teach children this song sung to the tune of "Five Little Ducks," and have the children with the cards act it out:

Five letter friends went out to play
Over the hill and far away. (*the five children go to the other side of the room*)
The other friends called /**a**/, /**a**/, /**a**/, (*hold up the matching alphabet card*)
But only letter **a** came running back. (*the child with the matching letter necklace comes back*)

Replace the boldfaced letter and repeat with other letters and children.

Art Activities

Friendship Rainbow

Materials
- butcher paper
- rainbow-colored paint (i.e., red, orange, yellow, green, blue, indigo, and violet)—each color on a separate paint pad (see Art Recipes, page 414)

Preparation

Use a pencil to lightly draw a large rainbow on butcher paper. Make rainbow-colored paint pads.

Directions

Invite children to place their hand on the red paint pad and fill in the top band of the rainbow with red handprints. Continue with other colors in order (i.e., orange, yellow, green, blue, indigo, violet) to cover the entire rainbow with handprints.

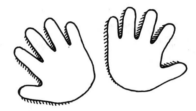

Friendship Collage

Materials
- butcher paper
- tape
- collage material (e.g., scraps of fabric, paper, and wallpaper; feathers; sequins; buttons; pipe cleaners)
- glue

Preparation

Divide a piece of butcher paper into sections—one section for every two children. Tape the butcher paper to the floor. Set out the collage material on a table.

Directions

Assign pairs to work together. (Try to pair up children who do not usually play together.) Invite partners to pick out five to ten collage items to glue in their section. If needed, help children label their section with their names.

🖌 Group Picture

Materials
- white construction paper
- crayons and markers
- bookbinding materials

Preparation

Set up a place for each child to sit at a table. Place a sheet of white construction paper and crayons and markers at each spot.

Directions

Explain to children that they will work on an art project together. Invite children to sit down and start drawing on the paper in front of them. After about a minute, have children pass their paper to their left. Continue in the same manner until all children at the table have contributed to each picture. Bind the pages together to make a class book. The book can be sent home with a different child every night to share with his or her family, or it can be placed in the reading center.

🖌 Friendship String Art

Materials
- paint (assorted colors)
- pie tins
- yarn
- scissors
- empty thread spools (1 for every pair of children)
- construction paper
- newspaper

Preparation

Pour different colors of paint into separate pie tins. Cut yarn into 2-foot (61-cm) sections so there is one piece for every two children. Tie a spool to one end of each piece of yarn. Fold construction paper in half widthwise so there is one sheet for every two children. Cover the work area with newspaper.

Directions

Divide the class into pairs. Give one child in each pair the yarn with the spool and the other the construction paper. Have the child with the paper place it on the floor. Show children how to open their paper so the creased edge is touching the floor. Tell the child with the yarn to hold it by the spool, dip the yarn in paint, and lower the yarn into the fold of the paper. Have the child holding the paper close it around the yarn. Have children unfold the paper, remove the yarn, and switch roles.

Cooking Activities

🥣 Friendship Munchies

Ingredients
- favorite dry snacks sent in by families (see Family Letter: Theme Introduction, page 241)

Other Supplies
- large bowl
- serving spoon
- small paper cups

Directions

Invite each child to pour his or her snack from home into a large bowl. Mix the snacks together. Spoon the mix into a cup for each child to give to another child.

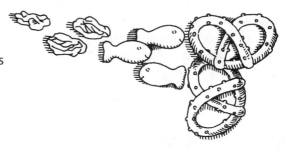

🥣 Friendly Faces

Ingredients
- small tortillas (1 per child)
- low-fat cream cheese
- fruit (e.g., apples, bananas, kiwi, pear, pineapple, raisins)

Other Supplies
- kitchen knife (teacher use only)
- plastic spoons

Directions

In advance, wash and slice fruit into various shapes and sizes. Give each child a tortilla and a spoonful of cream cheese. Tell children to use the back of their spoon to spread the cream cheese over the tortilla. Have children use pieces of fruit to create a friendly face.

Juicy, Jiggly Friends

Ingredients

- 3 packets of unflavored gelatin
- ¾ cup (177 mL) boiling water
- 12-ounce (355-mL) can of frozen apple, orange, grape, or other juice concentrate

Other Supplies

- saucepan
- spoon
- 9" x 13" (23 cm x 33 cm) pan
- people-shaped or gingerbread man cookie cutters

Directions

Dissolve gelatin in boiling water. Add juice, and stir until well mixed. Pour gelatin mixture into a 9" x 13" pan. Chill at least 2 hours. Invite children to use the cookie cutters to cut out friendly figures from the gelatin. When children eat their treat, remind them to take small bites and not swallow it whole.

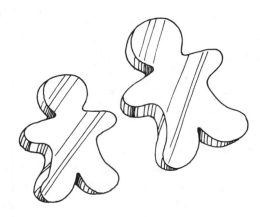

Graham Cracker Gifts

Ingredients

- graham crackers
- flavored cream cheese

Other Supplies

- craft sticks
- aluminum foil

Directions

Break graham crackers in half, and give each child two halves. Have children wash their hands and then use craft sticks to spread cream cheese on one half. Tell children to put the other half of the graham cracker on top of the cream cheese. Show children how to wrap each graham cracker "sandwich" in foil. Have children give their sandwich to a friend.

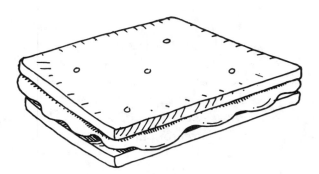

Fingerplays and Flannel Board Activities

Making Friends

(Fingerplay)

One little child standing on his own. (*holding up one finger*)
Two little children, now they're not alone. (*holding up two fingers*)
Three little children happy as can be. (*holding up three fingers*)
Four little children playing in a tree. (*holding up four fingers*)
Five little children, they're all friends. (*holding up five fingers*)
Wave good-bye 'cause that's the end. (*waving*)

Five Little Friends

(Fingerplay)

Five little friends playing on the floor, (*holding up five fingers*)
One got tired, and then there were four. (*stretching and yawning, holding up four fingers*)
Four little friends climbing up a tree, (*pretending to climb a tree*)
One jumped down, and then there were three. (*jumping, holding up three fingers*)
Three little friends running at the zoo, (*running in place*)
One fell down, and then there were two. (*sitting on floor, holding up two fingers*)
Two little friends sitting in the sun, (*using hand as a visor over eyes*)
One got hungry, and then there was one. (*placing hand on tummy, holding up one finger*)
One little friend looking for some fun, (*looking around*)
He fell asleep, and then there were none. (*pretending to sleep*)

You Are Special

(Flannel Board—sung to the tune of "One Elephant Went Out to Play")

Create these flannel board pieces: a photograph of each child backed with the rough side of Velcro. Add a different child's photo before singing each verse. Continue until all the children's pictures are displayed. The following are two examples of how to do the activity:

One fun child went out to play (*putting up the child's photo*)
On a bright and sunny day.
He had so much fun,
He wanted to share it with someone.

Two fun children went out to play
(*adding the new child's photo*)
On a bright and sunny day.
They had so much fun,
They wanted to share it with someone.

Songs

Friendship Boogie

(Sung to the tune of "The Hokey Pokey")

You give your friend a high five.
You give your friend a big smile.
You give your friend a quick wink,
And then you dance for a while.
You do the friendship boogie,
And you turn yourself around.
Making friends is what it's all about.

🎵 Friends Go Marching

(Sung to the tune of "The Ants Go Marching)

Have children march in a circle and have those who fit the characteristic you name sit down in the middle of the circle. Continue singing by replacing the boldfaced word until all children sit down.

My friends are marching round and round.
Hurrah, hurrah.
My friends are marching round and round.
Hurrah, hurrah.
My friends are marching round and round.
Those wearing **black** must sit down.
We'll march around until we all sit down!

🎵 Best Friend

(Sung to the tune of "You Are My Sunshine")

You are my best friend,
My very best friend.
You make me happy,
Every day.
You share your tasty snacks,
You share your best toys,
So don't take
My best friend away.

🎵 This is . . .

(Sung to the tune of "London Bridges")

This is **Cole**. **He's** our friend,
He's our friend, **he's** our friend.
This is **Cole**. **He's** our friend.
He's so special!

Continue singing by replacing the boldfaced name and pronoun until all children have been named.

♫ Ten Special Friends

(Sung to the tune of "Ten Little Indians")

One special, two special, three special friends,
Four special, five special, six special friends,
Seven special, eight special, nine special friends,
Ten special friends are we!

♫ Where Is . . .?

(Sung to the tune of "Where Is Thumbkin?")

Where is **Mia**? Where is **Mia**?
There **she** is, there **she** is.
Dance and spin around.
Dance and spin around.
Now sit down, now sit down.

Continue singing by replacing the boldfaced name and pronoun until all children have been named. Other actions can be substituted such as jump up and down and skip around the circle.

♫ If You're Friendly and You Know It

(Sung to the tune of "If You're Happy and You Know It")

If you're friendly and you know it,
Wave hello. (*waving*)
If you're friendly and you know it,
Wave hello. (*waving*)
If you're friendly and you know it,
And you really want to show it,
If you're friendly and you know it,
Wave hello. (*waving*)

Additional verses:
Shake a hand.
Blow a kiss.
Give a hug.
Shout, "Hooray!"

Counting Friends

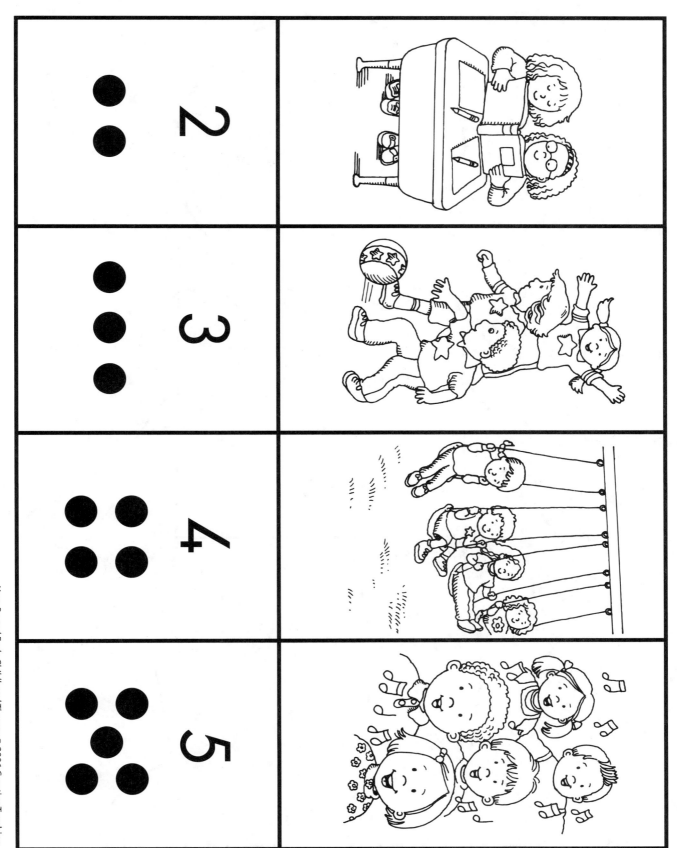

Making Friends

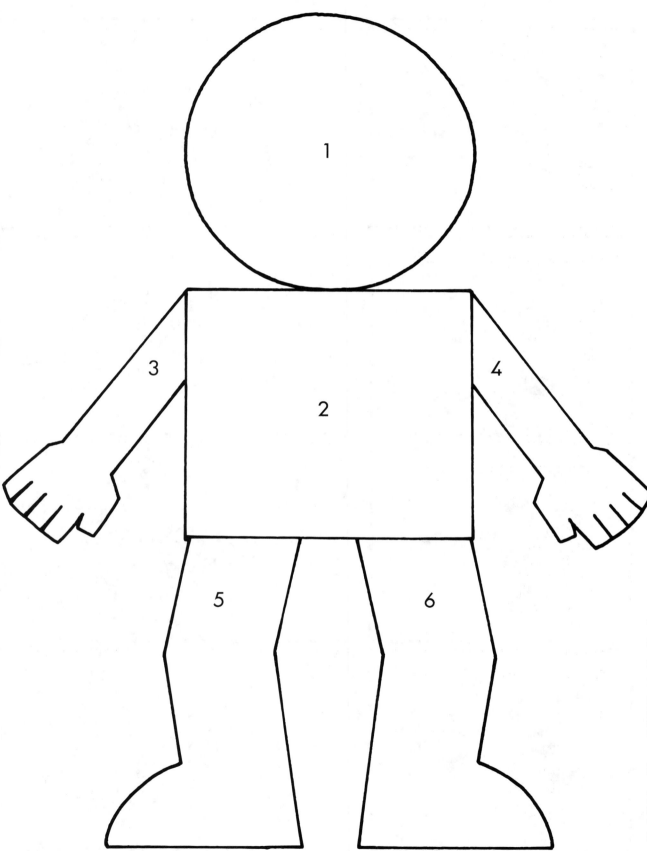

Year-Round Early Childhood Themes © 2006 Creative Teaching Press

Scavenger Hunt Lists

Scavenger Hunt List #1

1. pencil

2. crayon

3. book

Scavenger Hunt List #2

1. block

2. paper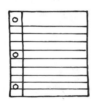

3. marker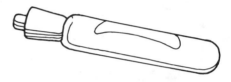

Scavenger Hunt List #3

1. doll

2. paintbrush

3. tape

Scavenger Hunt List #4

1. ball

2. ruler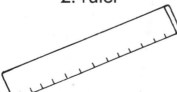

3. eraser

Who Do You See?

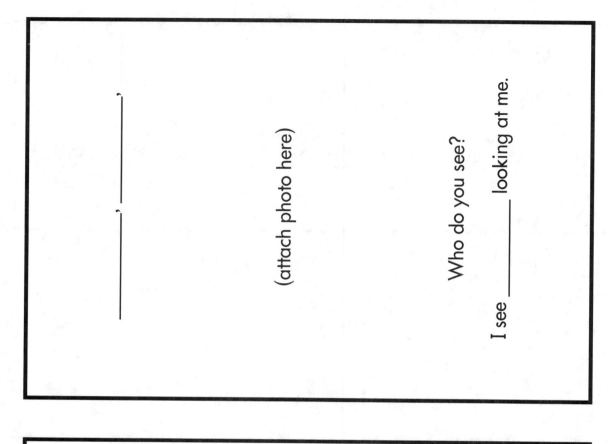

(attach photo here)

Who do you see?

I see _____ looking at me.

(attach photo here)

Who do you see?

I see _____ looking at me.

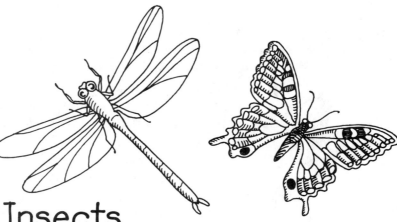

Insects

Concepts

The concepts covered in this unit include the following:
- All insects have three body parts and six legs.
- Spiders are not insects; they have eight legs.
- There are many types of insects. Ants, aphids, bees, ladybugs, butterflies, caterpillars, crickets, fireflies, houseflies, dragonflies, mosquitoes, cockroaches, and grasshoppers are some types of insects.
- Insects move in different ways. Some fly, while others walk, crawl, hop, or swim.
- Bees and ants live in large communities, and each bee or ant has its own special job.
- Some insects camouflage themselves for protection.
- Insects live in many different places.
- Insects communicate in many ways.
- Caterpillars go through a metamorphosis or change and become butterflies.
- Insects can be helpful and harmful.

Vocabulary

abdomen—the final body section of an insect

antennae—the pair of feelers on the head of insects

camouflage—coloring that helps insects blend into their surroundings for protection

chrysalis—the protective covering during the pupa stage of a butterfly's metamorphosis

larva—the stage of an immature insect's metamorphosis between egg and pupa when it feeds and molts

metamorphosis—a change in physical form

pollinate—the process of insects transferring pollen to help plants grow

pupa—the stage in an insect's metamorphosis between larva and adult where it is usually enclosed in a protective covering to undergo changes

thorax—the middle body section of an insect

Date _____

Dear Family:

"Insects" will be the theme for our next unit. Children are fascinated by these small creatures all around us and the changes they undergo.

Classroom Activities

Children will participate in the following activities:
- Learning how to identify insects.
- Singing songs and doing fingerplays about insects.
- Conducting an experiment to find out what food ants like best.
- Listening to and discussing *The Very Hungry Caterpillar* by Eric Carle.
- Making a beautiful "butterfly snack."

Home Activities

Here are some activities for your family to try at home to complement what children are doing in the classroom:
- Take a family walk or visit a park and observe several insects. Encourage your child to describe the physical characteristics of each insect and how it moves.
- Make bug puppets out of socks and other craft materials. Your child is welcome to bring the puppets to school to share.

Have fun as you explore all of the interesting Insect activities with your child.

Thank you for all you do!

Sincerely,

Dear Family:

We will use the following items during our Insects unit. We would appreciate any help you could give us. We will begin this unit on _____, so please sign and return the form below if you can donate items by _____.

- new flyswatters
- picnic supplies
- cotton balls
- dry dog food
- cheesecloth
- fruit—red apples, pears, plums, strawberries, oranges
- turkey basters
- craft supplies—sequins, ribbon, yarn
- pasta—rotini, shell, and bowtie
- small pretzel sticks and knots

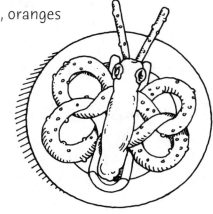

Thanks!

• •

I would like to contribute the following items for this unit:

_____

Please contact me at _____ (phone number or e-mail) to let me know how I can help.

_____
(parent's name)

Year-Round Early Childhood Themes © 2006 Creative Teaching Press

Center Ideas

The following are suggestions for different Insect centers. The activities provided in this unit can be used or modified for these centers:

- **Art Center**—insect templates, stencils, clay or play dough (see Art Recipes, page 409), insect-shaped easel paper

- **Block and Building Center**—plastic insects, toilet paper tubes, egg cartons, clay, glue

- **Dramatic Play Center**—insect puppets, plastic insects, magnifying glass, insect nets, insect costumes

- **Listening Center**—tapes of books about insects, tapes of insect sounds, tapes of stories written in class

- **Manipulatives Center**—insect puzzles, variety of plastic insects

- **Math and Science Center**—secure habitats with live insects such as ladybugs, caterpillars, and butterflies (with proper care); models or pictures of insects; honeycomb; magnifying glasses

- **Reading Center**—insect books and stories (see recommended read-alouds, page 274), stories written in class

- **Sand and Water Tables**—plastic insects, tongs, tweezers

- **Writing Center**—insect stamps and stickers, paint pads (see Art Recipes, page 414) to make fingerprint insects

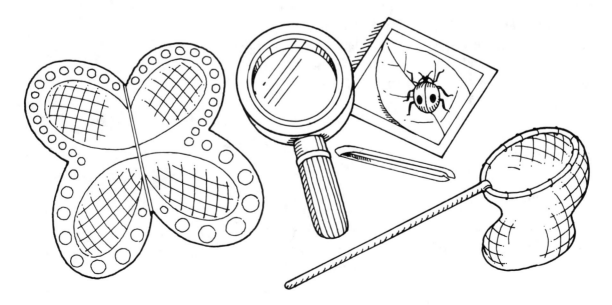

Language Development

Recommended Read-Alouds

Are You a Bee? by Judy Allen (Kingfisher)

Are You a Ladybug? by Judy Allen (Kingfisher)

Are You an Ant? by Judy Allen (Kingfisher)

Caterpillar Spring, Butterfly Summer by Susan Hood (Reader's Digest)

From Caterpillar to Butterfly by Deborah Heiligman (HarperCollins)

How to Hide a Butterfly: And Other Insects by Ruth Heller (Grosset & Dunlap)

The Napping House by Audrey Wood (Red Wagon Books)

Quick as a Cricket by Audrey Wood (Child's Play)

Ten Little Ladybugs by Melanie Gerth (Piggy Toes Press)

There Was an Old Lady Who Swallowed a Fly by Simms Taback (Viking)

The Very Clumsy Click Beetle by Eric Carle (Philomel)

The Very Hungry Caterpillar by Eric Carle (Philomel)*

The Very Lonely Firefly by Eric Carle (Philomel)

The Very Quiet Cricket by Eric Carle (Philomel)

What Do Insects Do? by Susan Canizares (Scholastic)

*Read-aloud used in an activity

Read-Aloud Activity

Read a book to the children. Ask children what new things they have learned about insects from the book. Ask recall questions from the story. Make a "story bag" with flannel board pieces that relate to the story, and store them in a resealable plastic bag. Invite children to retell the story by themselves or in a group using the flannel board pieces.

Discussion Starters

Use these suggestions to promote discussions or to motivate children to tell a story. These can be discussed and then used to write group stories for children to illustrate.

1. Invite children to share their favorite characteristics of different insects. Have children complete the sentence *If I could have any kind of insect for a pet, I would have a _____ because _____.*

2. Help children see life from an insect's perspective. Ask them to tell you *If I were an ant, I would be afraid of _____ because _____.*

3. Ask children to share their preferences. Have them complete the following sentences:
   If I were a bee...
   I would like _____(color) flowers.
   I would build my hive _____ (where) because _____.
   I would hide _____(where) during a storm.
   I wouldn't be yellow and black; I would be _____ and _____.
   I wouldn't buzz, I would _____.

4. Invite children to draw a picture of their favorite insect. Have children complete the sentence as you write down their dictation: *My bug is a _____. It can _____. It eats _____.*

5. On butterfly-shaped paper, invite children to complete the sentence *If I were a butterfly, I _____.*

6. At the end of the unit, have children complete the sentence *If I were a bug, I would be a _____ because _____.*

Math Activities

Spot the Dots

Skills: counting, one-to-one correspondence, symmetry

Materials
- Spot the Dots reproducible (page 299)
- red paper
- black markers

Preparation
Copy a class set of the Spot the Dots reproducible on red paper.

Directions
Give each child a copy of the reproducible. Ask children to help you count the dots on each ladybug. Give each child a black marker. Have children use it to make the same number of dots on the other side of each ladybug.

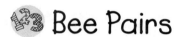 Favorite Insects Graph

Skills: counting, data collection and display

Materials
- overhead transparency
- overhead markers
- overhead projector
- pictures of insects

Preparation

Create a graph on an overhead transparency. Write the names of different insects and make a simple drawing of each on the graph. Title it *Our Favorite Insects*.

Directions

Show children pictures of insects, and ask which one is their favorite. Record children's responses on the graph. Discuss the results with children. Ask them questions such as *Which insect got the most votes? The least votes?*

Bee Pairs

Skills: counting, matching, one-to-one correspondence, ordering

Materials
- Bee Pairs reproducible (page 300)
- yellow paper
- scissors

Preparation

Copy a class set of the Bee Pairs reproducible on yellow paper, and cut out each bee.

Directions

Divide the class into pairs, and give each pair two sets of bee cutouts. Invite pairs to mix up the bees and then group them by number of stripes. Challenge children to put their bees in counting order.

Ladybug Spots

Skills: counting, matching, one-to-one correspondence

Materials
- Ladybug Spots Cards (page 301)
- red paper
- scissors
- paper clips

Preparation

Copy a class set of the Ladybug Spots Cards on red paper. (For more advanced children, make a copy of the cards, and cover the spots on the cards that have the numerals written on them.) Cut apart each set of cards, and paper-clip the sets together.

Directions

Give each child a set of cards. Invite children to match the cards that have the same number of spots on them.

Ants at the Picnic

Skills: counting, one-to-one correspondence, subtraction

Materials
- dice
- plastic ants (raisins can be used if plastic ants are not available)
- picnic supplies (e.g., paper plates, plastic utensils, tablecloth, pretend food)

Preparation

Directions

Divide the class into pairs for this game. Give each pair a die, 20–30 plastic ants, and picnic supplies. Have children set up their "picnic" and put the ants off to the side. Invite partners to take turns rolling the die and counting out that number of ants to place on their picnic plate. Explain to children that they must roll the exact number to put the last ant or ants on their plate. The game ends when both players put all of their ants on the plate.

 Ant Sizing

Skills: size comparison, ordering

Materials
- Ant Sizing reproducible (page 302)
- scissors

Preparation

Copy and cut apart a class set of the Ant Sizing reproducible.

Directions

Give each child a set of ant cutouts. (Vary the number of ants used in this activity based on children's ability.) Discuss with children how to use the terms *bigger* and *smaller* to compare the sizes of the ants. Ask them to hold up their largest ant and then their smallest ant. Invite children to put their ants in order from smallest to largest and then largest to smallest.

Butterfly Wing Hunt

Skill: matching colors

Materials
- Butterfly Wings reproducible (page 303)
- copy paper (assorted colors)
- scissors
- extra-long pipe cleaners (1 per child)
- clear tape

Preparation

Copy a class set of the Butterfly Wings reproducible so each pair is a different color (depending on class size, you may need to do this activity in smaller groups), and cut each pair of wings apart. Place one butterfly wing of each color somewhere in the classroom. Create the butterflies' bodies using pipe cleaners. Fold each pipe cleaner in half. Twist the two sides around each other about 1 inch (2.5 cm) in from the end to make the antennae.

Directions

Give each child one butterfly wing. Help children find the matching wing. Give each child a pipe-cleaner body, and tape both wings to the body. Show children how to hold the bottom of the butterfly's body and wave it around to make it "fly." Invite children to sit in a circle. Call out two different colors, and have the children with the corresponding butterflies stand up and fly their butterfly to the other child's spot and sit down. Repeat until all children have had a chance to switch places.

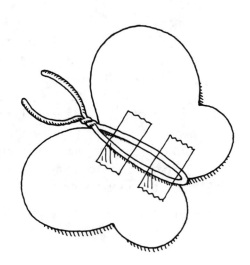

Sensory Activities

 ## Bug Club

M a t e r i a l s   • magnifying glasses (1 per child)

Preparation

Plan to take children to an outside area to look for insects on a nice day.

Directions

Explain to children that they are going to be part of a "bug club." Tell them the bug club looks for places insects might live. Remind children that insects often find good hiding places to live where they will not get eaten or stepped on. Give each child a magnifying glass. Take the class outside to find insects. Invite children to look for insects under rocks and sticks and in bushes and grass. Remind children to look at the insects but not touch them. Point out how some insects blend in with their background. Tell children that this is called *camouflage* and it keeps the insects safe because they are hard to see.

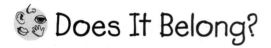 ## Does It Belong?

M a t e r i a l s   • pictures of animals and insects

Preparation

Directions

Have children sit in a circle. In the middle of the circle, place pictures of three insects and one animal. Encourage children to discuss the similarities and differences between the creatures in the pictures. Have children decide which pictures belong together and which picture does not. Invite them to share the reasons why that picture does not belong. Repeat this activity with other combinations of insects and an animal.

What Do Ants Like to Eat?

Materials
- food items (e.g., cracker, lettuce leaf, sugar, piece of fruit, cookie)
- paper plate

Preparation

Directions

Display each food item. Have children identify the different foods and share with the class which ones they like to eat. Explain to children that they are going to find out if ants like to eat the same foods that they do. Place the food on a paper plate, and set it outside for a few hours on a warm day. (For best results, put the plate where you see some ants.) Take the class out periodically to observe which foods the ants did and did not eat.

Camouflaged Insect Hunt

Materials
- sand table or tub
- sand, colored rice, or colored pasta (the color of dirt)
- plastic insects
- hand shovels
- sieves
- tweezers

Preparation

Put sand, colored rice, or colored pasta (see Art Recipes: Rice and Pasta Dye, page 416) in a sand table or tub, and hide plastic insects in it.

Directions

Tell children that insects are sometimes hard to see because their colors blend into the background. Explain that this is called *camouflage*. Invite children to use hand shovels and sieves to sift through the "dirt" to find camouflaged "insects." Invite them to remove the insects with tweezers. Ask children if they can count the number of legs on each insect and identify it.

Cricket Habitat

Materials

- crickets (available at pet stores)
- small aquarium
- dirt
- grass clippings
- branches
- egg carton cut into separate pieces
- lid from a jar
- wet cotton balls
- small pieces of fruit
- pieces of dry dog food
- cheesecloth

Preparation

Gather all of the items listed above for use in a habitat for crickets.

Directions

Explain to children that all living creatures need four elements to survive: shelter, water, food, and air. Tell children that they are going to help build a home or habitat for crickets. Discuss with children each element the crickets need as you build the different parts of the crickets' home:

- Put dirt, grass clippings, branches, and egg carton pieces into the aquarium (shelter).
- Place a lid with wet cotton balls on top of the dirt (water).
- Add fruit and dry dog food pieces (food).
- Add the crickets.
- Cover the aquarium with cheesecloth (to allow air in).

Encourage children to observe the crickets for a week, and then release them.

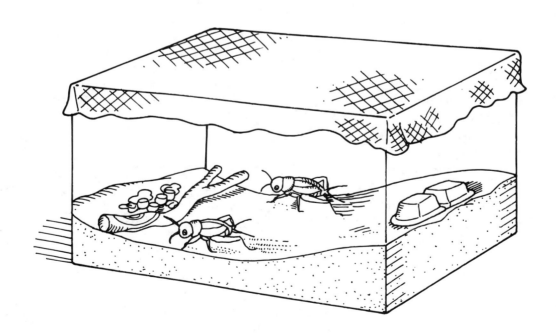

Motor Skills Activities

 Three Body Parts and Six Legs

Materials • none

Preparation

Directions

Divide the class into groups of three, and assign each child in the group a different insect body part—head, thorax, or abdomen. Have children line up in their groups and place their hands on the shoulders of the child in front of them. Tell the child at the front of the line to put his or her arms in the air to make "antennae." Sing the song below to the tune of "Mary Had a Little Lamb," and have children follow the directions.

Insects have three body parts,
Body parts, body parts.
Insects have three body parts,
And this is what they are:

Insects have a head that moves,
    (*first child moves*)
Head that moves, head that moves.
Insects have a head that moves
And wiggles to and fro.

Insects have a thorax,
A thorax, a thorax.
Insects have a thorax
That wiggles to and fro.
    (*second child wiggles*)

Insects have an abdomen,
An abdomen, an abdomen.
Insects have an abdomen
That wiggles to and fro.
    (*third child wiggles*)

Insects have six legs to move, (*all three children move their legs*)
Legs to move, legs to move.
Insects have six legs to move
To take them to and fro. (*all three children walk forward together*)

 Move Like a Bug

Materials • none

Preparation

Find a large open area for this activity.

Directions

Invite children to perform the following movements:
- butterfly—pretend to fly, flutter
- grasshopper, flea, and cricket—hop, jump, spring
- ant and roach—scurry and hurry
- bee and mosquito—buzz and pretend to fly
- caterpillar—crawl

Stages of a Butterfly's Life

Materials
- Butterfly Life Cycle Cards (page 304)
- *The Very Hungry Caterpillar* by Eric Carle
- crayons or markers
- scissors

Preparation

Copy, color, and cut apart one set of the Butterfly Life Cycle Cards.

Directions

Read to children *The Very Hungry Caterpillar*. Show children the Butterfly Life Cycle Cards, and review with them the different stages the caterpillar went through during its metamorphosis. Invite children to act out the stages of a butterfly's life:
- egg—lie in a tight ball on the ground
- caterpillar—crawl, eat grass and leaves
- chrysalis—wrap all up and stand very still
- butterfly—come out of the chrysalis, dry wings, and fly away

"Bee" a Dancer

Materials • none

Preparation

Find a large open area for this activity.

Directions

Explain to children that bees talk to each other by dancing. Invite children to play a version of Mother, May I? Have children stand against a wall and face you. Tell children that if you dance in a circle, they may move one step toward you. If you shake your hips, they may move five steps. (These are the actual movements of the bees—they may be replaced with other movements.) Once the children have reached you, start the game over with a child in charge.

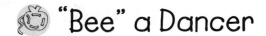 # Alphabet Activities

Caterpillar Name Puzzles

Materials
- green construction paper
- scissors
- sentence strips
- glue
- crayons or markers

Preparation

Cut several circles out of green paper. Label separate circles with the letters of each child's name. Write each child's name on a separate sentence strip. (Space out the letters so they will match up with the letters on the paper circles.)

Directions

Have children sit in a circle. Give each child his or her name strip and glue. Put the circles with the letters of the children's names faceup in the middle of the circle. Invite children to find the letters in their name and glue them on top of their sentence strip to make a caterpillar body. Provide blank paper circles for children to draw a caterpillar's face for them to glue to their caterpillar's body.

 # Insect Initials

Materials
- paper
- several plastic ants or raisins

Preparation

Label separate sheets of paper with the beginning letter of each child's name.

Directions

Give each child the paper with his or her first initial on it and several plastic ants or raisins. (Tell children that the raisins are pretend ants.) Invite children to outline the letter with the plastic ants or raisins.

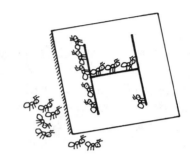

 # Letter Subtraction

Materials
- Insect Name Puzzles (pages 305–306)
- scissors
- counters
- alphabet cards

Preparation

Make enough copies of the Insect Name Puzzles so most children have the name of a different insect. Cut apart each name.

Directions

Give each child a name strip and a handful of counters. (Give children who have an insect with a short name more than one name strip.) Mix up a set of alphabet cards, choose a card, and read aloud the letter while you show the card to the class. If any children have the name of an insect with that letter, tell them to place a counter on it. Play continues until every child has covered all of his or her letters.

 # Swat!

Materials
- butcher paper
- tape
- flyswatters

Preparation

Write several large letters on butcher paper. Tape the paper to the wall at a height so child can touch all of the letters.

Directions

Show children the different letters on the butcher paper. Ask them to help you identify the letters. Once children are familiar with the letters, tell them that they will be using flyswatters to swat letters that you call out. Invite three volunteers to come up to the paper. Name one of the letters on the paper, and have the volunteers find that letter and swat it with their flyswatter. Have the volunteers swat a few more letters, and then repeat the activity with a different group of children.

 # Art Activities

Shiny Beetle

Materials
- orange or brown paint
- paint containers
- plastic spoons
- corn syrup
- white card stock
- paintbrushes

Preparation

Pour the different colors of paint into separate paint containers. Use a plastic spoon to stir a spoonful of corn syrup into each paint container.

Directions

Give each child a piece of card stock and a paintbrush. Invite children to paint a beetle with the "shiny paint." Set aside the paintings to dry. They will dry shiny.

Ladybug Puppets

Materials
- Ladybug Puppet Legs reproducible (page 307)
- black construction paper
- scissors
- stapler
- red paper plates (2 per child)
- newspaper
- black markers

Preparation

Copy a class set of the Ladybug Puppet Legs reproducible on black construction paper. Cut out each sheet so there are two sets of three legs for each child. Staple each set of legs to the opposite sides of the rim of a paper plate. Staple the rims of the two paper plates together so there is a hollow space between the two plates. Leave the bottom part of the plates unstapled so children can insert their hand here. Tear newspaper into small strips.

Directions

Give each child a ladybug puppet. Invite children to use a black marker to add spots and a face to their ladybug. Give each child several small strips of newspaper to stuff inside their ladybug to fill up some of the space. Invite children to insert their hand in the opening at the bottom to manipulate their ladybug puppet.

Flighty Finger Painting

Materials
- finger-painting paper
- finger paint
- recording of "The Flight of the Bumblebee" by Nikolai Rimsky-Korsakov on CD/tape
- CD/tape player

Preparation

Prepare an area where children can finger-paint.

Directions

Explain to children that a composer wrote music that he called "The Flight of the Bumblebee" because it sounds like bumblebees flying around very quickly. Invite children to lie down and close their eyes. Play "The Flight of the Bumblebee." Then, invite children to go to the finger-painting area. Play the music again, and encourage children to paint to the music.

 Butterfly Squish

M a t e r i a l s
- Butterfly Wings reproducible (page 303)
- paint in assorted bright colors
- turkey basters
- rolling pins
- scissors

Preparation

Copy a class set of the Butterfly Wings reproducible. Fold each butteryfly shape in half, lengthwise.

Directions

Give each child a copy of the reproducible. Have children decide what colors they want their butterfly to be. Show children how to use a turkey baster to put paint on one half of their butterfly. Have children fold their butterfly in half along the original fold. Invite children to use a rolling pin to roll over their butterfly shape. Have children open their butterfly and set it aside to dry. Cut out each child's butterfly shape and display it on a bulletin board.

Giant Anthill

M a t e r i a l s
- Anthill reproducible (page 308)
- light brown butcher paper
- scissors
- black markers
- black inkpads

Preparation

Cut a large outline of an anthill out of butcher paper. Make a copy of the Anthill reproducible.

Directions

Show children the Anthill reproducible. Discuss with children the different tunnels and chambers in the anthill. Have children use black markers to draw tunnels and chambers inside the anthill on the butcher paper. Help them add "ants" to the anthill. Show them how to press their index finger on an inkpad and print on the anthill three fingerprints in a row for an ant's head, thorax, and abdomen. Invite children to draw six legs and two antennae on their ant.

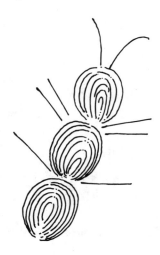

Flyswatter Painting

Materials
- light-colored butcher paper
- heavy-duty tape
- pie tins
- paint in assorted colors
- flyswatters (1 per child)

Preparation

Outside, tape butcher paper to a fence, and fill pie tins with different colors of paint. (This activity is great for a "water day" when children are wearing swimsuits.)

Directions

Tell children that they are going to paint using a flyswatter as their paintbrush. Invite children to "paint" on the paper by dipping a flyswatter into paint and slapping it on the paper.

Butterfly Life Cycle

Materials
- Butterfly Life Cycle Cards (page 304)
- paper plates
- leaves
- rice
- spiral rotini, shell, and bowtie pasta
- resealable plastic bags
- scissors
- glue

Preparation

Draw two perpendicular lines across each paper plate to divide it in fourths. Draw an arrow between each of the four sections in a clockwise direction. Place four leaves, several grains of rice, and one of each type of pasta in a plastic bag for each child. Copy and cut apart one set of Butterfly Life Cycle Cards.

Directions

Show children the life cycle cards, and tell them that butterflies start as eggs (show the rice), hatch into hungry caterpillars (show the rotini), wrap up in a chrysalis (show the shell pasta), and then turn into butterflies (show the bowtie pasta). Give each child a paper plate and a life cycle bag. Help children glue a leaf in each section of their paper plate. Help children glue each type of pasta in the correct section of the life cycle diagram. The pasta should be glued down starting in the top, righthand corner with the rice (eggs) and continuing in a clockwise pattern for the rotini (caterpillar), shell (chrysalis), and bowtie (butterfly).

Cooking Activities

🥣 Ants in Dirt

Ingredients
- graham crackers
- chocolate chips or raisins

Other Supplies
- resealable plastic bags
- rolling pins
- small bowls
- spoons

Directions

Place a graham cracker in a plastic bag for each child, release the air, and seal the bag. Give one bag to each child. Have children crush the graham cracker with a rolling pin or their hands to make "dirt." Give each child a bowl, and have children pour their dirt into it. Invite children to add "ants" (chocolate chips or raisins) to their dirt.

🥣 The Very Hungry Caterpillar Fruit Salad

Ingredients
- 1 apple
- 2 pears
- 3 plums
- 4 strawberries
- 5 oranges

Other Supplies
- *The Very Hungry Caterpillar* by Eric Carle
- kitchen knife (teacher use only)
- large bowl
- serving spoon
- small paper plates

Directions

Give each child one or more of the fruits listed above. Read aloud *The Very Hungry Caterpillar*. As you come to a fruit the caterpillar ate, have the children with that fruit hold it up. After the story is finished, wash the fruit, and slice it into bite-size pieces. Place the fruit in a large bowl to make the salad, and then serve it for the "very hungry" children to enjoy.

Jiggling Ladybugs

Ingredients

- black string licorice
- package (8-serving size) of red Jell-O
- boiling water
- raisins

Other Supplies

- clean scissors
- saucepan
- muffin tin with small cups
- paper plates

Directions

Use clean scissors to cut licorice into approximately 2" (5 cm) pieces. Cut enough for each child to have eight pieces. In advance, prepare Jell-O according to the Jigglers recipe on the box. Do not let it set. Put raisins in the cups of a muffin tin. Pour the Jell-O over the raisins. Refrigerate the Jell-O until it has set. Dip the bottom of the muffin tin in warm water for about 15 seconds. Remove the jigglers, and place each one with eight black licorice pieces on a separate plate. Have children add black licorice pieces for the ladybug's legs and antennae. When children eat their ladybug, remind them to take small bites and not swallow it whole.

Caterpillars

Ingredients

- ½ cup (118 mL) peanut butter
- ¼ cup (59 mL) honey
- 2 cups (473 mL) powdered milk
- green food coloring

Other Supplies

- mixing bowl
- spoon
- waxed paper

Directions

Mix together the first three ingredients in a bowl, and then add a few drops of green food coloring. (**Note:** Be mindful of any children with peanut allergies.) Give each child a spoonful of the mixture on waxed paper to roll into a "caterpillar."

Ladybugs

Ingredients
- small red apples
- pretzel sticks
- peanut butter
- raisins

Other Supplies
- kitchen knife (teacher use only)
- small paper plates
- spoon

Directions

In advance, cut apples in half lengthwise and break pretzel sticks in half. Give each child a plate with an apple half, a spoonful of peanut butter, several raisins, and six pretzel pieces. (**Note:** Be mindful of any children with peanut allergies.) Show children how to make a ladybug using the apple for the body, the raisins as the spots (use peanut butter to attach the raisins to the apple), and the pretzel pieces as the six legs.

Butterfly

Ingredients
- celery sticks
- cream cheese
- raisins
- pretzel sticks and knots

Other Supplies
- small paper plates
- plastic spoons

Directions

Give each child a paper plate with a celery stick, a spoonful of cream cheese, two raisins, two pretzel sticks, two pretzel knots, and a spoon. Show children how to use the back of the spoon to spread the cream cheese on their celery stick. Invite children to add two pretzel knots for the wings, two raisins for the eyes, and two pretzel sticks for the antennae.

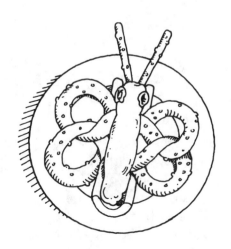

 Caterpillar Chrysalis

Ingredients
- can of crescent roll dough
- smoked mini-sausage links

Other Supplies
- baking sheet
- waxed paper
- permanent marker

Directions

Give each child a triangle of dough and a sausage link. Show children how to roll the dough around the link. Explain that the sausage link represents a caterpillar and the dough represents the chrysalis. Place each "chrysalis" on a waxed paper–lined baking sheet. Use a permanent marker to write each child's name next to his or her chrysalis. Bake the rolls for 10–15 minutes at 400°F (204°C).

Fingerplays and Flannel Board Activities

Caterpillars Changing

(Fingerplay)

One little caterpillar crawled on my shoe. (*placing one finger on shoe*)
Another came along and then there were two. (*placing two fingers on shoe*)
Two little caterpillars crawled on my knee. (*placing two fingers on knee*)
Another came along and then there were three. (*placing three fingers on knee*)
Three little caterpillars crawled on the floor. (*placing three fingers on floor*)
Another came along and then there were four. (*placing four fingers on floor*)
Four little caterpillars, watch them crawl today. (*placing four fingers on floor, "crawling" away*)
Because soon they'll turn into butterflies and fly away. (*waving hands with thumbs together to simulate butterflies flying*)

Five Little Grasshoppers

(Fingerplay)

Five little grasshoppers playing near my door. (*holding up five fingers*)
One saw a honeybee, then there were four. (*holding up four fingers*)
Four little grasshoppers playing near a tree.
One chased a busy fly, then there were three. (*holding up three fingers*)
Three little grasshoppers looked for something new.
One met a cricket, then there were two. (*holding up two fingers*)
Two little grasshoppers sitting in the sun.
A ladybug called, "Play with me," then there was one. (*holding up one finger*)
One little grasshopper said, "I'll have some fun."
She went to find her brothers, and then there were none. (*placing hand behind back*)

Ladybugs

(Flannel Board)

Create the following flannel board pieces: five ladybugs, leaves or a tree, and a flower.

I saw a little ladybug flying in the air, (*placing one ladybug on the board*)
But when I tried to catch her, two ladybugs were there. (*adding another ladybug*)
Two little ladybugs flew up in a tree. (*adding leaves or a tree*)
I tiptoed very quietly, and then I saw three. (*adding another ladybug*)
Three little ladybugs—I looked for one more.
I saw one sitting on the ground, and that made four. (*adding another ladybug at the bottom of board*)
Four little ladybugs—then another one arrived.
I saw her sitting on a flower, and that made five. (*adding a flower and placing last ladybug on it*)
Five little ladybugs, all red and black—
I clapped my hands and shouted, and they all flew back! (*removing all ladybugs*)

What Am I?

(Flannel Board)

Create the following flannel board pieces: bee, butterfly, grasshopper, fly, and spider.

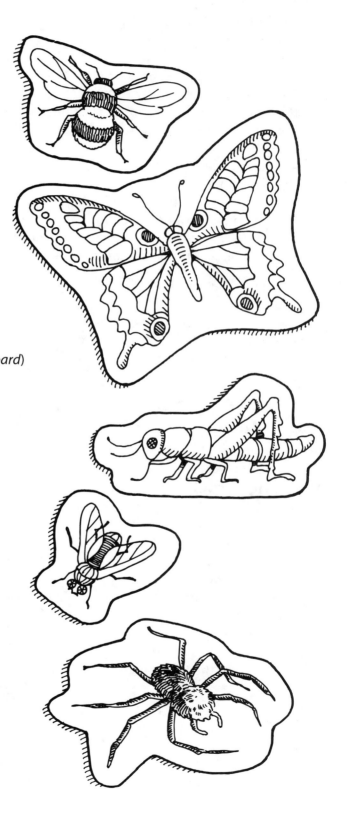

I make honey so sticky and sweet
That bears and people like to eat.
I mix a pollen-nectar batch
And store it in a special wax.
What am I?
A bee! (*adding bee to board*)

I flutter by the flowers,
Sipping up my lunch.
My babies look like little worms,
And leaves are what they munch.
What am I?
A butterfly! (*adding butterfly to board*)

I hop about in meadows,
Where grass is green and tall.
I make a cheerful chirping sound,
In summer, spring, and fall.
What am I?
A grasshopper! (*adding grasshopper to board*)

I buzz by your screen door.
I land on your clothes.
I sample your lunch,
And I tickle your nose.
I fly by so fast that I'm hard to swat.
Some call me a pest and dislike me a lot.
What am I?
A fly! (*adding fly to board*)

I'm not an insect,
But I spin an insect trap.
I have eight legs
That I like to tap.
What am I?
A spider! (*adding spider to board*)

🎵 The Insects in the Garden

(Sung to the tune of "The Wheels on the Bus")

The bees in the garden go buzz, buzz, buzz,
Buzz, buzz, buzz, buzz, buzz, buzz.
The bees in the garden go buzz, buzz, buzz
Out in the garden.

Additional verses:
The fireflies at night go blink, blink, blink
The crickets in the field go chirp, chirp, chirp
The ants in the grass go march, march, march
The caterpillars on the leaves go munch, munch, munch
The mosquitoes outside get smacked, smacked, smacked

🎵 Bumblebee

(Sung to the chorus of "Jingle Bells")

Bumblebee, bumblebee,
Landing on my toes.
Bumblebee, bumblebee,
Now he's on my nose.
On my arms, on my legs,
And also on my elbows.
Bumblebee, oh, bumblebee,
He lands and then he goes.

🎵 The Butterfly Song

(Sung to the tune of "Up on the Housetop")

First comes a butterfly that lays an egg.
Out comes a caterpillar with many a leg.
Oh, see the caterpillar spin and spin
A little chrysalis to sleep in.

Oh, oh, oh! Wait and see.
Oh, oh, oh! Wait and see.
Oh, out of the chrysalis, my oh my!
Out comes a pretty butterfly.

🎵 Fireflies

(Sung to the tune of "Twinkle, Twinkle Little Star")

Twinkle, twinkle firefly,
Flying in the evening sky.
Flashing on and off your light,
Adding beauty to the night.
Twinkle, twinkle firefly,
Flying in the evening sky.

🎵 A Caterpillar's Dream

(Sung to the tune of "The Itsy Bitsy Spider")

A caterpillar in a chrysalis
Dreamed of what she would become.
How about a fly,
Or an ant eating a crumb?
How about a beetle,
Or a bee buzzing by?
But she found when she woke up
She was a butterfly!

🎵 I'm a Little Firefly

(Sung to the tune of "I'm a Little Teapot")

I'm a little firefly shining bright.
Here are my wings, and here is my light. (*flapping arms and pointing to back*)
When the day is gone and it is night,
I twinkle and glow—oh what a sight! (*pretending to fly around room*)

Spot the Dots

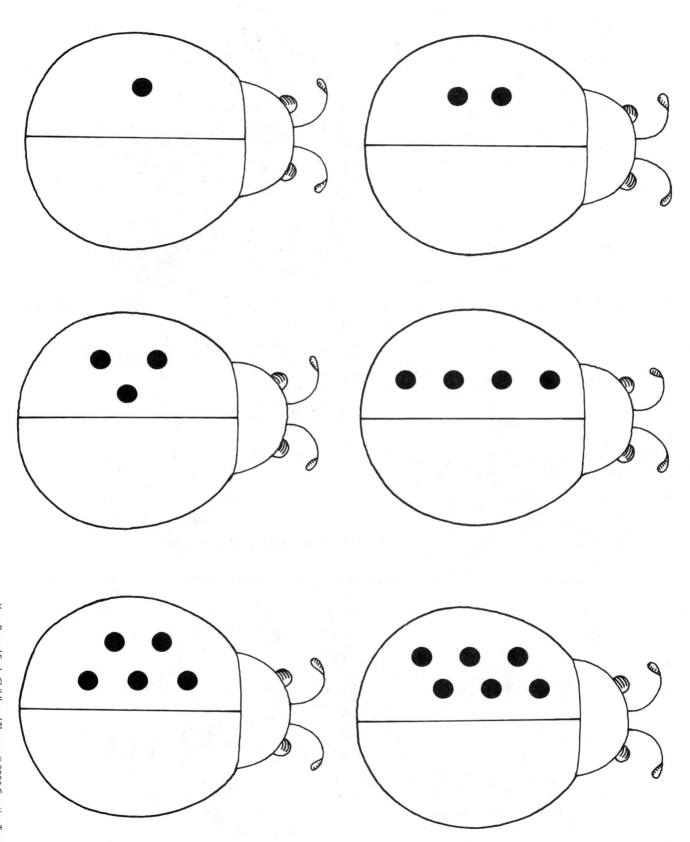

Bee Pairs

Year-Round Early Childhood Themes © 2006 Creative Teaching Press

Ladybug Spots Cards

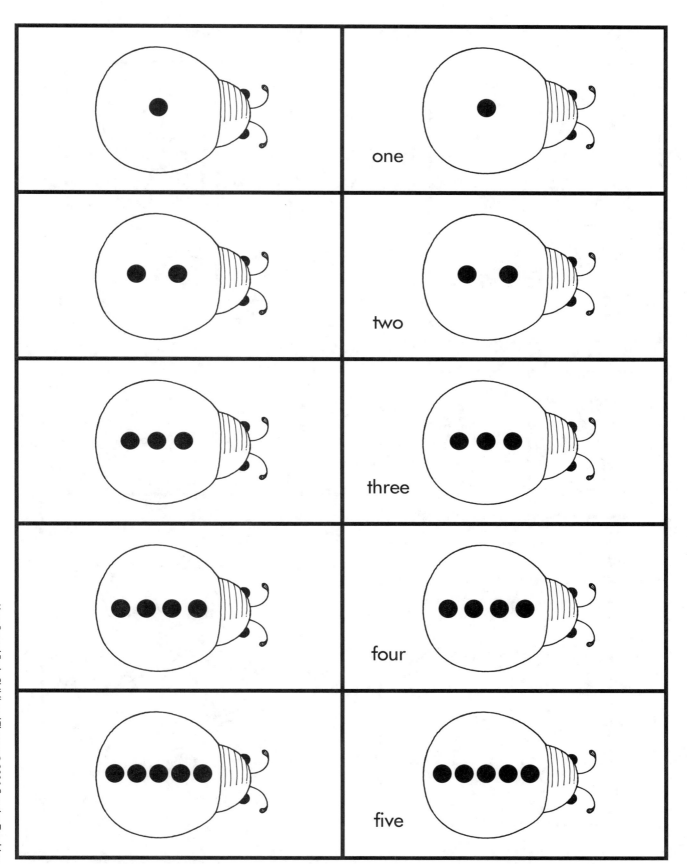

one

two

three

four

five

Ant Sizing

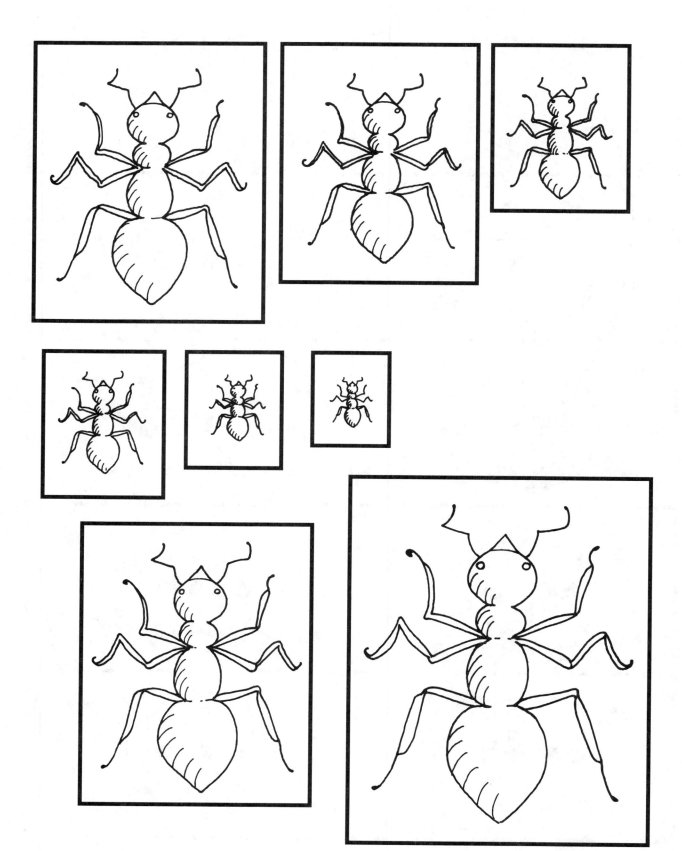

Butterfly Wings

Butterfly Life Cycle Cards

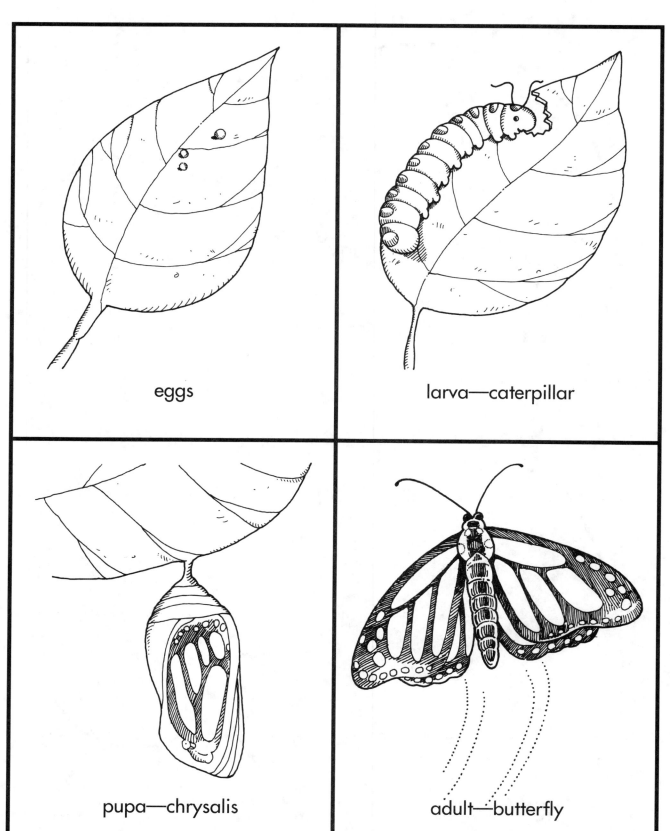

eggs

larva—caterpillar

pupa—chrysalis

adult—butterfly

Insect Name Puzzles

ant

aphid

beetle

bumblebee

butterfly

caterpillar

cockroach

Insect Name Puzzles

cricket

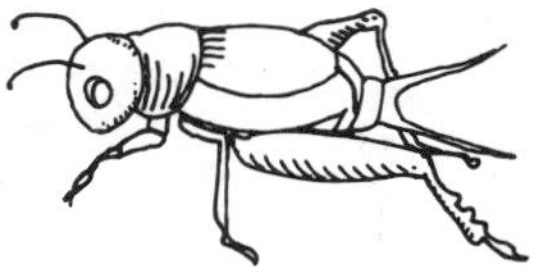

dragonfly

firefly

flea

housefly

grasshopper

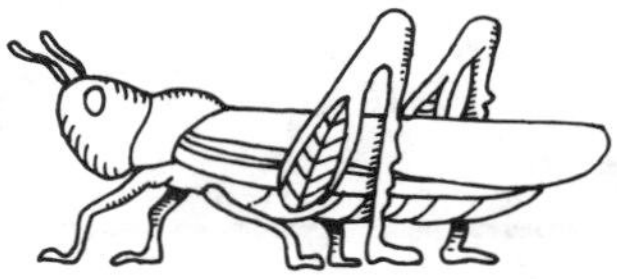

ladybug

mosquito

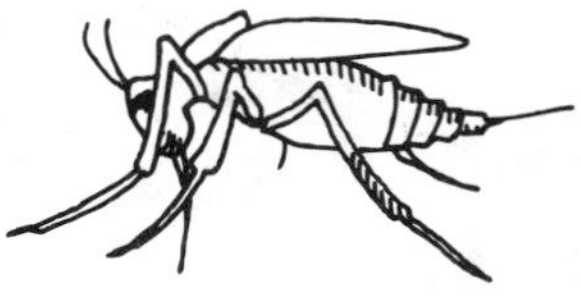

Ladybug Puppet Legs

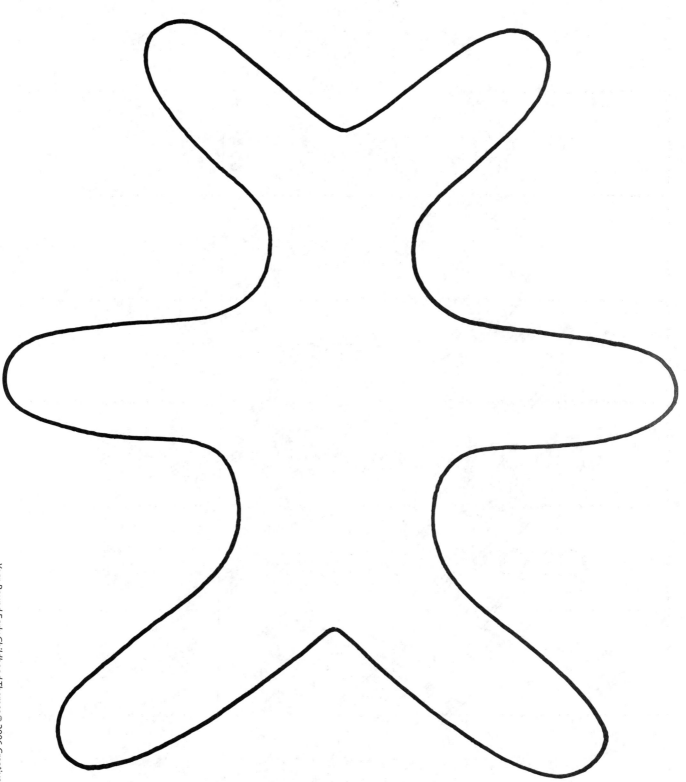

Anthill

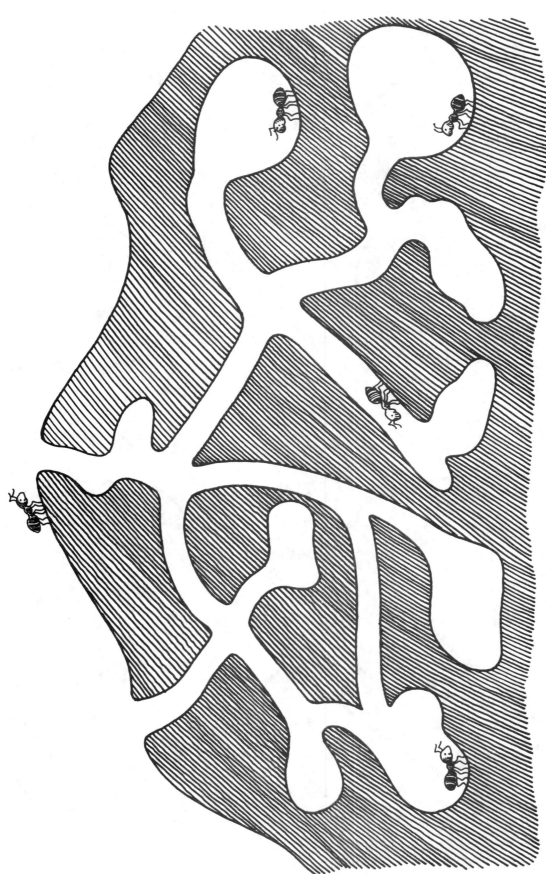

Year-Round Early Childhood Themes © 2006 Creative Teaching Press

Nursery Rhymes

Concepts

The concepts covered in this unit include the following:
- Hundreds of nursery rhymes have been written by many different people.
- Mother Goose nursery rhymes are the best known.
- Nursery rhymes are imaginary stories.
- Nursery rhymes help us learn about the difference between what is real and what is imaginary.
- Some nursery rhymes are funny.
- Some nursery rhymes help us learn about life.
- Some nursery rhymes help us learn to count.

Vocabulary

nursery rhyme—a traditional song or poem written for young children

The nursery rhymes in this unit include the following:
- Baa, Baa, Black Sheep
- Hey, Diddle Diddle
- Humpty Dumpty
- The Itsy Bitsy Spider
- Jack and Jill
- Jack Be Nimble
- Little Bo Peep
- Little Boy Blue
- Little Miss Muffet
- Mary Had a Little Lamb
- The Muffin Man
- Old Mother Hubbard
- One, Two, Buckle My Shoe
- Pat-a-Cake
- The Queen of Hearts
- Rub-a-Dub-Dub
- Simple Simon
- Sing a Song of Six Pence
- There Was an Old Woman Who Lived in a Shoe

Date _____

Dear Family:

"Nursery Rhymes" will be the theme for our next unit. We will be doing all kinds of fun activities with these cherished rhymes.

Classroom Activities

Children will participate in the following activities:
- Experimenting to find a way to protect Humpty Dumpty.
- Creating the old woman's shoe.
- Seeing which items sink or float.
- Working independently or in groups with story bags.
- Listening to and discussing *The Itsy Bitsy Spider* by Iza Trapani.

Home Activities

Here are some activities for your family to try at home to complement what children are doing in the classroom:
- Have your child tell you a bedtime nursery rhyme.
- Read some nursery rhymes to your child before bedtime. If you need some nursery rhymes, let me know.
- Invite your child to describe different nursery rhyme characters as you draw them together.

Have fun as you explore all of the neat Nursery Rhyme activities with your child.

Thank you for all you do!

Sincerely,

Dear Family:

We will use the following items during our Nursery Rhymes unit. We would appreciate any help you could give us. We will begin this unit on _____, so please sign and return the form below if you can donate items by _____.

- newspapers
- magazines and catalogs
- small bag of cotton balls
- bubble wrap
- sheet protectors
- spaghetti
- plastic spiders or Halloween spider rings
- clean, crushed eggshells
- toilet paper tubes

- string licorice
- double-stuffed chocolate sandwich cookies
- M&M's
- can of cherry pie filling
- small bag of butterscotch morsels

Thanks!

• •

I would like to contribute the following items for this unit:

_____

Please contact me at _____ (phone number or e-mail) to let me know how I can help.

_____
(parent's name)

Year-Round Early Childhood Themes © 2006 Creative Teaching Press

Center Ideas

The following are suggestions for different Nursery Rhyme centers. The activities provided in this unit can be used or modified for these centers:

- **Art Center**—chart paper cut into a shoe, an egg, and other shapes mentioned in nursery rhymes; clay or play dough (see Art Recipes, page 409); cookie cutters

- **Block and Building Center**—blocks, small plastic nursery rhyme characters, Styrofoam bricks to build a wall for Humpty Dumpty, plastic Easter eggs

- **Dramatic Play Center**—puppets of nursery rhyme characters, dress-up clothes

- **Listening Center**—tapes of nursery rhymes, tapes of stories written in class

- **Manipulatives Center**—nursery rhyme puzzles

- **Math and Science Center**—copies of the Lambs reproducible (page 339), real spider in a container, magnifying glass

- **Reading Center**—books of illustrated nursery rhymes (see recommended read-alouds, page 314), nursery rhyme story bags

- **Sand and Water Tables**—plastic spiders, colored pasta (see Art Recipes: Pasta and Rice Dye, page 416), sand, water

- **Writing Center**—nursery rhyme stickers and stamps

Language Development

Recommended Read-Alouds

The Arnold Lobel Book of Mother Goose by Arnold Lobel (Alfred A. Knopf Books)

Bad Egg: The True Story of Humpty Dumpty by Sarah Hayes (Little, Brown and Company)

Hey, Diddle Diddle by Kin Eagle (Charlesbridge Publishing)

Humpty Dumpty by Daniel Kirk (G. P. Putnam's Sons)

The Itsy Bitsy Spider by Iza Trapani (Charlesbridge Publishing)

Jack and Jill by Daniel Kirk (G. P. Putnam's Sons)

Mary Had a Little Jam and Other Silly Rhymes by Bruce Lansky (Meadowbrook Press)

Mary Had a Little Lamb by Iza Trapani (Charlesbridge Publishing)

The New Adventures of Mother Goose by Bruce Lansky (Meadowbrook Press)

Nursery Classics: A Galdone Treasury by Paul Galdone (Clarion Books)

The Random House Children's Treasury: Fairy Tales, Nursery Rhymes & Nonsense Verse by Alice Mills (Gramercy Books)

Rub a Dub Dub by Kin Eagle (Charlesbridge Publishing)

Read-Aloud Activity

Read a book or nursery rhyme to children. Have children discuss their reactions, ideas, and feelings about the book or rhyme. Create a story bag with flannel board pieces that represent the characters and events. Invite children to use the story bag to retell the story or rhyme.

Discussion Starters

Use these suggestions to promote discussions about a nursery rhyme. These ideas can be discussed and then used to write a variation of a nursery rhyme for children to illustrate.

Little Miss Muffet
- What are curds and whey? (*cottage cheese*)
- What is a tuffet? (*a small clump or mound of grass, a low seat*)
- A spider scared Miss Muffet. What scares you?
- Where do you think Miss Muffet went when she ran away?

Humpty Dumpty
- Why do you think Humpty Dumpty was sitting on a wall?
- What made Humpty Dumpty fall down?
- Why couldn't anyone put Humpty together again?

Little Bo Peep
- Where do you think Little Bo Peep lost her sheep?
- Do you think the sheep were just hiding from her?

There Was an Old Woman Who Lived in a Shoe
- How many children do you think the old woman had?
- Could you live in a shoe?
- Would it be fun to live in a shoe?

Hey, Diddle Diddle
- Why did a cow jump over the moon?
- Where do you think the dish and the spoon went when they ran away?

Old Mother Hubbard
- Was there any food in the cupboard for Old Mother Hubbard? How do you know?

Math Activities

 Put Humpty Together Again

(Use with "Humpty Dumpty," page 331)

Skill: color matching

Materials
- Humpty Dumpty reproducible (page 338)
- white card stock
- scissors
- gray butcher paper
- tape
- crayons

Preparation

Copy a class set of the Humpty Dumpty reproducible on card stock, and cut out each Humpty Dumpty. Draw a small stone wall on butcher paper and tape it to the wall.

Directions

Give each child a Humpty Dumpty cutout and a different color crayon. Invite children to color their cutout, and then cut each cutout in half. Place one half below the butcher paper wall, and give one of the other halves to each child. Invite children to find the matching half of their Humpty Dumpty and use tape to "put Humpty Dumpty together again."

 Noodle Numbering

(Use with "One, Two, Buckle My Shoe," page 334)

Skill: number recognition

Materials
- paper
- sheet protectors (optional)
- spaghetti
- colander

Preparation

Write in large print a different number from 1 to 10 on separate sheets of paper. Make several sets of numbers. Laminate the papers or place them in sheet protectors. Cook spaghetti according to package directions. Drain the spaghetti, and set it aside.

Directions

Give each child a few numbered papers and some spaghetti noodles. Invite children to use the noodles to form the numbers on their papers.

Little Lamb Sequencing

(Use with "Baa, Baa, Black Sheep," page 330, "Little Bo Peep," page 332, or "Mary Had a Little Lamb," page 333)

Skills: sequencing, measurement, size comparison

Materials
- Lambs reproducible (page 339)
- scissors
- glue

Preparation

Copy and cut out a class set of the Lambs reproducible.

Directions

Give each child a lamb cutout of each size. (Vary the number of lambs used in this activity based on children's ability.) Have children compare the sizes of the lambs using the terms *bigger* and *smaller*. Ask children to hold up their largest lamb and then their smallest lamb. Invite children to put the lambs in order by size: smallest to largest and largest to smallest. Place the lambs at a center for children to repeat the activity on their own.

Spider Addition and Subtraction

(Use with "The Itsy Bitsy Spider," page 331, or "Little Miss Muffet," page 333)

Skills: counting, number sense, estimating

Materials
- plastic spiders (can be cut from Halloween rings)
- resealable plastic bags (optional)

Preparation

Directions

Pass out five spiders to each child, and invite children to count the number of spiders that they have. Ask mathematical questions such as *How many spiders would you have if you took away two? How many will you have if you add one?* Invite children to estimate the answer and then carry out the process and count their spiders.

Variation

Place between one to five spiders in separate resealable plastic bags. (Leave some spiders out to complete the activity.) Label each bag with a numeral that is either one or two less or one or two more than the number of spiders in the bag. (As an option, draw the corresponding number of dots beside the numeral.) Invite children to add or remove spiders from the bags so the number of spiders matches the label on the bag.

Jack and Jill Go Up the Hill Game

(Use with "Jack and Jill," page 332)

Skills: counting, one-to-one correspondence

Materials
- Jack and Jill Game reproducible (page 340)
- dice
- counters

Preparation

Make a copy of the Jack and Jill Game reproducible for every two children.

Directions

Divide the class into pairs. Give each pair a game board, a die, and two counters. Invite partners to take turns rolling the die and moving their counter the number of spaces indicated on the die. The game is over when both players reach the well. Tell children they must roll the exact number to get to the well.

Sensory Activities

 # Humpty Dumpty Experiment

(Use with "Humpty Dumpty," page 331)

Materials
- hard-boiled eggs (1 per "experiment surface")
- experiment surfaces: pillow, fabric, newspaper, cardboard, bubble wrap

Preparation

Directions

Explain to children that they will test which surfaces an egg can fall on without breaking. Show children a pillow, a piece of fabric, newspaper, cardboard, and bubble wrap. Ask them to predict which of the items will prevent an egg from breaking. Drop an egg from waist height onto each surface. Compare with children the predictions to the results. Ask them to explain the results.

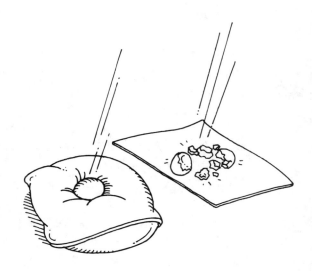

Rub-a-Dub-Dub

(Use with "Rub-a-Dub-Dub," page 335)

Materials
- water table or small tub of water
- small items (e.g., stones, balls of aluminum foil, blocks, counters, plastic animals or people)
- paper
- hula hoops

Preparation

Set up a table near the water, and set out the items. Label one sheet of paper *Float* and the other *Sink*. Set two hula hoops beside each other on the floor, and put one paper above each hoop to create a Venn diagram that does not overlap.

Directions

Recite with children the nursery rhyme "Rub-a-Dub-Dub." Invite children to gather around the table to feel each item, and encourage them to predict which items will float and which items will sink. Invite children to add three items, one at a time, to the water as you recite this variation of the rhyme:

> *Rub-a-dub-dub,*
> *Three things in a tub,*
> *And do you think they will float?*

After each item is tested, have the child who conducted the experiment place that item in the correct hula-hoop circle of the Venn diagram.

Favorite Nursery Rhymes

Materials
- audiotape
- tape recorder/player

Preparation

Directions

Invite each child to pick his or her favorite nursery rhyme. Ask an adult volunteer to record each child saying a portion of his or her favorite rhyme. Gather the class together, and have them listen to the recordings. Ask children to guess who is reciting each rhyme.

Spiderweb Rubbings

(Use with "The Itsy Bitsy Spider," page 331, or "Little Miss Muffet," page 333)

Materials
- Spiderweb reproducible (page 341)
- glue
- tape
- black paper
- unwrapped white crayons

Preparation

Make several copies of the Spiderweb reproducible. Trace a thick line of glue along the outline of each spiderweb to make a rubbing plate, and then set it aside to fully dry. Tape each rubbing plate to a table.

Directions

Demonstrate how rubbings are done. Place a piece of black paper over the rubbing plate, secure the paper to the table with tape, and rub the side of a white crayon over the paper. Invite children to make their own rubbings.

Motor Skills Activities

Eight Great Jumps

(Use with "Little Miss Muffet," page 333)

Materials
- construction paper
- scissors
- tape

Preparation

Cut out eight construction-paper circles, and tape them in a path on the floor so children can jump from one to the next.

Directions

Chant with children "Little Miss Muffet." Tell children to stand in a line behind the first circle. Explain to children that the circles are eight of Miss Muffet's tuffets and that they are the spiders who chase Miss Muffet away. Invite each child to jump from one "tuffet" to the next as the class counts to eight.

Humpty Dumpty Race

(Use with "Humpty Dumpty," page 331)

Materials
- masking tape
- play dough (see Art Recipes, page 409)
- plastic Easter eggs (the kind that open)
- large spoons (e.g., serving spoons, ladles)

Preparation

Use tape to make two lines on the floor to mark the two ends of a course. Place a ball of play dough in each plastic egg to add weight.

Directions

Divide the class into teams. Have half of each team stand behind one line and the other half stand behind the other line. Explain to children that they will carry an egg on a spoon as they run or walk as fast as they can between the two lines. Tell children to give the spoon with the egg to the next child in line to repeat the process in the opposite direction. Let children know that if their egg falls off the spoon, they can put "Humpty Dumpty" together again and continue the race. As the race takes place, have children chant "Humpty Dumpty."

Jack and Jill Race

(Use with "Jack and Jill," page 332)

Materials
- 4 large buckets
- 2 small buckets
- water

Preparation

This is a good activity to do outside with older children. Fill two large buckets with water, and set them beside each other. Set two more large buckets where you would like the race to end. Set a small bucket next to each large bucket filled with water.

Directions

Recite with children "Jack and Jill." Tell children that they are going to see how many pails of water they can fetch. Walk children through the race course. Show them how to dip a small bucket into a large bucket of water, walk quickly from one end of the course to the other, and pour the water from the small bucket into the large bucket at the end of the course. Divide the class into "Jacks" and "Jills" (boys and girls). Remind children to be quick yet careful as they race.

Let's Jump Over the Candlesticks

(Use with "Jack Be Nimble," page 332)

Materials
- orange or yellow tissue paper
- toilet paper tubes
- play dough (see Art Recipes, page 409)
- masking tape (optional)

Preparation

Insert tissue paper in the top of toilet paper tubes to create the "flame" of "candlesticks." Place a ball of play dough in the bottom of each tube to make a base. Arrange the candlesticks in a path around the room. (You may want to create a masking tape path on the floor for children to follow.)

Directions

Chant with children "Jack Be Nimble." Have children line up at the beginning of the path. Invite them to recite the rhyme as they follow the path and jump over the candlesticks along the way.

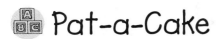

Alphabet Activities

Pat-a-Cake

(Use with "Pat-a-Cake," page 335)

Materials
- Cake reproducible (page 342)
- scissors
- alphabet stickers (enough to spell out each child's name)
- name tags
- large resealable plastic bags

Preparation

Copy and cut out a class set of the Cake reproducible. Collect the alphabet stickers needed for each child's name. Place each child's "cake," stickers, and a name tag in a separate plastic bag.

Directions

Give each child his or her bag. Invite children to remove the cake, stickers, and name tag from the bag. Have them place each sticker on their cake to spell their name, using their name tag as a guide. Display the cakes on a bulletin board along with the rhyme.

Humpty Dumpty Alphabet

(Use with "Humpty Dumpty," page 331)

Materials
- Humpty Dumpty reproducible (page 338)
- scissors

Preparation

Copy the Humpty Dumpty reproducible. (Make just a few for youngest children and increase the number as children's abilities improve). On the back of each egg, write an uppercase letter on the top half and the matching lowercase letter on the bottom half. Cut out each egg, and then cut apart each egg between the two letters with a unique puzzle cut.

Directions

Scatter the egg halves with the letters faceup on a tabletop. Invite each child to reassemble an egg as he or she chants "Humpty Dumpty." Have children continue until all of the eggs have been reassembled.

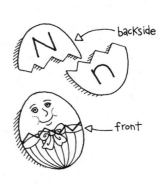

Find a Letter in Your Name

(Use with "Mary Had a Little Lamb," page 333)

Materials
- sentence strips
- large alphabet cards

Preparation

Write each child's name on a separate sentence strip. Make a sentence strip with your name.

Directions

Have children sit in a circle, and scatter a set of alphabet cards faceup in the middle of the circle. Give each child the sentence strip with his or her name. Sing the following song to the tune of "Mary Had a Little Lamb":

Find a letter in your name,
In your name, in your name.
Find a letter in your name
And show it to the class.

Find an alphabet card with a letter in your own name. Display it, and then return it to the floor. Repeat the song. Point to a child, and have him or her locate a letter in his or her name. Continue until each child has had a turn.

Oh, Do You Know the Letter...?

(Use with "The Muffin Man," page 334)

Materials　• large alphabet cards

Preparation

Directions

Have children sit in a circle. Invite a child to choose an alphabet card (this example is for the letter *b*) for the class to use in the following song, sung to the tune of "The Muffin Man":

> *Oh, do you know the letter **b**,*
> *The letter **b**, the letter **b**?*
> *Oh, do you know the letter **b***
> *That makes a sound like this—/**b**/?*

Invite another child to choose a different alphabet card. Continue singing by replacing the boldfaced letter with the new letter until all children have had a turn.

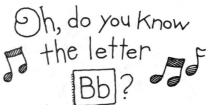

Jack Be Nimble Letter Jump

(Use with "Jack Be Nimble," page 332)

Materials　• paper
　　　　　　　• tape

Preparation

Write each letter of the alphabet in large print on a separate sheet of paper, and tape the papers to the floor in one section of the room.

Directions

Choose the name of a child and a letter, and then recite the following rhyme:

> ***Heather*** *be nimble,* ***Heather*** *be quick.*
> ***Heather*** *jump over the **i** real quick.*

Invite the child to jump over that letter. Replace the boldfaced name and letter to continue the rhyme until every child has had a turn.

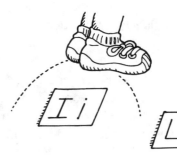

Art Activities

The Old Woman's Shoe

(Use with "There Was an Old Woman Who Lived in a Shoe," page 337)

Materials
- white butcher paper
- scissors
- magazines or catalogs
- paintbrushes
- brown paint
- glue

Preparation

Cut a very large boot from butcher paper. Cut pictures of children from magazines or catalogs.

Directions

Recite with children "There Was an Old Woman Who Lived in a Shoe." Give each child a paintbrush. Invite children to paint the shoe brown. When the paint is dry, have children glue the pictures of children on the shoe. Display the shoe in the classroom along with the rhyme.

Old Mother Hubbard's Cupboard

(Use with "Old Mother Hubbard," page 334)

Materials
- 12" x 18" (30.5 cm x 46 cm) sheets of white and brown construction paper
- stapler
- scissors
- grocery store advertisements
- glue

Preparation

For each child place a brown paper on top of a white paper. Hold the papers in landscape orientation. Staple them together along the left and right sides. Cut down the center of the brown paper to create "cupboard doors" that open.

Directions

Recite with children "Old Mother Hubbard." Give each child a grocery store ad. Invite children to cut out pictures of healthy foods for Old Mother Hubbard and her dog and glue them to the white paper "cupboard."

Simple Simon Met a Pieman

(Use with "Simple Simon," page 336)

Materials
- newspaper
- pumpkin pie paint (see Art Recipes, page 413)
- paint smocks
- white, uncoated paper plates
- paintbrushes
- light brown paint

Preparation

Set up a painting area covered with newspaper, and make pumpkin pie paint.

Directions

Recite with children "Simple Simon." Give each child a smock, a paper plate, and a paintbrush. Invite children to paint the edges of their plate with light brown paint and the center portion with pumpkin pie paint. Recite the rhyme again with children. Encourage them to use their "pie" to act out the verse.

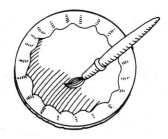

Four and Twenty Blackbirds Baked in a Pie

(Use with "Sing a Song of Sixpence," page 337)

Materials
- Pie reproducible (page 343)
- tan paper
- scissors
- black inkpads
- yellow crayons or markers
- stapler

Preparation

Copy a class set of the Pie reproducible on tan paper. Cut out each pie shape with another piece of tan paper underneath it so each child will have a top and an inside of a pie.

Directions

Recite with children "Sing a Song of Sixpence." Give each child a blank pie shape (inside of the pie). Have children press their thumb on a black inkpad and print six thumbprints on the pie shape. Have them repeat this process until there are 24 thumbprints to represent the birds' heads. Invite children to use a yellow crayon or marker to draw beaks on the "birds." Staple a copy of the reproducible on the top of each child's "blackbird pie." Make sure to staple just the top of the papers so children can look inside their pie.

 # Humpty Dumpty Eggshell Art

(Use with "Humpty Dumpty," page 331)

Materials
- Humpty Dumpty reproducible (page 338)
- card stock
- food coloring
- water
- bowl
- crushed eggshells
- paper towels
- black and red construction paper
- scissors
- glue
- paintbrushes
- wiggly eyes

Preparation

Copy a class set of the Humpty Dumpty reproducible on card stock, and cut them out. Pour water and a few drops of food coloring into a bowl. Color eggshells in the water mixture, and set the shells on paper towels to dry. Cut black construction paper into strips to make arms and legs for Humpty Dumpty. Cut red construction paper into mouth shapes.

Directions

Recite with children "Humpty Dumpty." Give each child a copy of the reproducible, glue, a paintbrush, and some crushed eggshells. Invite children to paint Humpty Dumpty (the front or back side) with glue. Have them add the colored eggshells and facial features to the egg. Show children how to accordion-fold the black paper strips to make arms and legs. Tell them to glue the arms, legs, a mouth, and wiggly eyes on their egg. Display the artwork on a bulletin board along with the rhyme.

Baa, Baa, Black Sheep

(Use with "Baa, Baa, Black Sheep," page 330)

Materials
- cotton balls
- powdered black tempera paint
- plastic bag
- white card stock
- glue
- crayons or markers

Preparation

Place cotton balls (each child will need a handful) and powdered black tempera paint in a plastic bag. Shake the bag until the cotton balls are coated with powdered paint.

Directions

 Trace on card stock each child's hand with the thumb sticking out to create a sheep's body. (The thumb is the face, the palm is the body, and the fingers are the legs.) Invite children to dip cotton balls into glue and attach them to their sheep's body. Have children use crayons or markers to add facial features to their sheep.

Cooking Activities

 # Little Boy Blue's Haystacks

(Use with "Little Boy Blue," page 333)

Ingredients
- 2 tablespoons (30 mL) peanut butter
- 6-ounce (170-g) package butterscotch morsels
- 3-ounce (85-g) can chow mein noodles

Other Supplies

- electric skillet
- spoon
- waxed paper

Directions

Add peanut butter, butterscotch morsels, and noodles to a skillet on low heat. (**Note**: Be mindful of any children with peanut allergies.) Cook until morsels melt and noodles are well coated. Drop mixture by spoonfuls onto waxed paper and let it cool slightly. Give each child a spoonful to mold with their fingers into a "haystack."

Queen of Hearts Tarts

(Use with "The Queen of Hearts," page 335)

Ingredients
- cans of refrigerated biscuits (1 biscuit per child)
- cherry pie filling

Other Supplies
- paper plates
- plastic spoons
- waxed paper
- baking sheet
- permanent marker

Directions

Give each child an uncooked biscuit on a paper plate. Have children use their hands to flatten their biscuit. Tell children to add a small spoonful of cherry pie filling in the middle of their biscuit. Help children fold their biscuit over and pinch the edges shut. Place the biscuits on a waxed paper–lined baking sheet. Use a permanent marker to write each child's name on the waxed paper beside his or her biscuit. Bake the biscuits according to the directions on the package.

Spider Cookies

(Use with "The Itsy Bitsy Spider," page 331, or "Little Miss Muffet," page 333)

Ingredients
- double-stuffed chocolate sandwich cookies
- 2-inch (5-cm) pieces of string licorice
- M&M's
- frosting in a resealable plastic bag

Other Supplies
- small paper plates
- scissors

Directions

Give each child a small paper plate with a sandwich cookie, eight licorice pieces, and two M&M's. Tell children to press one end of each licorice piece into the frosted portion of their cookie to make "spider legs." Cut off a corner of the bag of frosting and squeeze two dabs of frosting on the top of each child's cookie. Have children place M&M's over the frosting to make "spider eyes."

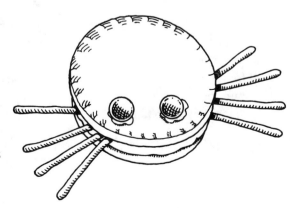

Pat-a-Cake Biscuits

(Use with "Pat-a-Cake," page 335)

Ingredients
- food coloring
- egg whites
- cans of refrigerated biscuits (1 biscuit per child)

Other Supplies
- bowl
- spoon
- paper plates
- new paintbrushes
- baking sheet

Directions

Right before this activity, mix a few drops of food coloring with egg whites in a bowl. Give each child a paper plate with an uncooked biscuit. Have children "pat" their biscuit until it is flat. Help children use the egg-white mixture to "paint" their initial on their biscuit. Bake the biscuits according to the directions on the package.

Nursery Rhymes

Baa, Baa, Black Sheep

Baa, baa, black sheep,
Have you any wool?
Yes, sir,
Yes sir,
Three bags full.
One for my master.
One for my dame,
And one for the little boy
Who lives down the lane.

Hey, Diddle Diddle

Hey, diddle diddle,
The cat and the fiddle,
The cow jumped over the moon.
The little dog laughed to see such a sight,
And the dish ran away with the spoon.

Humpty Dumpty

Humpty Dumpty sat on a wall.
Humpty Dumpty had a great fall.
All the king's horses and all the king's men
Couldn't put Humpty together again.

The Itsy Bitsy Spider

The itsy bitsy spider
Went up the water spout.
Down came the rain
And washed the spider out.
Out came the sun
And dried up all the rain.
And the itsy bitsy spider
Went up the spout again.

Jack and Jill

Jack and Jill
Went up the hill
To fetch a pail of water.
Jack fell down
And broke his crown
And Jill came tumbling after.

Jack Be Nimble

Jack be nimble.
Jack be quick.
Jack jump over the candlestick.

Little Bo Peep

Little Bo Peep has lost her sheep,
And can't tell where to find them.
Leave them alone, and they'll come home,
Wagging their tails behind them.

Then she took her little crook,
Determined for to find them;
What a joy to behold them nigh,
Wagging their tails behind them.

Little Boy Blue

Little Boy Blue, come blow your horn,
The sheep's in the meadow. The cow's in the corn.
Where is the boy who looks after the sheep?
He's under a haystack, fast asleep.

Little Miss Muffet

Little Miss Muffet sat on her tuffet,
Eating her curds and whey.
Along came a spider
Who sat down beside her,
And frightened Miss Muffet away!

Mary Had a Little Lamb

Mary had a little lamb,
Little lamb, little lamb.
Mary had a little lamb,
Its fleece was white as snow.

Everywhere that Mary went,
Mary went, Mary went,
Everywhere that Mary went,
The lamb was sure to go.

The Muffin Man

Oh, do you know the muffin man,
The muffin man, the muffin man?
Oh, do you know the muffin man
Who lives on Drury Lane?

Old Mother Hubbard

Old Mother Hubbard went to the cupboard
To fetch the poor dog a bone.
But when she came there,
The cupboard was bare,
And so the poor dog had none.

One, Two, Buckle My Shoe

One, two, buckle my shoe.
Three, four, shut the door.
Five, six, pick up sticks.
Seven, eight, lay them straight.
Nine, ten, a big fat hen.
Let's get up and count again!

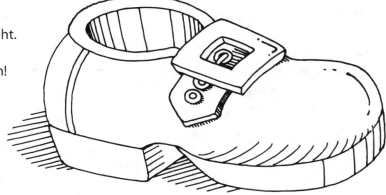

Pat-a-Cake

Pat-a-cake, pat-a-cake, baker's man.
Bake me a cake as fast as you can!
Roll it, and pat it,
And mark it with a *B*.
Put it in the oven for baby and me.

The Queen of Hearts

The Queen of Hearts,
She made some tarts
All on a summer's day.
The Knave of Hearts,
He stole the tarts,
And took them clean away.

The King of Hearts
Called for the tarts
And scolded the knave full bore.
The Knave of Hearts
Brought back the tarts,
And vowed he'd steal no more.

Rub-a-Dub-Dub

Rub-a-dub-dub,
Three men in a tub,
And who do you think they be?
The butcher, the baker, the candlestick maker.
They have all gone off to sea!
Turn 'em out knaves all three.

Simple Simon

Simple Simon met a pieman
Going to the fair.
Said Simple Simon to the pieman,
"Let me taste your ware."

Said the pieman to Simon,
"Show me first your penny."
Said Simple Simon to the pieman,
"Indeed I have not any."

Simple Simon went a-fishing
For to catch a whale;
But all the water he had got
Was in his mother's pail.

Simple Simon went to look
If plums grew on a thistle;
He pricked his fingers very much,
Which made poor Simon whistle.

He went for water in a sieve,
But soon it all fell through;
And now poor Simple Simon
Bids you all adieu.

Sing a Song of Sixpence

Sing a song of six pence,
A pocket full of rye;
Four and twenty blackbirds
Baked in a pie.

When the pie was opened,
The birds began to sing.
Now wasn't that a dainty dish
To put before the king?

The king was in the counting house
Counting out the money.
The queen was in the parlor
Eating bread and honey.

The maid was in the garden
Hanging out the clothes.
Along came a blackbird
And bit her on the nose.

 # There Was an Old Woman Who Lived in a Shoe

There was an old woman who lived in a shoe.
She had so many children, she didn't know what to do,
So she gave them some broth without any bread,
And kissed them all gently and sent them to bed.

Humpty Dumpty

Year-Round Early Childhood Themes © 2006 Creative Teaching Press

Lambs

Jack and Jill Game

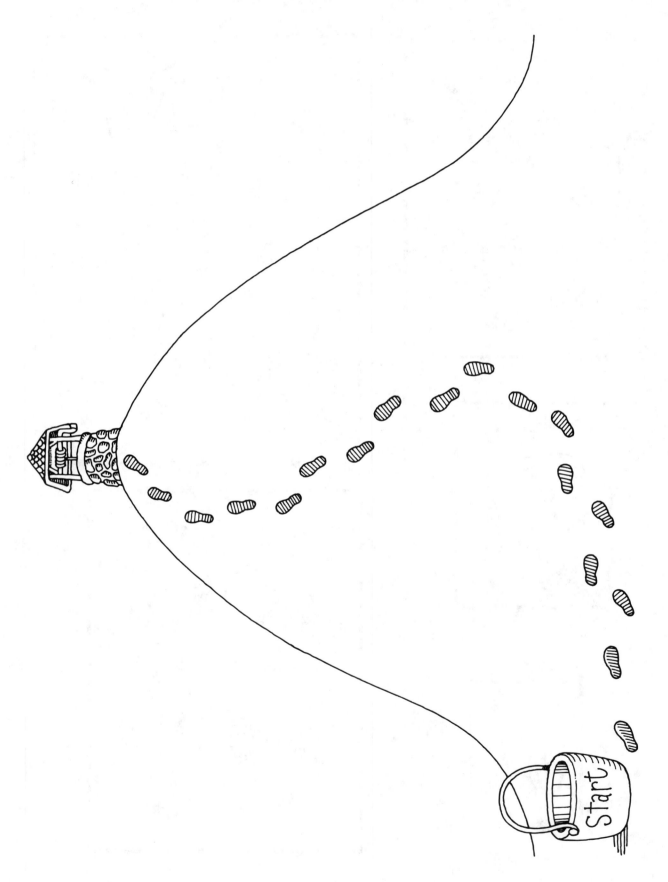

Year-Round Early Childhood Themes © 2006 Creative Teaching Press

Spiderweb

Cake

Year-Round Early Childhood Themes © 2006 Creative Teaching Press

Pie

Shapes and Colors

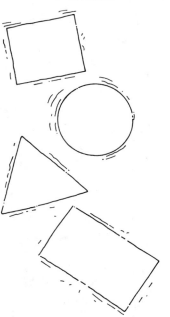

Concepts

The concepts covered in this unit include the following:
- Shapes are all around us in different objects.
- Some basic shapes are circle, square, triangle, and rectangle.
- Other shapes include oval, pentagon, diamond, heart, star, and crescent.
- Different shapes have different numbers of sides, lengths of sides, and angles.
- A circle is round.
- A square has four equal sides.
- A triangle has three sides.
- A rectangle has four sides.
- An oval is a stretched-out circle.
- A pentagon has five sides and can look like a house.
- The three primary colors are red, yellow, and blue.
- New colors can be made by mixing two primary colors together: red and yellow make orange, red and blue make purple, and blue and yellow make green.

Vocabulary

circle—a shape with a curved line that stays the same distance from the center

primary colors—the colors red, yellow, and blue; make up all the other colors

rectangle—a four-sided, four-cornered shape with the opposite sides the same length and 90° angles

triangle—a shape with three sides and three corners

secondary colors—the colors orange, purple, and green that are made from combinations of two primary colors

shape—the form of an object

square—a four-sided, four-cornered shape with all of the sides the same length and 90° angles

The shapes and colors in this unit include the following:

• circle	• pentagon	• blue	• purple
• crescent	• rectangle	• gray	• red
• diamond	• square	• green	• white
• heart	• star	• orange	• yellow
• oval	• triangle		

Date _____

Dear Family:

"Shapes and Colors" will be the theme for our next unit. We will discuss and explore many of the basic shapes and colors.

Classroom Activities

Children will participate in the following activities:
- Learning about primary colors.
- Mixing primary colors to make secondary colors.
- Listening to and discussing *Mouse Paint* by Ellen Stoll Walsh.
- Finding shapes and colors in our environment.
- Exploring some new and different art materials.

Home Activities

Here are some activities for your family to try at home to complement what children are doing in the classroom:
- Plan a meal around a certain color and invite your child to help plan and prepare it. Take a trip to the grocery store and have your child look for items that could be included in the meal.
- Have a daily shape and color hunt. Let your child know what shape and color to look for each day and identify different objects with that shape or color.

Have fun as you explore all of the spectacular Shape and Color activities with your child.

Thank you for all you do!

Sincerely,

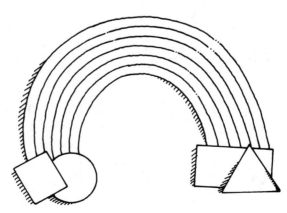

Year-Round Early Childhood Themes © 2006 Creative Teaching Press

Dear Family:

We will use the following items during our Shapes and Colors unit. We would appreciate any help you could give us. We will begin this unit on _____, so please sign and return the form below if you can donate items by _____.

- bottle of shampoo
- bubble wrap
- colorful streamers, ribbons, and tissue paper
- empty cardboard egg cartons
- old white sheet
- clear, plastic water bottles
- spray bottles
- new bunion or corn pads
- weather stripping scraps
- unflavored gelatin packet
- shaped crackers

Thanks!

• •

I would like to contribute the following items for this unit:

_____

Please contact me at _____ (phone number or e-mail) to let me know how I can help.

_____
(parent's name)

Center Ideas

The following are suggestions for different Shape and Color centers. The activities provided in this unit can be used or modified for these centers:

- **Art Center**—easel with paper cut in various shapes, play dough (see Art Recipes, page 409), cookie cutters of various shapes

- **Block and Building Center**—unit blocks, pattern blocks to play matching games with, shaped wood scraps, glue, Styrofoam shapes

- **Dramatic Play Center**—colorful scarves and clothes for dress up

- **Listening Center**—tapes of stories about shapes and colors

- **Manipulatives Center**—pattern blocks and matching games to play with them, puzzles

- **Math and Science Center**—prisms, glasses with cellophane lenses

- **Reading Center**—books about shapes and colors (see recommended read-alouds, page 349), flannel board activities

- **Sand and Water Tables**—colored water, colored pasta or rice (see Art Recipes: Pasta and Rice Dye, page 416)

- **Writing Center**—shape and color stickers, shape stamps

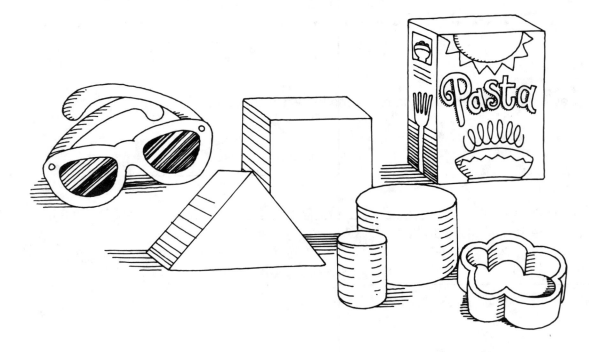

Language Development

Recommended Read-Alouds

Color Dance by Ann Jonas (Greenwillow Books)

Color Farm by Lois Ehlert (HarperCollins)

A Color of His Own by Leo Lionni (Alfred A. Knopf Books)

Color Zoo by Lois Ehlert (HarperCollins)

Colors Everywhere by Tana Hoban (Greenwillow Books)

Is It Red? Is It Yellow? Is It Blue? by Tana Hoban (Greenwillow Books)

It Looked Like Spilt Milk by Charles G. Shaw (HarperCollins)

Lunch by Denise Fleming (Henry Holt and Company)

Mouse Paint by Ellen Stoll Walsh (Harcourt)

Of Colors and Things by Tana Hoban (Greenwillow Books)

A Rainbow of My Own by Don Freeman (Puffin)

Red, Blue, Yellow Shoe by Tana Hoban (Greenwillow Books)

Shapes, Shapes, Shapes by Tana Hoban (Greenwillow Books)

So Many Circles, So Many Squares by Tana Hoban (Greenwillow Books)

Read-Aloud Activity

After reading aloud a book, discuss with children their ideas, thoughts, and feelings about the book. Invite children to act out the book or a scene from it using different props.

Discussion Starters

Use these suggestions to promote discussions about a read-aloud or to motivate children to tell a story. These ideas can be discussed and then used to write group stories for children to illustrate.

1. After children learn about primary and secondary colors, ask them *If there were only three colors, which three would you choose? Why?* See if children understand that other colors can be made by mixing primary colors together.

2. Have children explore their imagination. Ask questions similar to the following:
   - *What if, suddenly, all the squares and rectangles in the world disappeared? What would happen? What shape would we make our doors and windows? Could we fit through them? What shape would our houses become?*
   - *What would happen if everything that is round turned square? Could our cars get anywhere on square wheels? Could we drink out of square cups?*
   - *What if there were no colors in the world? What do you think it would be like if everything was gray? If all the people and all the animals turned gray, could we tell them apart? Do you think it would be a pretty place to live?*

3. Describe objects of a certain shape or color, and ask children to identify what shape or color you are thinking of.

Math Activities

 ## Shapes and Numerals

Skills: counting, numeral recognition, matching sets

Materials
- Shape and Numeral Cards (page 370)
- card stock
- scissors

Preparation

Copy two sets of the Shape and Numeral Cards on card stock. Cut apart each card. Then cut the cards in one set in half, separating the shapes from the numeral. Put the intact deck of cards in a pile on a table, and spread out the remaining cards faceup.

Directions

Invite children to draw a card from the deck and recreate that card by picking out the correct numeral card and shape card. Repeat the activity until all cards are matched.

 # How Many?

Skills: estimating, data collection and display, counting

Materials
- M&M's
- small, clear jar with a lid
- chart paper

Preparation

Count the M&M's. Pour them into a jar, and secure the lid.

Directions

Show children the jar of M&M's, and ask *How many M&M's do you think there are in this jar?* Record their estimates on chart paper. Pour the M&M's on a table and give each child a small handful to count. Have children help you add up the M&M's (you already know the actual number), and compare this number to the children's estimates.

Extension

Have children list the colors of the M&M's and then sort them into groups by color. Graph the colors, and then invite children to eat their candies.

 # Colors Rock!

Skills: matching colors, one-to-one correspondence

Materials
- cardboard egg carton
- scissors
- 6 colors of paint (e.g., red, orange, yellow, green, blue, purple)
- paintbrushes
- 12 small rocks (should be able to fit into egg carton cups)
- beads (optional)

Preparation

Cut the egg carton in half, and paint each egg cup in the two halves a different color.

Directions

Have children help paint the rocks. There should only be two of each color. Place the egg cartons and rocks in a center. Invite children to put each rock in the matching color cup of the egg carton.

Variation

Children can sort beads into the colored cups of the egg carton.

Parking Colored Cars

Skills: sorting, counting, comparing

Materials
- toy cars in four colors (several of the same color)
- construction paper (same color as the cars)

Preparation

Place the collection of cars in the center of a playing area. Put four different colored sheets of construction paper at four corners to make "parking garages."

Directions

Invite children to sort the toy cars by color. Tell them to "drive" the cars to the matching color garage. Have children count how many cars they have in each garage. Ask *Which color did you have the most of? Which color did you have the least of?*

Pattern Paths

Skill: patterning

Materials
- Shapes reproducibles (pages 371–375)
- construction paper (assorted colors)
- scissors
- tape

Preparation

Make several copies of the Shapes reproducibles on construction paper. Each shape should have its own color of paper. Cut out the shapes, and attach loops of tape to the back of each shape. Place some the shapes on the floor to create three crisscrossing AB-patterned paths. The shapes should be close enough for children to step from shape to shape. Scatter the remaining shapes among the patterned paths.

Directions

Invite a child to stand at the beginning of each path. Tell each child the pattern he or she will be following (e.g., *Your AB pattern goes red square, blue circle, red square, blue circle*). Challenge the children to step on only the shapes that would make their AB pattern and follow the path to the end. Have a new set of children repeat the activity.

Variation

To save preparation time, base the activity on color patterns only and use sheets of colored construction paper.

Sensory Activities

👁️ Shampoo Shapes

Materials
- Shapes reproducibles (pages 371–375)
- shampoo
- food coloring
- resealable freezer bags
- spoon

Preparation

For each child put about four spoonfuls of shampoo (there should be a thin layer of shampoo spread out when you lay the bag flat) and a few drops of food coloring in a freezer bag. Make sure the air is removed from the bag before placing it in another bag to prevent leakage. Copy a class set of the Shapes reproducibles.

Directions

Give each child a bag with shampoo and a set of shapes. Have children push the shampoo around until the color mixes in. Have them place their circle shape in front of them and trace their finger around the outline of the circle. Invite children to place their bag on top of the circle and use the circle as a template to trace the shape in the shampoo. Have them run their hand over the bag to smooth out the contents and repeat the process with the other shapes. Once children have traced all of the shapes, invite them to make the shapes on their own.

👁️ Rainbow Recognition

Materials
- prisms
- string
- white butcher paper (optional)
- tape (optional)

Preparation

Attach each prism to a string, and display the prisms in a sunny window. If needed, tape white butcher paper where the prisms' reflections fall for better observation.

Directions

Encourage children to observe the colors on the prisms and their reflections on the opposite wall. Invite children to move the prisms around and see what happens and if the colors change. Have children share their observations, and invite them to think of new experiments they could do with the prisms.

Surprise Play Dough

Materials
- play dough (see Art Recipes, page 409)
- red, yellow, and blue food coloring

Preparation

Separate play dough into three batches, and mix one color of food coloring with each.

Directions

Give each child a play dough ball. Have children group themselves according to the color of their dough. Pair up children with different colors of dough (i.e., red and yellow, red and blue, yellow and blue). Assist children in giving half of their dough to their partner. Ask them what they think will happen when they mix their dough with another color dough, and then have them carry out the process. Discuss with children the new colors they formed by mixing the primary colors.

Coloring Gelatin Experiment

Materials
- unflavored gelatin packets
- 9" x 13" (23 cm x 33 cm) baking dish
- baking sheet
- food coloring
- small cups
- paint smocks
- eyedroppers (1 per child)

Preparation

Prepare gelatin according to the directions on the package, pour it into a dish, and refrigerate it for at least 12 hours. Once the gelatin is set, turn the dish over and slide the gelatin onto a baking sheet. Pour food coloring into small cups.

Directions

Give children paint smocks to wear to protect their clothing. Invite each child to fill an eyedropper with food coloring and then stick the eyedropper into the gelatin and insert the color. Encourage children to discuss what they discover.

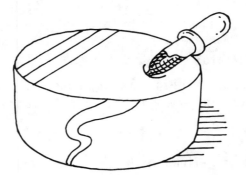

Motor Skills Activities

Shape of Things

Materials
- Shape of Things reproducible (page 376)
- scissors

Preparation

Copy a class set of the Shape of Things reproducible. Cut off the bottom portion with the individual shapes, and then cut out each shape.

Directions

Give each child a set of the shape cutouts and a beach picture from the reproducible. Encourage children to name the shapes they see in the picture. Invite children to place each shape cutout on top of the correct shape in the picture.

Outlining Shapes

Materials
- Shapes reproducibles (pages 371–375)
- small items (e.g., buttons, beans, sequins, counters, raisins, M&M's)
- glue

Preparation

Copy a class set of the Shapes reproducibles.

Directions

Give each child a set of Shapes reproducibles and a handful of small items. Invite children to place the small items around the perimeter of each shape to create an outline of the shape and then glue the items to the paper.

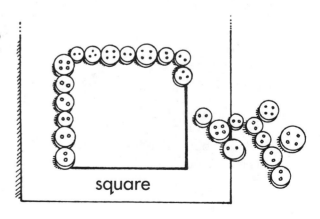

square

Bean Bag Toss

Materials
- different colored bean bags
- construction paper (the same colors as the bean bags)
- masking tape

Preparation

Laminate each piece of construction paper. Tape the pieces of construction paper next to each other on the floor. Use masking tape to make a line for children to stand behind to toss the bean bags.

Directions

Invite children to stand behind the masking tape line and throw the bean bags on the paper of the same color.

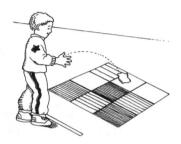

String Shapes

Materials
- Shapes reproducibles (pages 371–375)
- scissors
- string

Preparation

Copy and cut out the Shapes reproducibles. Cut a 5-foot (1.5-m) piece of string for every two children. Tie the ends of each piece together to create a loop.

Directions

Divide the class into pairs, and give each pair a loop of string. Hold up a shape as you say its name, and invite partners to use their string to make the shape. Prompt children to identify their shape using the geometric term (e.g., triangle, rectangle) or the name of a real object (e.g., a mountain, a door). Repeat with the remaining shapes.

Variation

Challenge children to play a version of Simon Says. Have children create the shapes you announce. For example, say *Simon says make a triangle*, and have partners use their string to make a triangle.

Dancing Rainbows

Materials
- streamers, scarves, and ribbons in assorted colors
- music on CD/tape
- CD/tape player

Preparation

Directions

Invite each child to choose a streamer, scarf, or ribbon. Play music and encourage children to dance.

Alphabet Activities

First and Last Name Puzzles

Materials
- Shapes reproducibles (pages 371–375)
- colored paper
- scissors
- tape
- crayons

Preparation

Copy the Shapes reproducibles (one shape per child) on different colors of paper so there is only one of each shape in a certain color. Label each shape with a different child's first and last name. Cut out each shape, and then cut each shape in half between the first and last name using a unique puzzle cut.

Directions

Mix up the cutouts, and place them on a table. Invite children to search for their first name and last name and tape the two pieces together to form a shape. Challenge children to think of an object that is the same shape. Have them draw a picture of it on the back of the shape. Invite older children to help you write the name of the object underneath the drawing.

Shape and Color Names

M a t e r i a l s
- Shapes reproducibles (pages 371–375)
- colored paper
- scissors
- tape

Preparation

Copy on colored paper enough of the Shapes reproducibles so there is one shape for every two children. Label the top of the shape with the name of the color of paper and the bottom with the shape's name. Cut out each shape, and then cut each shape in half between the two words using a unique puzzle cut.

Directions

Pass out one half of each shape cutout to each child. Invite children to search for the child with the other half of their shape. Invite children to tape the two halves together to make the shape.

Alphabet Hearts

M a t e r i a l s
- Alphabet Hearts reproducible (page 377)
- scissors or paper cutter

Preparation

Copy and cut apart a class set of the Alphabet Hearts reproducible.

Directions

Give each child a set of alphabet hearts. (Base the number of hearts given on children's ability.) Show children how to create a row of hearts by putting matching letters of the alphabet next to each other. Invite children to string along the letters of the alphabet in order.

Colorful Words

Materials • construction paper (assorted colors)

Preparation

Label each sheet of construction paper with the name of its color.

Directions

Show children one color of paper at a time. Invite children to name different things that are that color as you write down their responses on the paper. You may want to add a simple drawing next to each word. Repeat the activity with the remaining colors.

Art Activities

Colorful Handprints

Materials
- red, yellow, and blue paint
- shallow paint trays
- bucket
- water
- liquid dish soap
- paint smocks
- white construction paper
- paper towels

Preparation

Pour paint into shallow trays. Fill a bucket with warm soapy water.

Directions

Have each child put on a paint smock. Place a piece of construction paper (landscape orientation) in front of each child. Help children dip each hand in a different paint color of their choice. Have them print one hand on each end of the paper. Invite children to rub their hands together to create a new color. Have them print the new color between the other two handprints. Help children wash and dry their hands immediately.

Tissue Paper Magic

Materials
- tissue paper (assorted colors)
- scissors
- bowls
- water
- paintbrushes
- white construction paper

Preparation

Cut tissue paper into small squares for younger children. Fill bowls with water, and set the art supplies on a table.

Directions

Invite older children to cut tissue paper into squares. Set aside the squares, and give each child a paintbrush and a sheet of white construction paper. Have children "paint" the paper with water. Invite children to lay squares of tissue paper over the wet paper. Have them paint over the entire surface with water again. When the paper is dry, have children remove the tissue paper. The color "magically" stays behind.

Paint Rollers

Materials
- paper towel tubes
- bubble wrap
- double-sided tape
- weather stripping
- bunion or corn pads
- paint
- large, shallow paint trays
- construction paper

Preparation

Create three different types of paint rollers using the following directions:
- Place double-sided tape along the edges of the bubble wrap. Wrap a paper towel tube with the bubble wrap, leaving a 1½" (4 cm) "handle" on each end.
- Make designs around a tube using weather stripping.
- Attach bunion and/or corn pads around a tube.

Pour different colors of paint into separate trays.

Directions

Give each child a sheet of construction paper. Invite children to pick a tube and roll it through a tray of paint. Have them roll their roller across their paper to make a design.

 # Color Swirl Experiment

Materials
- corn syrup
- spoon
- clear, plastic water bottles (1 per child)
- red, yellow, and blue food coloring
- glue gun (teacher use only)

Preparation

Put a spoonful of corn syrup in each plastic bottle. Add several drops of red, yellow, and blue food coloring to each bottle. Use the glue gun to secure the lids on the bottles.

Directions

Give each child a bottle. Invite children to tip and turn their bottle and watch the colors swirl, mix, and change. Have children set their bottle on its side and allow the colorful corn syrup to dry. Display the colorful bottles in a window.

 # Beautiful Table Cloth

Materials
- old white sheet
- black permanent marker
- spray bottles (1 per child)
- water
- food coloring

Preparation

Plan to take children outside for this activity. Use a permanent marker to draw many large shapes on a sheet. Fill spray bottles with water and a few drops of food coloring. Hang the sheet outside (a chain link fence works well), or set it on the grass.

Directions

Give each child a spray bottle. Invite children to choose a shape to color. Tell them to spray the colored water inside the shape's lines. Once children have painted one shape, they can move on to another or spray the areas outside the shapes. Once the sheet is dry, it makes a wonderful tablecloth.

Cooking Activities

🥣 Purple Cows

I n g r e d i e n t s
- vanilla ice cream
- grape juice

Other Supplies
- ice-cream scoop
- plastic cups
- straws

Directions

Drop a scoop of ice cream into a plastic cup for each child. Pour grape juice over the ice cream. Give a cup to each child, and have him or her stir it with a straw and then enjoy the tasty treat.

🥣 Rainbow Cake

I n g r e d i e n t s
- white cake mix
- recipe ingredients listed for cake mix
- food coloring
- ready-made white frosting

Other Supplies
- mixing bowl
- mixing spoon
- cake pan
- butter knife (teacher use only)

Directions

Prepare the cake according to the directions on the package. Pour the batter into a cake pan. Scatter drops of food coloring over the top of the cake. Put a knife into the batter. Move it in a swirling motion to spread and mix the colors. Bake the cake according to the directions, and set it aside to cool. Frost the cake with white frosting. Scatter drops of food coloring over the frosting. Use a knife to swirl the colors into the frosting.

Shape Sandwiches

Ingredients
- cheese, bread, and ham slices
- margarine or butter

Other Supplies
- shape cookie cutters (e.g., circle, star, square)

Directions

Invite children to use cookie cutters to cut the ingredients into different shapes. Have children assemble their sandwiches and eat them.

Biscuit Doughnuts

Ingredients
- can of refrigerated biscuits (1 biscuit per child)
- preserves or jelly

Other Supplies
- small paper plates
- cookie cutters (2 of each shape—1 large and 1 small)
- baking sheet
- waxed paper
- permanent marker
- plastic spoons

Directions

Give each child an uncooked biscuit on a paper plate. Have children use their hand to flatten out the dough. Have children use a large cookie cutter to cut out their biscuit. Show children how to use the smaller version of that cookie cutter to cut out the center of their biscuit. Place the biscuits on a waxed paper–lined baking sheet, and use a permanent marker to write each child's name next to his or her biscuit. Bake biscuits according to the directions on the package, and then set them aside to cool. Give each child his or her biscuit on a plate. Invite children to fill the hole in their biscuit with a spoonful of preserves or jelly.

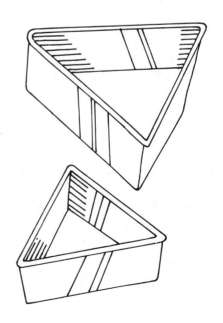

 Colorful Shape Kabobs

Ingredients • variety of fresh fruits, including melons

Other Supplies

- melon baller
- kitchen knife (teacher use only)
- wooden skewers
- paper plates

Directions

In advance, use a melon baller to cut round-shaped pieces of melon and a knife to cut other fruit into cubes. Give each child a wooden skewer and a paper plate. Invite children to slide fruit onto the skewer to make a colorful shape kabob.

Extension

Challenge children to make a pattern with the fruit as they place it on the skewer.

Cracker Patterning

Ingredients • variety of shaped crackers

Directions

Create a pattern with crackers in the middle of a table. Give each child a handful of crackers. Invite children to recreate the pattern. Have children eat the crackers as directed (e.g., *Eat a square cracker*).

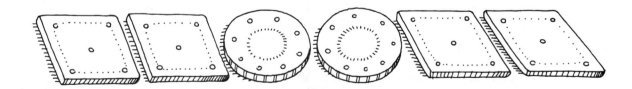

Fingerplays and Flannel Board Activities

🍄 A Beautiful Rainbow Came

(Fingerplay)

One day the sun was shining bright, (*using hand as a visor over eyes*)
But some clouds came along and made it black as night. (*holding up hands for clouds*)
The rain began to sprinkle on the ground, (*wiggling fingers for rain*)
And soon it was raining all over town.
But when the clouds had passed, (*moving hands to side*)
A big, beautiful rainbow stretched across the sky. (*making an arch with hands*)

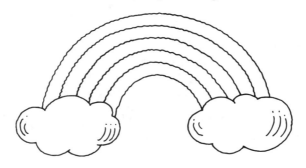

🍄 One Yellow Sun

(Fingerplay)

One yellow sun shining down on me. (*holding up one finger*)
Two red apples hanging in a tree. (*holding up two fingers*)
Three fish swimming in the ocean blue. (*holding up three fingers*)
Four pink piglets—they're brand new. (*holding up four fingers*)
Five green leaves hanging on a twig. (*holding up five fingers*)
Six purple grapes—they're juicy and big. (*holding up six fingers*)
Seven black bats flying late at night. (*holding up seven fingers*)
Eight orange butterflies took off in flight. (*holding up eight fingers*)
Nine brown dogs chasing ten white cats. (*holding up nine and then ten fingers*)
Now we're done and that is that.

Shapes

(Flannel Board—sung to the tune of "Frère Jacques")

Create the following flannel board pieces: square, circle, triangle, and rectangle.

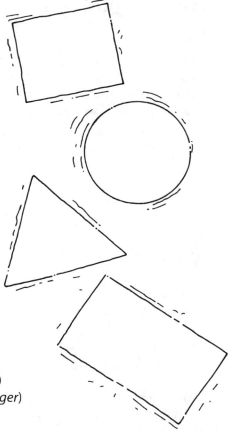

This is square. This is square. (*putting up square*)
How can you tell? How can you tell?
It has four sides, (*holding up four fingers*)
All the same size.
It's a square, it's a square. (*tracing sides with finger*)

This is circle. This is circle. (*putting up circle*)
How can you tell? How can you tell?
It goes round and round. (*tracing outline with finger*)
No end can be found.
It's a circle. It's circle. (*tracing outline with finger*)

This is triangle. This is triangle. (*putting up triangle*)
How can you tell? How can you tell?
It only has three sides, (*holding up three fingers*)
That join to make three points. (*touching three points*)
It's a triangle. It's a triangle. (*tracing sides with finger*)

This is rectangle. This is rectangle. (*putting up rectangle*)
How can you tell? How can you tell?
It has two short sides, (*touching shorter sides with finger*)
And it has two long sides. (*touching longer sides with finger*)
It's a rectangle. It's a rectangle. (*tracing all four sides with finger*)

Favorite Colors

(Flannel Board–sung to the tune of "Six Little Ducks")

Create the following flannel board pieces: assorted colors of crayons and a crayon box.

So many crayons in the box for you,
Red ones, yellow ones, blue ones, too. (*pointing to the crayons as they are named*)
But the one little crayon that rhymes with **bean** (*pulling out the green crayon*)
Is my favorite color. It's the color **green**.

Additional verses:
Replace the first boldfaced word with a new word that rhymes with the color of one of the flannel
crayons. For example, *But the one little crayon that rhymes with **shoe** is my favorite color. It's the color **blue**.*

Songs

🎵 Square Song

(Sung to the tune of "You Are My Sunshine")

I am a square, a lovely square.
I have four sides. They're all the same.
I have four corners, four lovely corners.
I am a square, and that is my name.

🎵 Triangle Song

(Sung to the tune of "Pop! Goes the Weasel")

I am a small triangle.
I have three sides you see.
I also have three corners.
They're just right for me.

🎵 Triangle

(Sung to the tune of "Bingo")

There is a shape that has three sides
And triangle is its name-o.
Three sides and three points.
Three sides and three points.
Three sides and three points—
And triangle is its name-o.

🎵 Rectangle

(Sung to the tune of "Bingo")

There is a shape that has four sides,
But it is not a square. NO!
It's a rectangle. It's a rectangle. It's a rectangle.
It is not a square. NO!

Two sides long and two sides short—
They are not the same. NO!
It's a rectangle. It's a rectangle. It's a rectangle
The sides are not the same. NO!

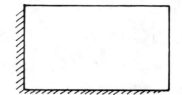

🎵 I'm a Lovely Rectangle

(Sung to the tune of "I'm a Little Teapot")

I'm a lovely rectangle, tall and thin.
I look like a door, that's the shape I'm in.
Two lines short and two lines tall—
That describes me to you all.

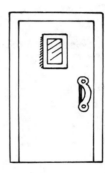

🎵 Colors

(Sung to the tune of "The Itsy, Bitsy Spider")

Orange is a pumpkin.
Purple is a plum.
Yellow is a lemon.
Green's a moldy bun.
Blue is the water and the big sky.
And red is a cherry in a yummy pie.

Brown is a teddy bear.
Pink is a rose.
White is the milk
That I drink to help me grow.
Black is a playful dog with a wet nose.
Now I'm out of colors. Which ones do you know?

What Shape Is This?

(Sung to the tune of "The Muffin Man")

Copy the Shapes reproducibles on pages 371–375 to use with this song.

Oh, do you know what shape this is,
What shape this is, what shape this is?
Oh, do you know what shape this is
I'm holding in my hand?

Repeat the song using different shapes. Have children name the shape at the end of each verse.

Rolling Circle

(Sung to the tune of "Did You Ever See a Lassie?")

Have you ever seen a circle, a circle, a circle?
Have you ever seen a circle that goes round and round?
It rolls this way and that way, and this way and that way.
Have you ever seen a circle that goes round and round?

If You're Wearing . . .

(Sung to the tune of "If You're Happy and You Know It")

If you're wearing something red, shake your head.
If you're wearing something red, shake your head.
If you're wearing something red, then please shake your head.
If you're wearing something red, shake your head.

Additional verses:
blue . . . touch your shoe
black . . . pat your back
green . . . bow like a queen
yellow . . . shake like Jell-O
brown . . . turn around
pink . . . give a wink

Shape and Numeral Cards

5 star	4 square	3 triangle	2 circle	1 rectangle
10 crescent	9 pentagon	8 diamond	7 oval	6 heart

Year-Round Early Childhood Themes © 2006 Creative Teaching Press

Shapes

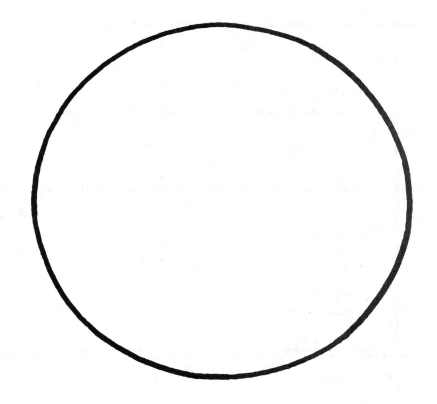

circle

square

Shapes

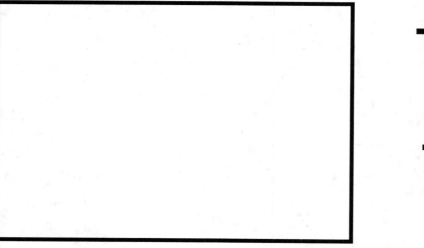

rectangle

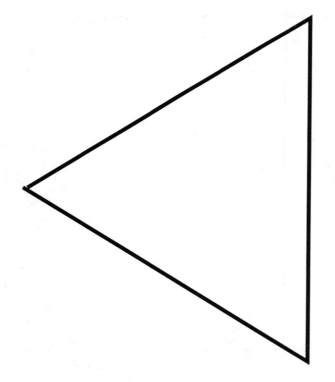

triangle

Year-Round Early Childhood Themes © 2006 Creative Teaching Press

Shapes

star

heart

Year-Round Early Childhood Themes © 2006 Creative Teaching Press

Shapes

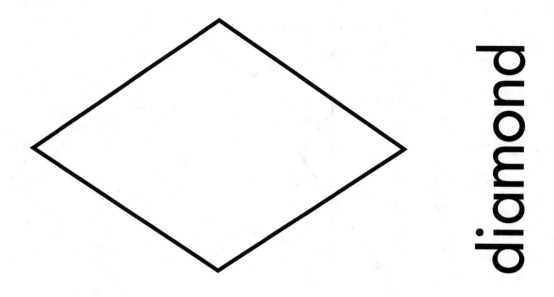

diamond

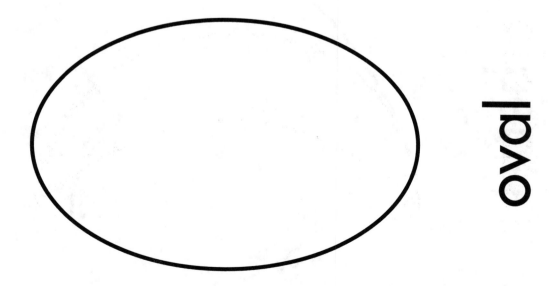

oval

Year-Round Early Childhood Themes © 2006 Creative Teaching Press

Shapes

pentagon

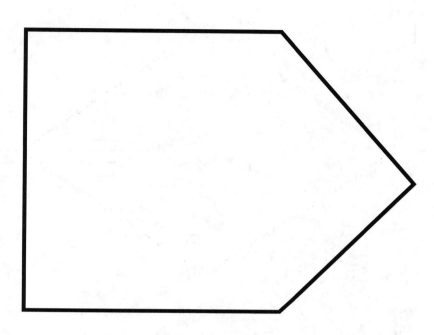

crescent

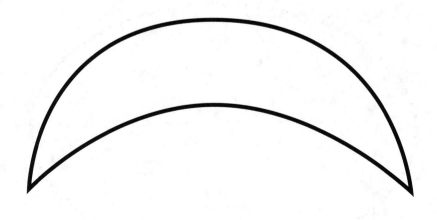

Shape of Things

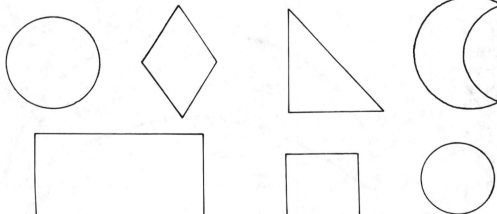

Year-Round Early Childhood Themes © 2006 Creative Teaching Press

Alphabet Hearts

a b

b c   c d   d e   e f

f g   g h   h i   i j

j k   k l   l m   m n

n o   o p   p q   q r

r s   s t   t u   u v

v w   w x   x y   y z

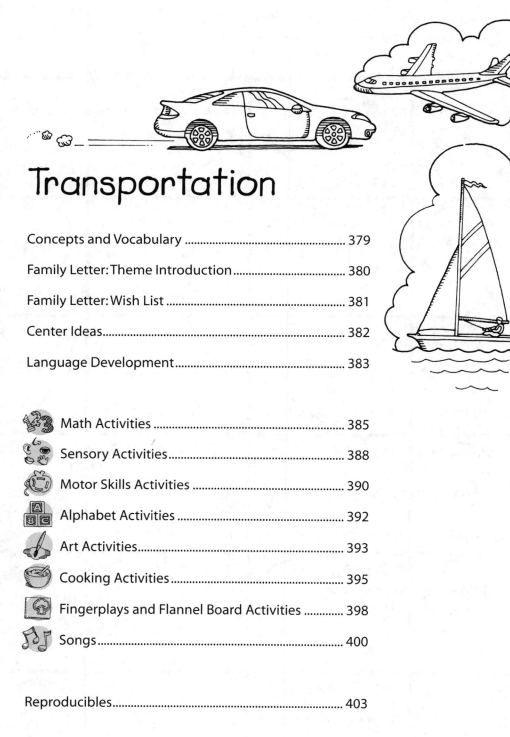

Transportation

Concepts

The concepts covered in this unit include the following:
- There are many forms of transportation.
- We need more than one form of transportation.
- Different forms of transportation can move us on the ground, in the water, and in the air.
- Forms of transportation can move us, move the things we need, help us, or entertain us.
- Some vehicles that help us are fire trucks, garbage trucks, tow trucks, and ambulances.
- We carry one means of transportation with us everywhere we go—our feet
- There are laws that make using different forms of transportation safer.
- Some forms of transportation require payment and tickets.
- Forms of transportation need a power source to work.

Vocabulary

freight—goods transported by land, water, or air

passenger—a person traveling in an automobile, a bus, a train, an airplane, or a boat

transportation—means of carrying someone or something from one place to another

vehicle—a means for transporting people or goods

The types of transportation covered in this unit include the following:
- air—airplane, helicopter, space shuttle
- land—car, bus, trucks, trains
- water—boats, ferries
- animals—horse, elephant, camel
- ourselves

Date _____

Dear Family:

"Transportation" will be the theme for our next unit. We will be learning about many types of transportation on land, on water, and in the air. For this unit we will need some assistance from you. Please help your child make a paper airplane (as described under "Home Activities").

Classroom Activities

Children will participate in the following activities:
- Singing songs and doing fingerplays about transportation.
- Listening to books about transportation, including *Freight Train* by Donald Crews.
- Discussing the necessity for many types of transportation.
- Racing cars.

Home Activities

Here are some activities for your family to try at home to complement what children are doing in the classroom:
- Help your child create a paper airplane. Decorate it, and label it with your child's name. Send it back to school for our Airplane Flying Contest. Categories will include longest and shortest flight, most beautiful, most colorful, most unusual, flies straightest, and flies in a circle. Please have your child bring his or her airplane on _____.
- Take a walk around your neighborhood. Keep track of how many different types of transportation you see such as cars, pickup trucks, SUVs, vans, boats, bicycles, and animals.

Have fun as you explore all of the terrific Transportation activities with your child.

Thank you for all you do!

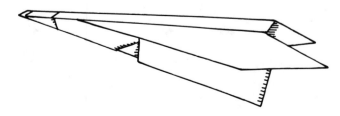

Sincerely,

Year-Round Early Childhood Themes © 2006 Creative Teaching Press

Dear Family:

We will use the following items during our Transportation unit. We would appreciate any help you could give us. We will begin this unit on _____, so please sign and return the form below if you can donate items by _____.

- toy vehicles (with child's name)
- Styrofoam packing "peanuts"
- shaving cream (non-menthol)
- license plates (out of use)
- old magazines with pictures of vehicles
- unopened box of graham crackers
- paper plates
- corks
- empty thread spools
- unopened bag of M&M's

Thanks!

• •

I would like to contribute the following items for this unit:

_____

Please contact me at _____ (phone number or e-mail) to let me know how I can help.

_____

(parent's name)

Center Ideas

The following are suggestions for different Transportation centers. The activities provided in this unit can be used or modified for these centers:

- **Art Center**—easel paper shaped like vehicles, vehicle cookie cutters, stencils, play dough (see Art Recipes, page 409), old maps

- **Block and Building Center**—train sets, cars, trucks, airplanes, toilet paper and paper towel tubes, PVC pipe, shoeboxes, sturdy glue, construction paper, spools

- **Dramatic Play Center**—hats and costumes for train conductors, pilots, and other transportation-related job clothing; toy train

- **Listening Center**—tapes of transportation books, tapes of transportation stories written in class

- **Manipulatives Center**—vehicle counters and puzzles

- **Math and Science Center**—pieces of a tire tred, magnifying glass

- **Reading Center**—transportation books (see recommended read-alouds, page 383), books and stories written in class, flannel board and pieces

- **Sand and Water Tables**—sand, water, and gravel tables/tubs; toy cars, trucks, and construction equipment

- **Writing Center**—transportation stamps and stickers, tickets to fill in

Language Development

Recommended Read-Alouds

Don't Let the Pigeon Drive the Bus! by Mo Willems (Hyperion Books for Children)

Down by the Station by Will Hillenbrand (Gulliver Books)

Freight Train by Donald Crews (Greenwillow Books)

I Stink by Kate McMullan (Joanna Cotler Books)

I Want to Be an Astronaut by Byron Barton (HarperCollins)

Inside Freight Train by Donald Crews (HarperFestival)

Mr. Gumpy's Motor Car by John Burningham (HarperCollins)

My Truck Is Stuck! by Kevin Lewis (Hyperion Books for Children)

Row Row Row Your Boat by Iza Trapani (Charlesbridge Publishing)

Sheep in a Jeep by Nancy Shaw (Houghton Mifflin)

Train Song by Diane Siebert (HarperCollins)*

*Read-aloud used in an activity

Read-Aloud Activity

Read a book to the class. Have children list the different characters and objects in the story. Record their responses on chart paper. Use the list to create a story bag (i.e., flannel board pieces children can use to tell the story). Invite children to retell the story on the flannel board.

Discussion Starters

Use these suggestions to promote discussions about a read-aloud or to motivate children to tell a story. These ideas can be discussed and then used to write group stories for children to illustrate.

1. Discuss various means of transportation (e.g., walking, strollers, wagons, cars, motorcycles, horses, trucks, planes) and when each might be used. Discuss children's experiences with different types of travel and why we need more than one form of transportation. Record children's responses on chart paper.

2. Discuss the various types of things that can be transported in different types of train cars. (Display pictures or flannel board pieces.) Include cars that carry people, fruits and vegetables, milk, vehicles, mail, chemicals, furniture, and livestock. Discuss what it might feel like to ride in a train and what you might see. Record children's responses on chart paper.

3. Create a flannel board with pictures of trucks made for hauling various items. Talk about things they might carry: items for stores, furniture for someone moving, livestock, milk, cars, or rides for carnivals. Discuss why trucks are so important. Draw a picture of a truck, and have children dictate a story about what it is hauling.

4. Set out replicas of various means of transportation (e.g., plastic cars, trucks, airplanes, trains). Describe places that someone might want to go (e.g., the library, the moon, Disneyland, Grandma's house). Discuss which type of transportation is the best to get there and why.

5. Tell children the beginning of the following story, and invite them to finish it: *We're going on a trip to outer space today. Let's climb into our space shuttle. Look at all of the seats in here. Climb in and buckle up. Look at that huge window. We'll be able to see everything we pass. Time to blast off. 10 – 9 – 8 – 7 – 6 – 5 – 4 – 3 – 2 – 1 – BLAST OFF! Here we go. Look out of the window. What do you see?*

6. Bring a suitcase with assorted items: some items that should be taken in a suitcase for a trip (e.g., clothing, shampoo, shoes) and others that should not (e.g., hammer, glue gun, ruler). Tell children that you are going on a trip. Display the items you packed. Have children decide what you should and should not take and why.

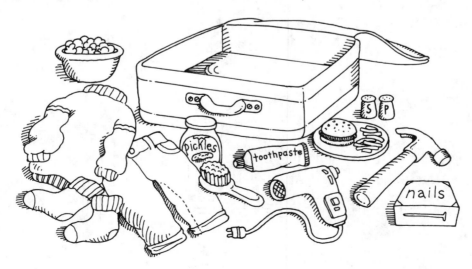

Math Activities

🎈 How Did We Come to School?

Skills: data collection and display, counting

M a t e r i a l s
- How Did We Come to School? reproducible (page 403)
- clipboards (1 per child)
- pencils

Preparation

Copy a class set of the How Did We Come to School? reproducible. Attach each copy to a clipboard.

Directions

Tell children that they will be asking each other the question *How did you come to school?* Have them practice asking the question with a partner. Give each child a clipboard with the copy of the reproducible and a pencil. Show children how to ask the question and use the pictures to fill in the correct box. Help children complete the poll by asking at least five other children the question. (You may want to have a parent volunteer help out.) Challenge children to count the boxes they shaded in each row.

🎈 Balloon-Powered Car

Skills: predicting, measurement

M a t e r i a l s
- masking tape
- small balloon
- drinking straw
- medium-sized toy car
- measuring tape

Preparation

Tape the opening of a balloon to one end of a straw so the balloon's opening is sealed around the straw. Tape the straw to the top of a toy car with the end of it hanging over. Use masking tape to create a starting line on the floor.

Directions

Invite a child to gently push the car from the starting line. Use tape to mark the distance it traveled. Encourage children to predict what they think will happen if the balloon is blown up and then the air is let out. Blow up the balloon through the straw, and pinch off the end of the straw. Put the car on the starting line, and let go of the straw. Use a measuring tape to measure the distance the car traveled, and mark it with masking tape. Ask children to describe what happened.

Transportation Patterning

Skills: color matching, sorting, patterning

Materials
- Transportation Patterning reproducible (page 404)
- scissors

Preparation

Copy the Transportation Patterning reproducible. Make enough copies so that each child will have two rows of vehicles. Cut out the vehicles. Leave a row intact for each child to use as a model. (The vehicles are laid out in an AB pattern.)

Directions

Give each child a row of the AB pattern and four individual pieces (two cars, two trucks). Invite children to use the row as a base and place the matching pieces on top. Then, give children more individual pieces, and have them extend the pattern. Invite older children to create other patterns for another child to copy.

Loading Trucks

Skills: counting, one-to-one correspondence, number recognition

Materials
- paper
- scissors
- large toy trucks (1 per child)
- tape
- "freight" (e.g., small cubes, plastic animals)

Preparation

Cut paper to fit on the side of toy trucks. Label each paper with a numeral from 1 to 5 and the corresponding number of dots. Tape one paper to the side of each truck. Set out the freight items.

Directions

Invite children to load their trucks with freight. Tell them to put the correct number of items on each truck as indicated by the numeral and dots on the side of the truck. Encourage children to make up what cargo their trucks are carrying and where their trucks are going to deliver the freight.

Variation

Make the numbered papers large enough to tape to a child's back. Choose five volunteers. Tape one paper on each volunteer's back. Have these children get on their hands and knees—they will be the "trucks." Have other children place the correct number of items on each child's back. Invite the trucks to "drive around" by crawling. Repeat the activity with other children.

Train Ride

Skill: number recognition

Materials
- Train Tickets reproducible (page 405)
- *Train Song* by Diane Siebert or another train-related book
- chairs
- sticky notes
- scissors

Preparation

Make enough copies of the Train Tickets reproducible so each child will have a ticket. Set up chairs like the interior of a passenger train car. Write a different number on each sticky note (one number per child). Place each sticky note on a different chair in numerical order. Number the tickets the same as the sticky notes, fill in the remaining information, and then cut apart the tickets.

Directions

Invite children to take an imaginary train ride with you. Give each child a train ticket. Invite children to find their seat by matching the number on their ticket to the sticky notes on the chairs. Read aloud *Train Song*.

All Aboard!

Skills: counting, number recognition

Materials
- index cards
- hole punch
- string
- scissors
- 4 engineer hats (optional)

Preparation

Make a class set of index-card necklaces. Use a hole punch to make a hole in the top corners of each card. Tie one end of a piece of string to each hole. Label four of the index cards with a numeral between 2 and 5. Draw two to five dots on each of the remaining necklaces. Set up four train stations around the room.

Directions

Choose four children as the engineers, and give each of them an engineer hat and a numeral necklace. Give an index-card necklace to each of the remaining children. Place an engineer at each train station, and have each engineer say *All aboard!* Tell children to "board the train" by placing their hands on the child in front of them if the number of dots on their necklace matches the number on the engineer's necklace. Have the engineers take their "train" to another station that does not have a train. Choose new engineers, have the remaining children switch necklaces, and repeat the activity.

Sensory Activities

Driving in the Suds

Materials
- non-menthol shaving cream
- plastic toy vehicles (1 per child)

Preparation

Directions

Gather children around a table, and squirt some shaving cream on the table in front of each child. Give each children a toy vehicle. Invite children to drive it around in the shaving cream.

Play Dough Badges

Materials
- baker's clay (see Art Recipes, page 410)
- rolling pins
- star cookie cutters
- dull pencils
- baking sheet
- waxed paper
- permanent marker
- paint
- paintbrushes

Preparation

Mix the ingredients for baker's clay (do not cook). Form the clay into a small ball for each child.

Directions

Give each child a ball of clay. Tell children that they will be making a star badge to give to a firefighter or police officer. Have children take turns rolling out their clay and using a cookie cutter to make a star-shaped badge. Show children how to drag a dull pencil through the clay to make a design on their badge. Place the badges on a waxed paper–lined baking sheet. Use a permanent marker to write each child's name on the waxed paper beside his or her badge. Bake the badges according to the directions on page 410. After the badges have cooled, invite children to paint their badge. Have children present their badge to a firefighter or police officer who visits the school.

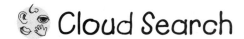 # Cloud Search

Materials

- large box
- Styrofoam packing peanuts
- pairs of airline-related items (e.g., plane tickets, wings, small toy airplanes, pilots' hats, small cases or other types of luggage)

Preparation

Fill a large box with packing peanuts. Gather matching items, and bury one of each item in the packing peanuts. Place the remaining items on a table.

Directions

Review with children the different items on the table and their connection to air travel. Tell children that the box of packing peanuts is a "cloud." Hold up one of the items from the table. Invite a child to reach into the cloud and feel around to find the same item as the one you held up. Invite the child to pull out the item and see if he or she is correct. Repeat the activity with a different child until each child has had a turn.

Paper Airplane Flying Contest

Materials

- Airplane Award (page 406)
- colored paper
- paper airplanes (see Family Letter: Theme Introduction, page 380)
- masking tape
- chart paper

Preparation

Copy a class set of the Airplane Award on colored paper. Remind children to bring the paper airplane they made at home with their families. Use masking tape to create a line on the floor from which children will fly their paper planes.

Directions

Ask children *Where do planes travel—in the air, on the water, or on the land?* Give children their paper airplane to release one at a time from the masking tape line. (This can be done as a whole class or small group. Younger children may need help throwing their airplane.) Have children observe which plane flies the shortest, the longest, in a circle, etc. Encourage them to comment positively on each paper plane (e.g., *Jordan's flew the highest*), and record their comments on chart paper. Use these comments to judge the airplanes in a variety of categories (e.g., longest flight, shortest flight, most beautiful, most colorful, most unusual, flies straightest, flies in a circle). Present a different airplane award to each child.

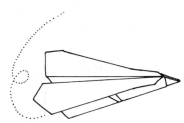

Motor Skills Activities

Traffic Signals

Materials
- 9" x 12" (23 cm x 30.5 cm) sheets of black, red, yellow, and green construction paper
- scissors
- glue

Preparation

Cut black construction paper in half lengthwise so each child will have a 4¹/₂" x 12" (11.5 cm x 30.5 cm) piece. Cut red, yellow, and green construction paper into 3" x 3" (7.5 cm x 7.5 cm) squares so each child has a square of each color. Create a completed traffic signal from the materials.

Directions

Show children the completed traffic signal, and discuss what each color means. Give each child a set of three squares. Invite children to cut off the corners of each paper square to make a circle. Have children glue the circles on their black paper in the correct place to make a traffic signal.

Red Light, Green Light

Materials
- paper plates
- red and green construction paper

Preparation

Teach children the song "Drive, Drive, Drive Your Car" on page 401.

Directions

Explain to children that they are going to play a game in which they are drivers who obey the traffic signal laws. Sing with children the song "Drive, Drive, Drive Your Car." Give each child a paper plate "steering wheel." Tell children that if you hold up the green paper they can "drive" and if you hold up the red paper they should stop. Give children who obey the laws a chance to direct the "traffic."

Traffic Jam

M a t e r i a l s

- green and black butcher paper
- tape
- scissors
- white chalk
- small toy cars (1–2 per child)
- drawing paper
- crayons or markers

Preparation

Tape green paper to a tabletop. Cut black paper into several strips of "road," and tape one road down the middle of the table. Use chalk to draw a dotted line down the middle of the road. Encourage children to bring small toy cars from home (labeled with the child's name).

Directions

Give each child one or two toy vehicles. Invite children to put their vehicles on the one road and drive the cars around. Ask children *Where can the cars go? Can you move them where you want them to go? What do we need to do so the cars can move?* Add one more road, and ask *Does that solve the problem?* Continue adding more roads until the cars can move freely. Invite children to draw on paper places they would like to visit. Discuss with children other modes of transportation (e.g., airplanes, boats, buses, subways).

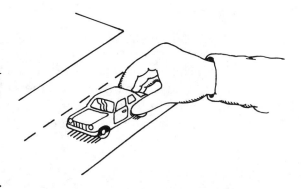

Traveling on the Map

M a t e r i a l s

- large regional or state map
- tape
- highlighter
- colored markers

Preparation

Tape a map to a tabletop, and highlight two cities.

Directions

Invite children to look at the map, and show them the different features (e.g., cities, roads, rivers, lakes). Point out the two highlighted cities. Invite a few children to use colored markers to trace the roads between the cities. Continue to have children trace the roads until all children have had a chance. Ask *How else could you travel to get from one place to another?*

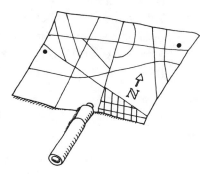

Alphabet Activities

 Alphabet Train

Materials
- Alphabet Train reproducible (page 407)
- scissors

Preparation

Copy and cut apart a class set of the Alphabet Train reproducible. Make sure there is an alphabet displayed in the classroom that is in order and easily visible.

Directions

Give each child an alphabet train. (Base the number of train cars given on children's abilities.) Show children how to create a line of train cars by putting matching letters of the alphabet next to each other. Invite children to string along the letters of the alphabet in order.

License Plate Rubbings

Materials
- several license plates (can be purchased on the Internet)
- tape
- white paper
- unwrapped, dark-colored crayons

Preparation

Tape each license plate to a table.

Directions

Demonstrate how rubbings are done. Give each child a piece of paper. Help children tape their paper over a license plate. Invite children to rub the side of a crayon over the paper. Have older children identify the letters (and numbers) in their rubbing.

School Bus Name Puzzle

Materials
- School Bus reproducible (page 408)
- yellow construction paper
- scissors
- name tags (optional)

Preparation

Copy a class set of the School Bus reproducible on yellow paper. Cut out each school bus, and label each bus with a different child's name. Cut buses into two or more pieces (between letters) depending on the children's abilities.

Directions

Put the bus pieces for four or five names on separate tables. Direct children to the correct table, and invite them to find and reassemble the pieces for their name. (You may want to provide a name tag for children to use as a guide.)

Art Activities

Land, Water, and Air Vehicles

Materials
- magazine pictures of different vehicles
- scissors
- butcher paper
- tape
- marker
- paint
- paintbrushes
- glue

Preparation

Cut out several pictures of different types of vehicles. Tape butcher paper to a table, and draw a landscape with a horizon, grass, roads, lakes, rivers, and other scenery as desired.

Directions

Invite children to paint the scenery. While the paint dries, discuss with children what types of vehicles could be put in this painting. Invite children to glue each vehicle cutout in the proper place (e.g., car on land, boat in water, helicopter in air).

Build a Better Vehicle

Materials
- construction paper (assorted colors)
- scissors or paper cutter
- glue
- bookbinding materials (optional)

Preparation

Cut out of construction paper several shapes that can be used as vehicle parts (e.g., circles, rectangles, squares, triangles).

Directions

Set out the paper shapes, and give each child a sheet of construction paper as a work mat. Invite children to invent their own vehicle using the shapes and then glue the shapes on their work mat. Encourage children to dictate a sentence or story about their new vehicle as you write it on their paper. Display the vehicles on a bulletin board, or bind the papers together to make a class book.

Painted Tracks

Materials
- old street maps
- scissors
- paint pads in assorted colors (see Art Recipes, page 414)
- washable toy cars

Preparation

Cut maps to about 18" x 11" (46 cm x 28 cm). Make paint pads in assorted colors.

Directions

Give each child a portion of a map and a toy car. Ask children to press the wheels of their car on a paint pad and then "drive" the car across the map. Invite children to repeat the process using a variety of colors.

Two-Dimensional Trains

Materials
- black paint pads (see Art Recipes, page 414)
- blue construction paper
- construction paper scraps (assorted colors)
- scissors
- glue
- corks or empty thread spools

Preparation

Make black paint pads.

Directions

Give each child a sheet of blue paper, paper scraps, and scissors. Challenge children to create three or four train cars by cutting scraps into squares, rectangles, and triangles. Tell children to glue their "train" on the blue paper. Invite children to press a cork or spool on a paint pad and then stamp the circle on the train cars to make wheels. For a language experience, have children dictate the ending to this sentence starter: *I am on the train. I am going to* _____ *.*

Cooking Activities

 # Sailboat

Ingredients
- squares of sliced cheese
- small tortillas
- string cheese

Other Supplies

- kitchen knife (teacher use only)
- blue paper plates

Directions

Slice cheese squares in half diagonally to make two triangles. Fold tortillas in half, and insert a cheese triangle between each fold. Place the tortillas in an oven until the cheese is melted. Give each child a plate (water) with a tortilla (boat), a piece of string cheese (mast), and the other half of cheese (sail) to assemble a "sailboat."

Train Engines

Ingredients
- graham crackers
- bananas, sliced widthwise
- peanut butter

Other Supplies
- paper plates
- craft sticks
- spoon

Directions

Give each child a plate with a craft stick, a whole graham cracker, one graham cracker half, one graham cracker fourth, two banana slices, and a spoonful of peanut butter. Tell children to use the craft stick to spread peanut butter on the whole cracker. (**Note:** Be mindful of any children with peanut allergies.) Show children how to add two banana slices to the bottom corners of the cracker for the wheels, the graham cracker half for the conductor's window, and the graham cracker fourth for the chimney.

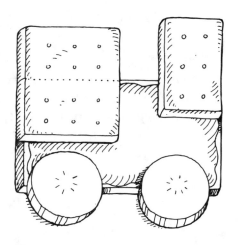

Traffic Signals

Ingredients
- graham crackers
- cream cheese
- red, yellow, and green M&M's

Other Supplies
- paper plates
- craft sticks
- spoon

Directions

Give each child a plate with a craft stick, a fourth of a graham cracker, a spoonful of cream cheese, and a red, yellow, and green M&M. Tell children to use the craft stick to spread the cream cheese on the cracker and put the red, yellow, and green M&M candies in proper order on their "traffic signal."

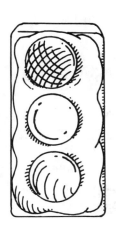

Hot Dog Canoes

Ingredients

- can of refrigerated biscuits (1 biscuit per child)
- hot dogs, cut widthwise

Other Supplies

- waxed paper
- baking sheet
- permanent marker

Directions

Give each child an uncooked biscuit and half of a hot dog. Have children flatten out the biscuit dough. It should be rectangular and slightly longer than the hot dog. Show children how to wrap the dough around their hot dog and pinch the ends together to look like a canoe. Place the "canoes" on a waxed paper–lined baking sheet. Use a permanent marker to write each child's name beside his or her canoe. Bake the biscuits according to the directions on the package.

Astronaut Treat

Ingredients

For each child:
- 2 tablespoons (30 mL) vanilla instant pudding mix
- ½ cup (118 mL) milk

Other Supplies

- resealable sandwich bags
- scissors

Directions

Pour dry pudding mix and milk into a resealable sandwich bag for each child. Seal each bag, trying to remove as much air as possible. Give each child a bag. Invite children to shake and squeeze the contents. Cut off a small corner of each bag, and invite children to squeeze the treat into their mouth.

Fingerplays and Flannel Board Activities

How Do I Get from Here to There?

(Fingerplay)

How do I get to the pet shop? (*scratching head in wonder*)
If I were a frog, I'd hop, hop, hop. (*hopping like a frog*)
How do I get to the sailboat's mast? (*scratching head in wonder*)
If I were a fish, I'd swim real fast. (*moving arms in a swimming motion*)
How do I get to the mountain so high? (*scratching head in wonder*)
If I were a bird, I'd fly through the sky. (*flapping arms*)
How do I get from here to there? (*scratching head in wonder*)
I can travel across land, water, and air.

Lonely Bus Driver

(Fingerplay)

One lonely bus driver all alone and blue, (*holding up one finger*)
He picked up a passenger and then there were two. (*holding up two fingers*)
Two people riding, they stopped by a tree.
They picked up a passenger and then there were three. (*holding up three fingers*)
Three people riding, they stopped by a store.
They picked up a passenger and then there were four. (*holding up four fingers*)
Four people riding, going for a drive.
They picked up a passenger and then there were five. (*holding up five fingers*)
Then the door swung open (*swinging out arms wide*) and out came four. (*putting down four fingers*)
Now the driver is all alone once more.

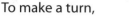 If I Were an Airplane

(Fingerplay)

If I were an airplane, (*holding arms straight out from shoulders*)
Flying way up high,
I'd tip my wings (*tilting one arm down, other arm up*)
To make a turn,
As I go zooming by. (*making zooming sound*)

Engine on the Track

(Fingerplay)

Here is the engine on the track. (*arms at side, bent at elbow, moving forward and backward*)
Here is the coal car, just in back. (*stepping back and pretending to shovel coal*)
Here is the boxcar to carry freight. (*stepping back and pretending to carry something heavy*)
Here is a mail car. Don't be late! (*stepping back and pointing to wrist*)
Way back here at the end of the train, (*stepping back*)
Rides the caboose through the sun and rain. (*raising hands over head in a circle for sun and
    moving wiggling fingers down for rain*)

The Little Boxcars

(Flannel Board—sung to the tune of "Ten Little Indians")

Create the following flannel board pieces: an engine, a caboose, and nine boxcars. Add train cars as directed in the song.

One little, two little, three little boxcars,
Four little, five little, six little boxcars,
Seven little, eight little, nine little boxcars
All behind the engine . . . Toot! Toot!

Songs

Transportation

(Sung to the tune of "Twinkle, Twinkle Little Star")

Take a bus or take a train.
Take a boat or take a plane.
Take a taxi, take a car,
Maybe near or maybe far.
Take a rocket to the moon,
But be sure to come back soon.

♫♪ Drive, Drive, Drive Your Car

(Sung to the tune of "Row, Row, Row Your Boat")

Drive, drive, drive your car,
All around the town.
Merrily, merrily, merrily, merrily,
Up the hills and down.

Turn, turn, turn the key,
Make the engine roar.
Merrily, merrily, merrily, merrily,
Let's go to the store.

Press, press, press the pedal,
Give the engine gas.
Merrily, merrily, merrily, merrily,
Now we're going fast.

Turn, turn, turn the wheel,
That is how we steer.
Merrily, merrily, merrily, merrily,
Make a turn right here.

Push, push, push the brake,
Make the car slow down.
Merrily, merrily, merrily, merrily,
Now we are in town.

♫♪ Airplane

(Sung to the tune of "The Wheels on the Bus")

The pilot in the airplane says, "Fasten your seat belts,
Fasten your seat belts, fasten your seat belts."
The pilot on the airplane says, "Fasten your seat belts,"
When flying through the sky.

Additional verses:
The children in the airplane go bumpity, bump.
The babies in the airplane go, "Waa, waa, waa."
The signs on the airplane go ding, ding, ding.
The drinks on the airplane go splish, splash, splish.
The armrests on the plane go up and down.

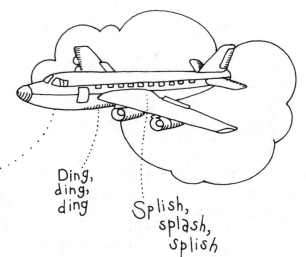

Fasten your seat belts

Ding, ding, ding

Splish, splash, splish

♫♪ The Wheels on the Bus

The wheels on the bus go round and round,
Round and round, round and round.
The wheels on the bus go round and round
All through the town.

Additional verses:
The people on the bus go up and down.
The driver on the bus says, "Move on back."
The wipers on the bus go swish, swish, swish.
The doors on the bus go open and shut.
The horn on the bus goes honk, honk, honk.
The babies on the bus go, "Waa, waa, waa."

Waa, waa, waa

Move on back

Honk, honk, honk

Swish, swish, swish

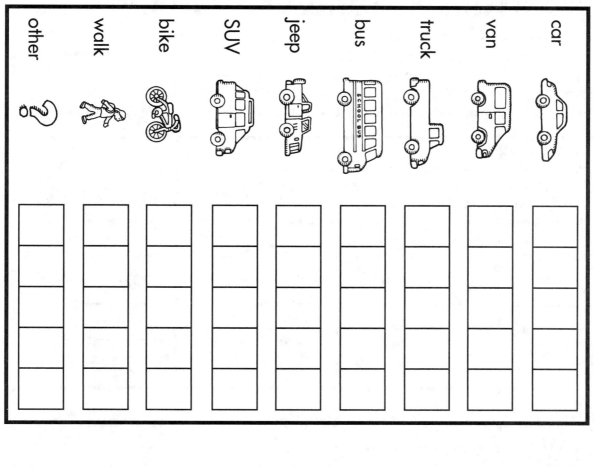

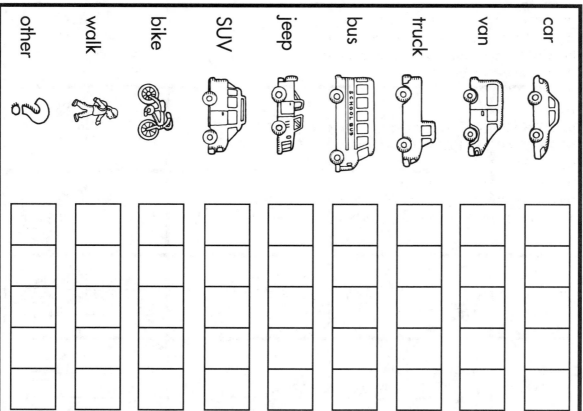

Transportation Patterning

Year-Round Early Childhood Themes © 2006 Creative Teaching Press

Train Tickets

Preschool Express

Seat _____

From _____

To _____

Preschool Express

Seat _____

From _____

To _____

Preschool Express

Seat _____

From _____

To _____

Preschool Express

Seat _____

From _____

To _____

Preschool Express

Seat _____

From _____

To _____

Preschool Express

Seat _____

From _____

To _____

Preschool Express

Seat _____

From _____

To _____

Preschool Express

Seat _____

From _____

To _____

Preschool Express

Seat _____

From _____

To _____

Preschool Express

Seat _____

From _____

To _____

Preschool Express

Seat _____

From _____

To _____

Preschool Express

Seat _____

From _____

To _____

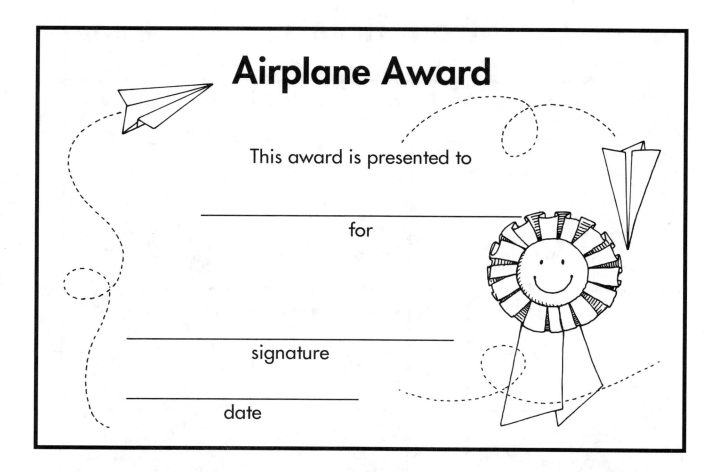

Airplane Award

This award is presented to

_____
for

_____
signature

_____
date

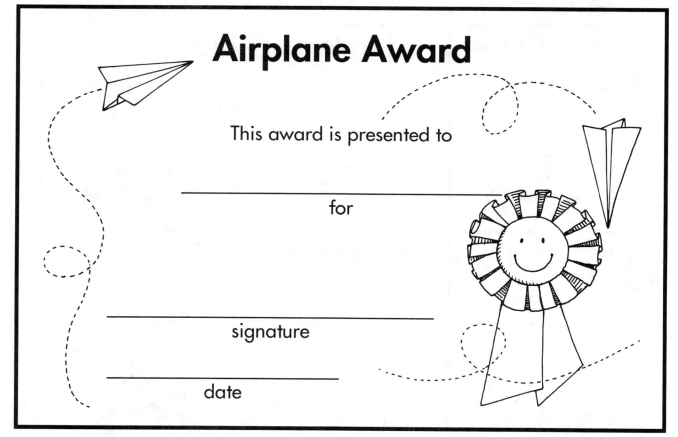

Airplane Award

This award is presented to

_____
for

_____
signature

_____
date

Year-Round Early Childhood Themes © 2006 Creative Teaching Press

Alphabet Train

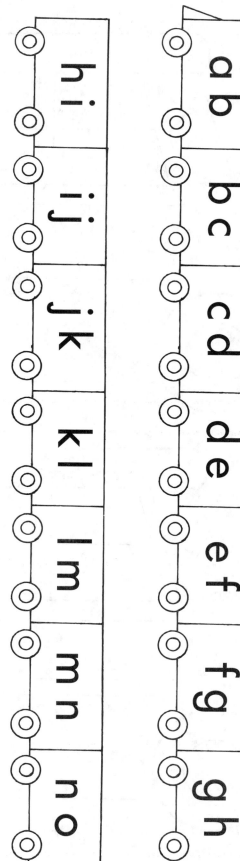

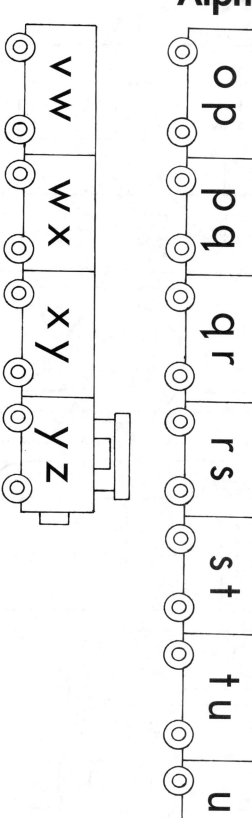

v w

w x

x y

y z

o p

p q

q r

r s

s t

t u

u v

h i

i j

j k

k l

l m

m n

n o

a b

b c

c d

d e

e f

f g

g h

School Bus

Year-Round Early Childhood Themes © 2006 Creative Teaching Press

Appendix: Art Recipes

Play Dough and Clay

Play Dough

Ingredients

- 4 cups (0.95 L) flour
- 4 cups (0.95 L) water
- 2 tablespoons (30 mL) oil
- 1 cup (237 mL) salt
- 4 teaspoons (30 mL) cream of tartar
- food coloring (optional)

Directions

Mix the dry ingredients together. In a saucepan, mix the wet ingredients. Combine the two mixtures over medium heat, stirring constantly, for about 5 minutes. The dough will pull away from the edge of the pan. (You should be able to pinch the dough without it sticking.) Knead until the mixture reaches play dough consistency. You can knead a few drops of food coloring into the dough to add color. Store play dough in an airtight container.

Apple Cinnamon Clay

Ingredients

- 1 cup (237 mL) cinnamon
- 1 cup (237 mL) applesauce
- ½ cup (118 mL) white glue

Directions

Mix all ingredients in a bowl. Knead the mixture until it feels like firm clay. Let it sit for 30 minutes before using.

Baker's Clay

Ingredients

- 4 cups (0.95 L) flour
- 1 cup (237 mL) salt
- 1 teaspoon (5 mL) powdered alum
- 1½ cups (355 mL) warm water

Directions

Mix all ingredients in a bowl. Mold as desired. Prick thicker areas with a toothpick, and then bake at 350°F (177°C) on an ungreased baking sheet for 30 minutes. Turn over clay and bake the other side for 1 hour. Paint as desired.

Crepe Paper Clay

Ingredients

- 1 cup (237 mL) crepe paper torn in tiny pieces
- 1 cup (237 mL) warm water
- ½ cup (118 mL) wheat flour

Directions

Put the crepe paper in a bowl, pour the water over it, and let it sit for several hours. Pour off the excess water, add flour, and stir until mixed thoroughly. Knead the clay on a floured surface.

Jell-O Play Dough

Ingredients

- 2 cups (0.5 L) water
- 2 tablespoons (30 mL) vegetable oil
- 0.3-oz (8.5-g) envelope of sugar-free JELL-O
- 2 cups (0.5 L) flour
- 1 cup (237 mL) salt
- 4 tablespoons (60 mL) cream of tartar

Directions

In a saucepan, heat water to a boil, then add vegetable oil. Combine dry ingredients and add them to the saucepan. Cook over medium to high heat, stirring constantly, until a ball of dough is formed. Cool the dough and store it in an airtight container.

Kool-Aid Play Dough

Ingredients

- 4 cups (0.95 L) flour
- 2 cups (0.5 L) salt
- 8 teaspoons (40 mL) cream of tartar
- 4 tablespoons (45 mL) vegetable oil
- 4 cups (0.95 L) water
- 4 envelopes of sugar-free Kool-Aid

Directions

Mix together the flour, salt, cream of tartar, and vegetable oil. Dissolve Kool-Aid in boiling water, and mix it with the other ingredients. When the dough is cool, knead it thoroughly and then store it in an airtight container.

Peanut Butter Play Dough

Ingredients

- 1 cup (237 mL) peanut butter
- 6 tablespoons (90 mL) honey
- 1½ cups (355 mL) nonfat dry milk

Directions

Combine all ingredients, and mix well. (**Note**: Be mindful of any children with peanut allergies.) Store dough in an airtight container.

Snow Play Dough

Ingredients

- 4 cups (0.95 L) flour
- 1 cup (237 mL) salt
- ²/₃ cup (158 mL) white powdered tempera paint
- ²/₃ cup (158 mL) silver glitter
- 2 cups (0.5 L) hot water
- 4 tablespoons (60 mL) oil
- 2 tablespoons (30 mL) cream of tartar

Directions

Mix together all the ingredients. Knead the mixture into a dough. Add more flour if dough is sticky. Store dough in an airtight container.

Paint and Painting Material

Condensed Milk Paint

Ingredients

- 1 cup (237 mL) condensed milk
- food coloring

Directions

Mix the milk with a few drops of food coloring to make a glossy paint.

Crystallizing Salt Paint

Ingredients
- $1/8$ cup (30 mL) liquid starch
- $1/8$ cup (30 mL) water
- 1 teaspoon (5 mL) powdered tempera paint
- $1/2$ cup (118 mL) salt

Directions

For each color of paint, mix all the ingredients together. Continue to stir paint while painting.

Puff Paint

Ingredients
- 2 parts non-menthol shaving cream
- 1 part white glue
- food coloring (optional)

Directions

Combine ingredients until stiff and shiny. As an option, add food coloring.

Pumpkin Pie Paint

Ingredients
- 1 cup (237 mL) white flour
- 1 cup (237 mL) wheat flour
- $1/4$ teaspoon (1.25 mL) ground cloves
- $1/4$ teaspoon (1.25 mL) nutmeg or ginger
- 2 teaspoons (10 mL) cinnamon
- 2 cups (0.5 L) water

Directions

Combine all ingredients, and mix well.

Paint Pad

Ingredients
- thin sponge
- shallow tray
- tempera paint

Directions

Moisten sponge. Put sponge in a shallow tray. Add paint. Store in an airtight container if you wish to reuse.

Sensory Bottles

Birdseed Bottle

Ingredients
- collection of items that fit inside a plastic soda bottle (e.g., buttons, sequins, paper clips, macaroni noodles, screws, nuts, bolts, marbles)
- birdseed

Directions

Add small items to a clear, plastic soda bottle, then fill bottle with birdseed. Use a glue gun to seal the lid to the bottle. Invite child to shake the bottle to find the "treasures."

Bubble Bottle

Ingredients
- water
- blue food coloring
- liquid dish soap

Directions

Fill a clear, plastic soda bottle one-half to two-thirds full with water. Color the water with blue food coloring. Add a squirt of dishwashing liquid. Use a glue gun to seal the lid to the bottle. Invite children to shake the bottle to see it fill with bubbles.

Glitter Bottle

Ingredients

- light corn syrup
- glitter
- food coloring

Directions

Fill a clear water bottle three-fourths full with light corn syrup. Add glitter and a few drops of food coloring. Use a glue gun to seal the lid to the bottle.

Miscellaneous

Clean Mud

Ingredients

- 6 rolls toilet paper
- 4 cups (0.95 L) bar soap flakes
- 3 quarts (85 mL) warm water

Directions

Tear up toilet paper, and place the pieces in a bucket. Add other ingredients, and mix well.

Modeling Goop

Ingredients

- 2 cups (0.5 L) salt
- 1 1/8 cup (267 L) water, divided
- 1 cup (237 mL) cornstarch

Directions

Heat salt and ½ cup water in saucepan over medium heat, stirring until salt dissolves. Add the remaining water and cornstarch to the salt water, and cook over low heat until it is thick and smooth. After mixture cools, it can be dried in the sun and painted.

Pasta and Rice Dye

Ingredients
- ½ cup (118 mL) rubbing alcohol
- food coloring
- ½ cup (118 mL) pasta or rice

Directions

Mix rubbing alcohol and food coloring in bowl with pasta or rice. Let rice soak for at least 10 minutes. Let noodles soak for at least 30 minutes. Drain and dry the pasta or rice on paper plates or layers of newspaper.

Plaster of Paris

Ingredients
- 1½ parts plaster of Paris
- 1 tablespoon (15 mL) alum
- 1 part water

Directions

Mix plaster of Paris and alum. Add water. Stir until smooth. The mixture can be poured into a disposable, plastic container. (**Note**: Never pour plaster of paris down the sink.)

Toothpaste Putty

Ingredients

For each child:
- ½ teaspoon (2.5 mL) toothpaste
- 1 teaspoon (5 mL) white glue
- 2 teaspoons (10 mL) cornstarch
- ½ teaspoon (2.5 mL) water

Directions

Mix toothpaste, white glue, and cornstarch with fingers. Add water. Mix until it forms a lump of putty.